W9-AEW-312

A S Q C

LIBRARY

HD38
.N2213
1987

A S Q C
LIBRARY

100 MANAGEMENT CHARTS

SOICHIRO NAGASHIMA

Revised Edition

1987

ASIAN PRODUCTIVITY ORGANIZATION

TOKYO

100 MANAGEMENT CHARTS

Revised Edition

ASIAN PRODUCTIVITY ORGANIZATION

Designed and Printed in Hong Kong by

NORDICA INTERNATIONAL LIMITED
for
ASIAN PRODUCTIVITY ORGANIZATION
4-14, Akasaka 8-chome
Minato-ku, Tokyo 107, Japan

Revised English Edition 1987
© Asian Productivity Organization

ISBN 92-833-1043-8 (Casebound)
ISBN 92-833-1044-6 (Limpbound)

PREFACE TO THE REVISED ENGLISH EDITION

What does top management really want today? Whether in the West or in the East, the competitive business environment can't afford to give management time for mental pause. The progress of internationalization, the heightened tempo of technological innovation, the changing profile of industrial structures, together with the mix of political, economic and social factors all contribute to the complexity of managing today's businesses.

The work of management has never been more demanding or multi-faceted. Whether they have studied business management or not, what type of book will serve the most managers in their day-to-day activities? It would be unrealistic to delve into high-flown theories laced with tedious and sophisticated terms. Many managers have been operating their businesses quite successfully, and have met the challenges of difficult industrial situations without the benefit of formalized or academic management training. This book has been developed with these considerations in mind. In other words, the aim of *100 Management Charts* is to help the manager to monitor the actual status of business through the use of concise graphs, charts and pictures, all of which will help him make sound decisions.

Let's indulge in a happy fantasy that a business manager could operate in the same kind of environment as that of a pilot flying a plane. For example, visualize the cockpit of the latest jumbo jet. There as many as a hundred different meters and instruments are displayed together on the instrument panel. They probably include an altimeter, an air speed indicator, measuring devices for wind velocity, wind direction, atmospheric pressure, weather, outside and inside temperatures and also oil pressure gauges, electric meters, fuel systems, etc. Pilots depend fully on these instruments to transport hundreds of passengers surprisingly quickly and safely to their destinations. How satisfying it would be if top management, like flight captains, could always study the actual status of their business as swiftly and accurately.

If top management could ascertain such figures as sales, cost of sales, gross profit, sales and general administrative expenses, operating profits, profit of the term and such management phenomena as marketing and sales, production and process control, organization and personnel control and other items, and investigate any failures at their source, how confident they would feel when they make their business decisions. The widespread acceptance of computers and computerization is one manifestation of the desires and hopes for scientific and reasonable management. It is an incomplete answer, however, to calculate, classify and list data efficiently. What is essential is to know how to utilize the various data of management for strategic decision making.

The 100 management charts that are introduced in this book are neither specially developed nor unique to Japanese business administration. On the contrary, most of them are known already on a universal basis to students of management. I am an Asian and a Japanese and at the same time a world citizen. Additionally, I am one of those who consider management consultancy as a God-given mission. Consequently, wherever the need arises, it is natural to try to utilize our formulae for industrial management and to systematize them. However, I did not select the management charts from academic manuscripts and various volumes on management for this book. It will become evident as you look through this book that it presents only charts which I personally have used and found practical. It also contains charts which I have developed during my actual management consultancy with more than 300 companies during the past twenty years.

There are several types of management charts:
(a) Charts for analysis
(b) Charts for strategic projects
(c) Charts for controlling daily activities

This book contains all three types of charts. As the last category (c) essentially relates to common sense management, most of the 100 charts represent types (a) and (b). The management charts are graphic representations of management and serve as visual educational materials. They help readers to understand intuitively the complicated and interrelated states of management by means of visual aids.

Graphs and pictures are a universal language. Pictures can say more than words. And, as an old proverb says, "Seeing is believing". These graphic charts present, convey, and even teach management control technology without the burden of ideologies and philosophies. In that sense, the charts can be used beneficially in all countries, developed as well as developing countries. In short, the actual thoughts and practical applications can be conveyed through a common medium such as graphic charts.

Forms suggest substance. When using these charts, you'll also receive the following advantages as by-products. The 100 management charts give practical benefits to those who have mastered business management, but will also inculcate the principles and theories of management through use. In other words, they also serve the purpose of education. The forms, designs, instructions and interpretations are, in themselves, techniques of management. Herein lies the evolution from forms to substance. The graphics present analytic project and control techniques; moreover, they also allow for readers' understanding of the varied underlying principles of management.

For example, Chart 1 on page 23 presents the profit and loss diagram which vividly illustrates, in graph form, the structure of a profit and loss statement. The chart explains very clearly how to compute the production cost in the present term by adjusting the inventory levels of work in process at the beginning and end of the term and relating them to the production expenses of the term. By relating the inventory levels at the beginning and end of the term to the production costs of the goods produced during the term, we can compute the cost of sales and this will teach us to set it side by side with the sales amount for the first time. In short, the gross profit can be obtained by subtracting the cost of sales from the volume, but it cannot be obtained by subtracting production expenses or the production costs from the sales amount of the term.

If you subtract general administration and sales expenses from the gross profit, you will get your operating profit. If you add operating profit to non-operating profit and subtract non-operating expenses from it, you'll get the current profit. Again, a chart will not only suggest the structure of the profit and loss statement but will also show how it is related to production cost accounting. If studied like this, the 100 charts, together with explanations of "the purposes of the charts", "how to make them", "various relations to one another," and "how to look at them", will be very useful for those who are not familiar with the principles and theories of management and its techniques. Each chart is numbered within each chapter. The charts are also numbered from 1 to 100 at the bottom right which corresponds to the number used in the Index to Charts, included at the end of the book.

In academic circles, this book is not likely to rank among some other more elaborate textbooks of management for it contains no difficult and puzzling terminology for beginners. On the other hand, this makes it ideal for beginners and those who want a quick and simple approach to business management and its techniques. The particular format of this book, which divides and subdivides various topics, lends itself well as an easily-referenced guide for many difficult situations that are likely to surface.

Conclusion

In preparation for the revised English edition of this book, I looked carefully through the original edition (Japanese version) once again from the beginning. If any charts were related to cases peculiar to Japan, I did my best to convert them and make them as universal as possible. Consequently, though this may be called an English version of the Japanese edition, in reality it is a revised edition of the original Japanese version.

Finally, I should like to express my sincere thanks to Dr. George C. Shen, former Head of Administration and Public Relations Division and Mr.

S. Nazim Zaidi, Head of Information and Public Relations Division of the Asian Productivity Organization for having keenly promoted the project whereby this book has been translated into English so that it may serve management and staff members throughout the world.

Soichiro Nagashima

January 1987

INTRODUCTION

The author wishes to express his gratitude for the encouragement and counsel of the president of Keirin Shobo, Mr. Hiroshi Fuwa, in the preparation of this book, and also to the Asian Productivity Organization for translating and publishing it.

This book has four objectives:

First, to create rudiments of rules for strategic management which go beyond simple routine planning.

Second, to provide continuous insight into the intangible nature of business administration and management.

Third, to act as a catalyst in effecting a transition from departmental specialization to integrated management, creating a multiplier effect in the process.

Fourth, to give a practical answer to those who may know the theories but request guides and techniques which they can put into operation immediately.

The First Objective: To create basic guidelines for strategic management which are more than simple rules.

All business strategies are born of knowledge which goes beyond everyday rules. Nevertheless, many people, as if they were seeking a philosopher's stone, look for a set of rules which they can use in all situations in order always to have a course of action which will lead them to success. Not only is there no such set of rules, but upon close examination or on testing actual applications, strategies are often found to consist of little more than a scattering of ideas.

If management strategy is to be successfully implemented, a fixed course of action suited to the particular situation must be plotted. The rules, guidelines and course followed will vary according to a myriad of factors, such as the type and size of the business, the market, environmental matters, and many others. Therefore, each business must establish its own rules, guidelines, and course of action to meet each specific situation.

The winds of change in the business environment are leaving in their wake enormous amounts of data and information. Computer printouts, reports, tables of statistics and engineering drawings have become several layers deep. File cabinets are on the verge of bursting and the office copy machine is about to overheat and break down. The real problem emerges when we stop to ponder to what extent and how well this vast volume of data and information is being utilized. Too many managers have found that business is generating information at a faster rate than the ability to handle and use the information.

The problems of handling business information are complex and varied. Sometimes the problem is availability of time. Sometimes the complexity of the data defies attempts to comprehend it. Sometimes the problem is in the application of the data.

During the past thirty years, the author has served as a consultant for several hundred companies. This experience has shown that data and information — and knowledge — are in ample supply, but that the ability to consolidate and apply to conclusions reached on the basis of analysis and understanding of the data is lacking.

The first objective is to establish principles for the organization of data, to facilitate its classification and consolidation according to purpose, and to provide rules which can govern the course of action. Managers, by using these rules, may identify pertinent problems, become capable of analysis and examination, and thus become capable of forming a plan for improvement. Policy can be established and strategy planned.

The Second Objective: To provide continuous insight into the intangible nature of business management.

When monitoring and evaluating business activities and effecting reforms, the universal units are monetary values and numerical quantities.

In business, monetary values and numerical quantities are recorded, re-recorded, compiled, classified, tabulated, and computerized. Records are routed from one department to another, from one person to another, from one computer to another. In very general terms, this is the information flow in a business enterprise.

By the time this endless flow of information reaches the top management echelon, considerable simplification and consolidation must be done in order that the people at the top may make suitable decisions, plan strategies, and devise tactics.

Top management, in deciding on policies and plans, makes the final selection from a variety of options. To facilitate and expedite this selection, middle management and the company's staff have the responsibility of sifting through information, structuring it, making generalizations, and preparing summaries. In doing this, middle management and the staff, must exhibit professionalism, as manifested by the use of graphs, drawings, tables, photographs, flipcharts, and other media for presenting the results of their work. In general, they must utilize all types of techniques and means of communication in order to help top management make decisions.

The Third Objective: To act as a catalyst in effecting a transition from

departmental specialization to integrated management, creating in the process a multiplier effect.

A business enterprise is a living entity involving many activities. These activities may at times be considered independently, but in reality they are closely related. The importance of these interrelationships is manifest by the increasing attention devoted to technological changes as well as the 'ecology' and total environment.

The third objective is to show how analytical procedures used in one area of management can be extremely valuable in other realms.

For example, the principles of industrial engineering are often used in sales and marketing, but may be useful in other areas as well:

Flow process charts and operation analysis in physical distribution;

Flow curves used in process control, for control of accounts receivable;

Cause and Effect diagram and Pareto analysis in quality control, for claims handling;

MEMO motion studies, in checking flow at supply centres;

PERT, in marketing new products.

There are many other possible applications. Moreover, marketing techniques may be applied to production improvement:

Advertising methods in forming a new company-wide system;

Motivation Research techniques and sales promotion techniques to convince superiors, fellow workers, and subordinates of the value of improvement plans;

Sales techniques oriented toward the workers for work methods improvement;

Seasonal sales fluctuation analysis in establishing anticipatory production policies.

The Fourth Objective: To give a practical answer to those who know the theories but request guides and techniques to put into operation immediately.

Many people criticize Picasso's works, but are not Picasso. There are many management consultants and management theoreticians who may — or may not — be able to function as managers. But just as Picasso may not be a great art critic, many managers may not be experts in management theories. Moreover, Picasso need not be an art critic, nor need a manager be a management theory expert.

In place of expertise, however, the manager must possess a high level of sensitivity. At the same time, departmental supervisors and staff members under the manager must acquire management techniques which will aid and enhance the manager's efforts. Applied techniques must be based on theory and sharpened by practice. The value of this theoretical foundation cannot be underestimated. Supervisors and others should master basic theory, but need not acquire advanced theory. As they are professionals, however, they must be able to exhibit and use management technology. In other words, they must be prepared in operational techniques, so that successful results can be obtained as quickly as possible and with minimal expenditure of capital and energy. This, then, is the meaning of management technology.

TABLE OF CONTENTS

Chapter 1

CHARTS FOR STRATEGY

In a book from ancient China, entitled "Ta Hsueh", it is written: "Without understanding we cannot see even if we look; we cannot hear even if we listen and we cannot taste even if we eat."

We cannot see the forest for the trees in using management charts, no matter how carefully they are prepared, if verbose passages or row upon row of complex figures are incorporated. In short, the major points must stand out, with the minor points clearly subordinated to them.

Let's take a look at the 100 MANAGEMENT CHARTS from the standpoint of their relation to the managerial function. This function is the core of classic business management. Although there are several methods of classification and handling, the 'plan-do-see' procedure, set forth by Alvin Brown (American management expert), enjoys the widest acceptance. A responsibility of the manager should be the implementation of this concept.

In brief, work should in all cases begin with a plan, proceed according to the plan and yield information which serves to monitor that plan. This last part is the 'see' phase, which consists of:

(1)   Analysis and evaluation of results

(2)   Correction in the event of unacceptable results

The 100 management charts involve not only the 'see' step, but explain how to form new plans on the basis of 'seen' results. The charts may be classified into three groups:

(1)   Charts for the evaluation of the present conditions and results of the plan

(2)   Charts for the incorporation into planning of tactics derived from analysis and evaluation

(3)   Charts to monitor goals (These charts form a small portion of the total.)

Take this example: The books have been closed for a particular tax accounting period, and tax returns have been completed and submitted. The chief accountant, satisfied that he has done his job, heaves a sigh of relief. All ends here.

This approach to management cannot be regarded as true management as it lacks the link joining 'see' to the 'plan-do-see' sequence. Accounting reports and other paperwork must be prepared to provide this link.

Interpretation of the available accounting paperwork is necessary, so that it may be converted into an easy-to-analyze form. Let us stress again that these charts have not been prepared merely as a means of evaluating results. Additionally, they contribute directly to the flow of tactical planning.

The initial course of action is the establishment of precise goals and objectives. There is always the danger of losing sight of the necessity for precision when the interwoven complexities of human relations in the business world come into play.

For instance, among system consultants many become so engrossed in dabbling with the system that they slip into a pattern of considering their work as an end in itself. A system should be a means to an end. The means should be established in accordance with objectives.

An organization, an order, a procedure or a standard may be a system itself or a link in a system. During the course of design, steps must be taken to eliminate inflexibility which may interfere with the realization of objectives.

This example is relevant:

Because another company or competitor has conducted a market survey, someone decides we must conduct one also, post-haste. Unfortunately, preparation of the questionnaire leaves something to be desired and unqualified personnel are assigned to the project. Consequently, results are predictably poor.

What is the problem? Simply, everyone involved lost sight of the goal, or there was no goal.

Before setting up a system, several questions must be answered: "What tactical benefit can be derived from the data in question?" Therefore, at the start, the first question to ask should be: "What kind of statistical information needs to be and can feasibly be derived?"

As soon as the exact nature and specification of the required tables has been established, we may proceed with a system for the acquisition of supportive data. In creating such a system, the only admissible concept is "control based on the objective". In this manner, efficient data control stripped of any unnecessary elements, is possible. In short, what is required is not "input first" (i.e. the system), but "requirements first".

THE ECONOMICS OF 100 MANAGEMENT CHARTS

There may be apprehension on the part of the reader on first encounter of the figure 100 in the title of this book. Please remember, however, that these charts cover the whole range of management, including general management, marketing and sales, production, industrial engineering and labour. These charts apply to discrete work areas and strata and may be classified to cover various time periods:

(1) Charts which, once prepared, may be used for an extended time
(2) Charts prepared on an annual basis
(3) Charts prepared on a quarterly basis
(4) Charts prepared on a monthly basis

The effort and time required to prepare the 100 charts is insignificant, even in medium-sized or small companies, measured against the profit which may be derived from their use. Their potential is literally enormous. They can provide indexes to curtail expenses, eliminate defects, boost profits, limit production time, boost sales, improve productivity and offer other stimuli to growth and development.

The System Approach

A company can be considered a living body, dedicated to attain such predetermined objectives as the pursuit of profit, creation of demand and the preservation of market position. This living body is a collection of special divisions, such as engineering, sales, production, materials and labour. To be most effective, its complex organization, labour relations and human relations must be skillfully managed and integrated.

Work involved in handling the complex monster is not simple. If careless, the president, managing staff or departmental managers may be drawn into the unpleasant position of always having to be on the defensive in trying to solve the problems which constantly surface. This situation can be likened to a game of chess in which your opponent keeps placing you in 'check' with each move. In the end, of course, there is no escape.

One expression we often hear is: "Management means looking at the trends," which means that the general or overall trends must be closely observed. Overall, however, this procedure leads nowhere as the complexity is overpowering. For this reason a systematic approach proves of value. The systematic approach may be defined as 'system approximation' of the problems.

Let's say we have a single management problem. Although it is only one problem, the fact that it is a management problem means there are complex elements and factors. Let a circle represent the problem.

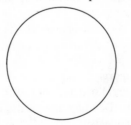

If we are to solve the problem, some method other than a direct approach must be used. Obviously, dividing the problem into small sections (elements, factors, subsystems) will be more effective.

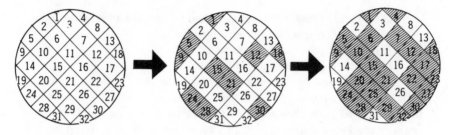

We now solve the minor problems one by one, without a confusing, massive effort. By solving the minor problems singly, the entire problem can eventually be resolved.

The 100 management charts presented in this book form a systematic route to handle the complex and sometimes mysterious problems that business management must solve.

We often hear that the balance sheet is "the face" of a business. In fact, the balance sheet does present broad view. At the same time, however, it lumps together many activities such as engineering, sales, production and labour.

To change the expression on that 'face', the entire structure must be changed. But each function must be attacked individually. Here, an efficient scalpel is necessary to separate each function from the whole for closer examination.

Consider sales. Sales activities consist of a chain of procedures. Unless action is directed along that chain, an impressive sales record cannot be achieved. Motor vehicle repairs also may be used for comparison. Here it is obvious that we must think in terms of systems (drive train, electrical system, power transmission system, etc.).

The mechanism of business management also requires consideration of systems. The individual aspects of business management should not be treated independently, in the interest of company growth and development.

The manager is a management expert, a specialist, who must be able to employ professionalism in controlling the company mechanism. Professionalism consists of analyzing the mechanism systematically and using the results to improve management.

This book and the 100 management charts have been prepared to assist the manager in the practice of the art of systematic management.

Function and Form of Reports

"Systematic (or organic) structure of the objectives" may be considered a communication system. Defining the relationship between organization and communication levels, yields:

(1) Supervisory level . . . . General status reports
(2) Managerial level . . . . Managerial reports
(3) Board level . . . . Data reports

A general status report reflects the actual state of work at the supervisory level. Information pertaining to the problems encountered may be passed along in verbal or written form. Areas covered, for example, may be production, reject rate, personnel attendance, accidents, daily sales and stock reports.

A managerial report, prepared primarily in tabular form, shows work achievements in the functional departments, budgets and differences between projected and actual costs.

The tendency to combine figures for various data categories generally increases with the management level. Typical end reports are the profit-loss statement and the balance sheet. Data reports, either verbal or written, are reports required in making management decisions. Prime examples are external reports, such as market, engineering, labour-wage and price fluctuation reports. Secondary examples include a wide range of reports concerning staff surveys and other items.

Many of the 100 charts in this book pertain to managerial reports. However, general and data reports are amply represented. In fact, the 100 management charts are based on the following types of reports:

(1) Reports for evaluating the present situation and results
(2) Reports showing the configuration of plans incorporating business strategies derived from analysis and evaluation
(3) Reports for controlling achievements

A breakdown of different types of reports is shown on page 7. This breakdown is similar to that applied to the 100 management charts.

Management Chart Requirements

The value of management charts can be judged by their:

(1) Accuracy
(2) Currency
(3) Efficiency
(4) Pertinence

Accuracy is a basic requirement for all data and communication and must not depend on the subjective or arbitrary discretion of the individual making the report.

Timeliness is a crucial element in any report. Decay sets in the moment data is generated. Failure to utilize data while it is current diminishes its value. Speed is vital.

The efficiency requirement covers economic aspects. In the case of managerial reports, timing and speed are of the utmost importance. Figures may be rounded off to three significant digits. Wherever possible, electronic processing should be utilized.

Pertinence relates to the relevance or usefulness of the charts or data. If their inclusion involves a borderline decision, the information probably should be deleted. For purposes of continuity and comparison, items should be represented in uniform measurements or values. This approach will also contribute to both comprehension and effect.

THE 100 MANAGEMENTS CHARTS: WHAT ARE THEY?

General requisites have just been described. Now let's define the charts themselves. The 100 management charts:

+ Represent a logical, procedural system for creating graphs and tabulations which may be used in analysis and planning, to strengthen the position of management and increase efficiency.
+ Are compiled in the sequence of 'see-plan-do' with 'see' as its starting point against the conventionally functional order of 'plan-do-see'.
+ Are designed so that the procedural steps induce real improvements within the corporate body, provide guidance, and assist in application.
+ Present a set of graphs which promote the application of managerial improvement techniques and strategic planning techniques, based on emphasis of the problems.

THE 100 MANAGEMENT CHARTS: WHO MAKES THEM? WHERE? WHO USES THEM?

Primary Responsibility Placed on the General Staff

Preparation and analysis work is the responsibility of the staff. Divide the staff into functional units. For example:

(1) Advisory staff (planning and survey sections, consultants)
(2) Coordinating staff (planning committees, staff conferences)
(3) Regulatory staff (controller, accounting department)
(4) Service staff (general affairs, personnel, transportation, building and repairs, and security)

Listing staff development in service order gives:

(1) Staff assistants (servants, stewards, secretaries, personal advisors)
(2) Staff (specialists) (tacticians, architects, engineers, military advisors)
(3) General staff (controllers, advisory group, planning department, survey section, president's office)

This list is not intended to show transformation, but rather augmentation with the passage of time.

Which staff should be charged with responsibility for the 100 management charts? As already explained, the management charts are:

(1) Charts for evaluating the present situation and results
(2) Charts showing the configuration of plans incorporating business strategies derived from analysis and evaluation

Types of Reports

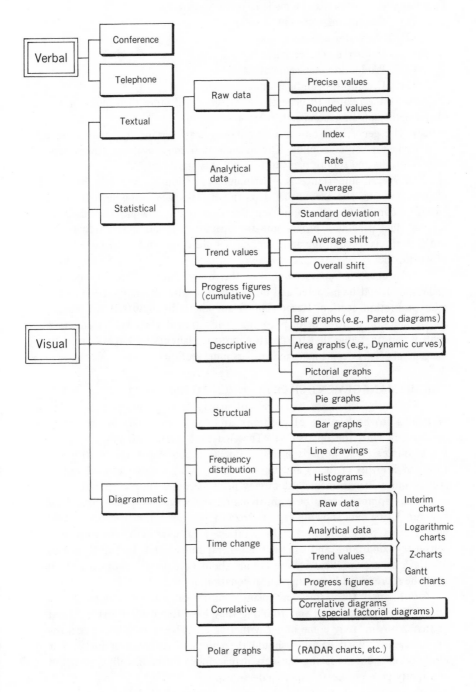

(3)   Charts for monitoring goals

Functionally, division may be made in the following manner:

(1)   General management

(2)   Marketing and sales

(3)   Industrial engineering

(4)   Production management

(5)   Organization and personnel

Anything related to general management will more than likely be the responsibility of the general staff (planning section, survey section, president's office). The general staff is also an advisory staff serving top management as a navigator serves a pilot. The general staff must evaluate the present state of affairs and submit plans to the company president.

Of special importance is a harmonious relationship between the planning section and the accounting department. The accounting department is basically concerned with preparing financial reports, while the planning section must provide a programme for turning materials into products. To avoid conflicts, accounting and planning should come under the jurisdiction of a controller.

Sales charts, of course, would be the responsibility of the sales department and should be prepared and utilized by the sales planning section or the sales promotion section. Responsibility for charts in industrial engineering and production control belongs to the production department (production control section, while that for charts concerning labour and wages belongs to the general affairs department and/or personnel section).

THE 100 MANAGEMENT CHARTS: WHEN TO USE THEM

Ordinarily there are two kinds of management problems. One is that pertaining to the 'capture of positions' and the other is that pertaining to 'encounters with the opposition'. The first kind deals with target control, for example. Desk work is involved, including combinations in different forms of knowns (a, b, c) and unknowns (x, y, z), so that general system tactics and a management system may be constructed on a corporate scale.

This approach may be compared to a war waged by a general and his advisors. Using data showing enemy strength, positions, and armament, along with factors pertaining to terrain, weather, local assistance, environs, miscellaneous conditions, and timing, the general and his staff lay out their plan of attack on a map. What we are talking about here are the problems which could be represented by mathematical equation.

But, apart from this desk plan, consider an infantry company in a jungle. They arrive at a river, thinking they have found their way out. But at that moment, they come under withering crossfire from pillboxes on the opposite bank. What decision should the company commander make? The kinds of encounters facing business management differ in refinement, but constantly pose problems requiring decisions.

Rejects pile up in the warehouse. When delivery dates are not met, customers seek compensation. The sales of new products slump. Employees quit in groups. An industrial spy steals technical data. A decision to purchase or not to purchase new products must be made. A strike for higher wages occurs.

In principle, 100 management charts are designed to satisfy the problem of the first kind, the 'capture of position'. These charts are used for the systematic solution of management problems. Their preparation should be regularly scheduled and periodically produced.

These charts can be applied to a solution of the second kind of management problem, that of 'encounter'. For a special objective, cost calculation is a problem of 'engineering economy' and 'special cost study' — processes external to the routine system. In such cases, there is an objective and a function. Results of analysis determine whether or not new products should be marketed, new facilities introduced to the plant, or new machines purchased.

Using management charts for both kinds of problems, capture of position and encounter, drastically cuts the costs of preparatory work in engineering and special costs surveys. Aside from problems arising periodically (annually, monthly, weekly, daily), the 100 management charts are very useful in the solution of random problems.

CREATION AND COMPREHENSION

McNamara Tactics and the 100 Management Charts

President John F. Kennedy surrounded himself with a number of capable men, thereby creating a shining epoch of governmental doctrines and processes in the history of the United States. These people were known as the Kennedy Machine, and highly admired. One of them, Robert S. McNamara, resigned his post as president of Ford Motor Company to join the Kennedy force, becoming the Secretary of Defense. The special tactics which McNamara devised will not soon be forgotten.

McNamara had been a statistical control officer in the Army Air Force during World War II. At the time, transporting supplies from India over the Himalaya range to B-29 bombing squadrons based in China became necessary. To determine what kind of supplies and volume were necessary was not an easy task. There was a limit to how much material could be transported by air. Here, McNamara put his own statistical control system into use, fully satisfying the requirements of the mission. Later, McNamara was ordered to the Pentagon to work in the Statistical Control Agency headed by a Colonel Thornton. At that time, he was promoted to captain.

At the end of the war, Colonel Thornton and ten of his men accepted positions in the Ford Motor Company. Henry Ford II was concerned about statistical control in industry. Colonel Thornton and his men became important and known as 'whiz kids'. Of all of them, Robert S. McNamara was most deserving of the name. He asked questions concerning anything and everything; he had an insatiable appetite for knowledge. One after another, he proposed new methods.

Examples of his untiring efforts include the time that Volkswagen sales began to threaten Detroit. On being told that Ford could not produce a compact car, McNamara immediately procured a Volkswagen and disassembled it completely. He examined the parts one by one and made a cost study. Later, he presented data which showed that a Ford compact could be produced at reasonable cost. The outcome was the Ford Falcon. It is interesting to note that 'value analysis', now an accepted procedure, was used by McNamara so many years ago.

McNamara received promotion after promotion, eventually becoming the president of Ford Motor Company on November 9, 1960.

What your company needs is thorough analysis based on the McNamara approach. In all projects and planning, statistical power must be demonstrated and cost and effect must be weighed against each other. The rules applying to management of a consumption-oriented organization such as the army are the same as those applicable to business management under a free competition system. McNamara's analysis involved graphs on which costs were plotted on the x axis. Effects were plotted on the y axis, and costs and effects were compared in graphs for the assessment of army projects.

The management charts presented in this book are designed to put dynamic logic into activities of your company and to introduce the effective tactics advocated by McNamara.

The Art of Management

Aside from technical knowledge directly related to management, the concept of the art of management is important. The art of management refers to common sense, something which most people feel is intrinsic and cannot be gained from books. The author strongly disagrees with this consensus.

Most intelligent persons have several common, basic abilities:
(1) 'Problem-sensitivity'
(2) Fluency of ideas
(3) Flexibility in relation to ideas
(4) Ability to use the ideas of others effectively, to improve and solidify the ideas of others
(5) A sharp sense of analysis and integration

Originality is quite helpful in systematic analysis and preparation of the 100 management charts, in order to create new costing procedures based on analysis and integration. The above assets may be developed through a creative thinking course.

Consider this example: By analyzing seasonal sales fluctuations, we have been able to determine the trends of individual product sales. We see that sales tend to drop during February and August (a common occurrence in Japan). Up to this point, we have the facts. Now come the problems.

This is the time to formulate and consider counter-measures, such as:

(1) Re-assign salesmen during February and August to bolster sales of slow-moving products

(2) Develop and market products suited to February and August (winter and summer peaks)

(3) Reduce expenses during these periods, making ample preparation for the following month in each case

(4) Conduct massive sales campaigns for these periods. (Many companies restrict sales campaigns during these periods, creating an opportunity for you).

Ideas such as these must be produced in rapid succession. When an idea is born, its merit must be determined immediately by weighing cost and effect against each other. If an idea is accepted as sound, steps must be taken to incorporate it into projects and planning.

The 100 management charts which reflect general management knowledge and creativity, are designed to show the value of proposals. The only step remaining is selection and decision by top management.

Prepared charts present a real potential for improving the company position. Requisites for preparing the charts are:

(1) A high degree of perception

(2) True logic

(3) High intellect, active imagination

(4) Outstanding ideas

(5) Exceptional organizational talent

(6) Correct tactics and measures

(7) Confidence

Finding all these qualities in a single person is unlikely. But, assembling the elite of the company into a 'think tank' will serve company needs. Setting up the think tank should not be delayed because of concern over expense. Many people apprehend the ratio of overhead to workers and expenses.

Time and money spent in planning are not wasted but pave the way to great profit.

THE 100 MANAGEMENT CHARTS: HOW TO MAKE AND USE THEM

Begin at a Practical and Realistic Point

In the suburbs of Tokyo, there is an electronics company which makes transistor radios and tape recorders. The president of this company became interested in and concerned with new management techniques. He obtained a computer, intending to use it initially for inventory control. Priority was given to obtaining direct material costs, so that individual product costs could be calculated.

11

This turned out to be more difficult than anticipated. There were many types of products and lots were small. In fact, from ten conveyor lines, some 25 to 30 types of products were produced monthly. Obviously, lots could not be assembled.

Let's assume that 500 different components were involved in each type of product. For one month's stock, this meant a total ot 25,000 to 28,000 items. With this stock level, the materials department was really overloaded. Due to export demand, designs had to be completed in very short periods of time. At the same time, the inventory list compiled by the computer included many components not actually in stock. This situation continued for some 15 to 18 months after computer operation was initiated. As computer operation during this period was not sufficient, material ledgers with manual entries also had to be maintained. Use of the computer did not reduce the number of personnel required. Actually, the system became more and more cumbersome.

Eventually, everyone concerned realized that this computer operation was impractical. For a company of its size (500 employees) the monthly computer bill came to around ¥1,000,000. Regrettably, a time came when the company was on the verge of giving up its computer. The manager of the accounting department, who was a management consultant, had been waiting for this moment. According to him, the time was not right for computerized inventory control, but the computer could be used for salary and accounts receivable calculations. After completion of programming, which required a month or two, salary calculation was shifted to the computer. Immediately, the work of four accountants was cut in half. Next, the accounts receivable problem was attacked, with equally gratifying results. All arguments against the computer collapsed.

From this example we can immediately perceive the underlying lesson: Begin at a reasonable and practical point.

To obtain full benefit from the 100 management charts, a coherent accounting system, covering the entire company, must exist.

Business activities cannot proceed as in a university laboratory. Business conditions and surroundings are quite different and furthermore, they are constantly changing. In business, there are limits as to what one may do. In an already developed final output system, initial activities must be limited to those areas which are accessible. From them, we may proceed to overhauling the entire system.

Report Control and Forms Management

Revamping the accounting and reporting system (a prerequisite to preparation of the 100 management charts) is a must, and directly relates to logical business management and business prosperity. As a starter, the *report control master sheet* should be prepared as follows.

1. Report control symbol	2. Name of report	3. Objective	4. Form space	5. Due date	6. Addressee

Originator		9. Hold time	10. Original material	11. Revisions	12.
7. Supervisor	8. Expediter				

This approach brings together the various reports presently being used in all departments and strata of the company, so that information concerning designations, objectives, due dates, addresses, and originators may be examined. Examinining these reports one by one will tell us whether they are directly or indirectly connected with the 100 management charts.

The next step is deciding whether or not all of the present reports are necessary. Reports having borderline value should be eliminated. There may be cases of duplication or partial duplication. Such reports should be either redesigned to eliminate duplication, or combined.

To smooth the flow of reports, originators, addresses, and due dates, where possible, should be rationalized. Simplification should be a guiding rule. In short, overhaul of the report system should be thorough. In addition to deletion, consolidation, re-arrangement, and simplification, proposed revisions should be included in the list, to provide information which may be used in standardizing the reports. Do not forget new reports required for preparation of the 100 management charts. The final step consists of assigning report control numbers (first column). Here, then, we have the foundation for a workable report system which will support the management programme described in this book.

The Management Data Book

Responsibility for preparation of the 100 management charts falls on the general staff, which submits analysis to top management. At the same time, however, the various departments in the company must be made aware of the value of management charts, by means of a suitable promotion programme. This step is necessary so that full cooperation may be obtained. In addition, ideas which may be useful in the solution of problems should be collected from all levels of the organization. Development of a management data book, which may be used for internal promotion of the management chart programme is also important.

PROCEDURES FOR PREPARING A MANAGEMENT DATA BOOK FROM 100 MANAGEMENT CHARTS

Definition of Management Data Book

1. The management data book contains information which helps top management to make decisions. The management data book can be said to correspond to the commander's data book (containing systematic information on tactical stratagems) which a commander at army headquarters uses.

   Objectives include:

   a. Preparation of management data in summary form, rounding off figures to a limited number of significant digits.

   b. Maintaining data in up-to-date form, so that properly timed management decisions may be made.

   c. Intuitive grasp of the status of management, so that proper management decisions may be made.

   d. Giving meaning to the internal control system, so that reports going to management can be assembled in management book form.

   e. Providing all management personnel with coherent uniform data, so that serious differences of opinion are minimized.

2. The management data book is a means by which the state of management can be determined, through systematic, logical organization of statistical data.

Contents of Management Data Book

The following policies should be observed in compiling the management data book:

1. Number of management charts should be limited to a minimum which will enable top management to make optimum decisions and to control company activities.

2. The present report system should be redesigned to conform to the minimum heading requirement.

3. The management data book should be oriented toward managers and higher ranking personnel.

4. In the preparation of original reports, the administrative staff of all departments should participate. The planning department (general staff) chief should be responsible for drafting and editing.

5. Initially, the management data book should be prepared on a quarterly basis. Later, as the system develops, a switch to monthly preparation may be made.

6. The management data book is based on actual data and projected plans. Left hand pages show interpretation and explanation of objectives. Right hand pages present all necessary graphic charts.

7. The management data book is a summary. It should be limited to the 100 management charts, so that it does not become unwieldy.

8. After the management data book has been prepared and distributed, arrangement should be made for early conferences among the personnel concerned. The design (planning) department (general staff) chief should be responsible for oral presentation of the data to top management. Top management should allow all concerned to participate in discussions.

9. The management data book is primarily intended for the president and top management. To bolster morale among low ranking personnel, however, distribution to everyone with a managerial title is desirable.

Chapter 2

CHARTS RELATING TO GENERAL MANAGEMENT

Management in general – Unification of management control and planning of management strategy

Management data show the actual state of activities and location of problems in the various fields of management. Most figures are expressed in monetary values, the standard measurement throughout the business world.

They clarify the complicated array of ever-changing individual management factors and can sometimes summarize them on the macro scale. When figures are analyzed and dissected systematically, the intrinsic interest and drama of management come alive.

As you can see the *organic chart of general management tools*, the techniques dealt with in managerial accounting appear frequently. In the system of techniques relating to general management, I have tried to cover general management thoroughly and widely, with managerial accounting as an axis going beyond the sphere of accounting techniques. Managerial accounting is an arithmetic function with profit projections, budget control, cost control and management analysis as the main tools. But general management here is dealt with more strategically, including marketing, sales, production control, IE, organization and personnel affairs, and relations with various other fields of management in addition to managerial accounting techniques.

For example, when we try to construct a product mix scenario by employing a marginal profit chart, if we have no concrete data on product life cycles, market-creating efficiency, merchandising, and utilities relating to the product, the completed "product mix" scenario has little value.

Cost control is an excellent system, combining cost accounting techniques with scientific management ideas. But however excellent it may be, it is of little value from the business point of view unless it is related to profit. For management to know how much it can lower production costs and how advantageously it can compete in a vigorously contested market, is more important than how precisely and accurately they can determine costs and prices. Though we are using the same basic figures, if we don't know how to treat cost reductions or how to employ VA or IE in order to effect cost reductions, we are losing some of the potential for improved profits.

Therefore, here we employ the same accounting techniques, but introduce general management considerations. The tables and charts mentioned here are ones from which we can draw strategic conclusions. Therefore, in general management techniques involving data calculations, we can only get a limited idea of management requirements by merely employing figures.

SEE, PLAN, DO

In order to obtain new ideas for managerial improvement and strategic planning, begin by looking directly at the realities of the situation. In this part of general management, everything begins with direct evaluation.

Of course, there is a management cycle, and even if you begin with the 'see, plan and do' method, you must repeat it continually in your daily management control. Here, for example, we analyze the cycle in order to achieve managerial improvement.

ORGANIC CHART OF GENERAL MANAGEMENT TOOLS

The chart is divided into parts by two break lines. The top is the 'see' area, namely the area of past results and analysis of the present situation. The second is the 'plan' area, the area where strategic targets and plans were established by freely employing creative ideas based on actual situation analysis.

Next is the 'do' area, to lead the staff to carry out projects to reach goals.

Area 1.

(1) *Profit and loss graph.* Track and dynamic life of the enterprise through the previous fiscal term. This indicates, in fact, the results of management in the previous term. We not only look at it as we would a formal balance sheet, but also trace its movement in the form of a graph so that we can appreciate it visually. By doing so, we can directly analyze the causes of low profit, the factors related to high cost items, etc.

Next, draw up a *graphic balance sheet* (2). This is regarded as the face of an enterprise. The profit and loss graph can be considered to be one facial expression, but the balance sheet is a photograph of the face at a certain moment. In that sense, it is static. Through this we can see the health and financial stability of an enterprise and when they are lacking, find out what causes the imbalance.

To make a *management analysis chart* (3), try to analyze the constitution of an enterprise by five dimensional phases. For this purpose, management analysis is performed on the data of the past three years, including

Organic Chart of General Management Tools

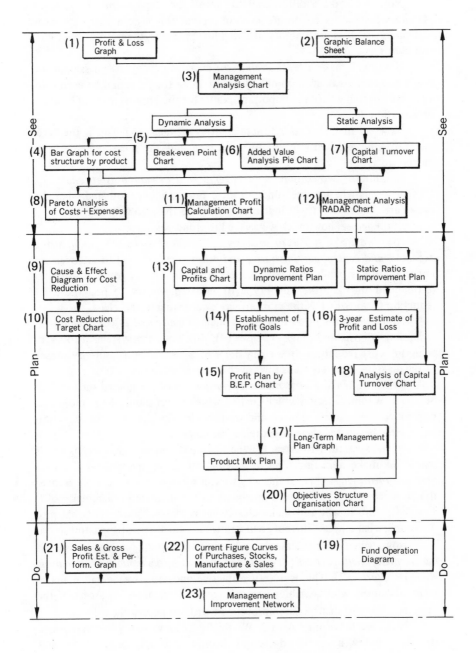

retroactive comparisons and inter-enterprise comparisons.

Now, we make a differential *bar graph for cost structure by product* (4) and we show its composite ratio in the bar graph. Some concrete ideas will emerge such as profitability of individual products, the possibility of cost reductions, etc.

Next, let's make a *break-even point chart* (5). What are our sales at the profit and loss break-even point? By ascertaining the form and behaviour of costs we can find where the important points for the improvement of business organization lie.

Now we make an *added value analysis pie chart* (6). This is the barometer of the productivity of an enterprise and the measurement of its modernization.

In addition, we compile a *turnover period of capital assets chart* (7). This shows us whether the fund turnover rate is high or low and what the causes are. Moreover, it will indicate, if we raise the revolving rate of a fund to a certain degree, how much we can reduce fund costs.

Also we make a *Pareto analysis of production costs, manufacturing expenses, and general administrative and selling expenses* (8) to discover the important items involved in cost reduction. Although not going so far as to recommend the 'kill the boss' type of solution, we try to find the chief reduction factor which is the most effective according to this chart.

Now, we move into Area 2 and make a *cause and effect diagram for reduction of costs and other expenses* (9), this being the system of tools for achieving cost reduction. If we can determine a suitable measure by means of the diagram, concrete steps toward cost reduction can be taken.

Next, we make a *cost reduction targets chart* (10) based on the data obtained. We must decide which cost of which items should be reduced and how much they can be reduced and who should take charge of the reduction work. Here begins the stage of strategic planning.

Now, we return to Area 1. When a product-wise cost analysis (8) is made, we make a marginal profit calculation graph and extend it into a *marginal profit chart* (11). In this way we can see exactly how fast we recover the fixed costs and how this contributes to the increase in marginal profit. For the future it will also make clear what composite products (what products and what amount thereof) will contribute most to profit maximization.

Now, when all the data have been presented like this, we use the *management analysis chart* (3) again and make it into a *management analysis RADAR chart* (12). This is a very attractive and effective overall management diagonsis, which enables top management personnel to ascertain the important parts of managerial improvement without leaving their desks.

Now, we move into Area 2. We finally make various plans and create strategies, and with the firm decision to avoid past errors, the real techniques of management begin here.

First, we draw up a *capital and profits chart* (13). When we are setting our profit goals, the past relation between total capital and operating profit makes us think in a time continuum. This technique corresponds to the deductive method in the setting of profit targets.

We must calculate a *table for establishing profit goals* (14). What would be the fairest and most appropriate profit rate and profit amount? Attack this problem from three angles, using deductive, semi-inductive and inductive methods. Finally we move into the stage of making a *chart for profit plan* (15). Here a *cost reduction target chart* (10) has been made and a *marginal profit chart* (11) has also been completed. Now we are in the position of having suitable conditions for actually establishing the profit goals.

By this technique the possible profit, the profit goals and fixed costs each will be finalized.

Next, a product mix plan is made. In the marketing sphere, linear programming is applied to this question. The basic principles and the way of making the chart are explained.

Going back a little, by the management analysis RADAR chart, an improvement programme for all ratios in dynamic and static state can be made. An *estimated profit and loss statement* and an *estimated balance sheet* (16), including a ratio improvement programme, should, if possible, be designed on a long-term basis of three, five and ten years. However, for the time being, we shall only make them for the near term. Here the *profit plan* (15) and the product mix plan must be well coordinated.

If the B/S and P/L can be estimated for a five-year period, a *long-term management plan graph* (17) needs to be made. This is tantamount to illustrating the future on paper. If you show this graph to your employees, they can anticipate how their living standards will go up and thus they can individually build up their own concepts of the future. Of course, the size of the enterprise, sales, costs, profits and income sources are all pictured.

Here, we return to a short-term plan (for the near term only). In accordance with the progress of a static ratio improvement plan, we make an *analysis of capital turnover chart* (18). From this, we obtain accurate hints about how money, the lifeblood of an enterprise, flows and stays fixed and about dangers existing in the fund composition of an enterprise and any signs of weakening of its financial health.

A target structure organization chart can now be constructed. This technique will most skillfully utilize target management. The total goals of the organization are related to the targets of individual persons. Moreover, it becomes apparent that attainment of the individuals' targets can lead to the satisfaction of individual interests and desires. Here ends Area 2 of strategic planning. Hereafter, only the process of Area 3 remains to be developed. In order to determine actual achievement a *graph of sales and gross profit estimate and performance* (21) is made next. This is made by the triangular graph method, which also constitutes a shrewd method for volume control of purchases, stock, production and sales on a graph showing *curves of current purchases, stocks, manufacturer and sales* (22).

When a *fund operation diagram* (19) is made, the movement of daily operating funds can be visually appreciated, and in this way we can firmly maintain the three major pillars of an enterprise, human achievement (20), the flow of goods (21) and the flow of money (18).

Last comes a *management improvement programme Gantt chart* (23). With this the integrated whole of the management improvement programme is revealed. Here, with the 'how' for achieving the 'what', the company starts en bloc on its own improvement programme.

1.   A PROFIT AND LOSS GRAPH

Purpose

The figures of a profit and loss statement often do not make the actual profit and loss situation clear. Even those familiar with statistics are often penny wise and pound foolish. If the profit and loss data are shown on a graph, mistakes and misunderstanding can be minimized. Furthermore, what should be done becomes evident, e.g., what item costs should be reduced first in order to enhance profits.

How to draw this graph

First look at the total sales, gross profit, operating profit, nonoperating profit, recurring profit and special profit on the profit and loss statement. Make the highest reading of the ordinate the total amount of these profits. Break down expenditure as shown on the sample and your graph is ready. Round off figures to thousands.

The graph's relationship with other documents

First of all, various documents regarding settlement of accounts must be complete. Take the profit and loss statement from the documents and base the graph on the statement. This graph is good for presenting essentials before you prepare the management analysis chart, which will be explained later.

How to use the graph

As this chart is a graphic presentation of profit and loss in reporting style, giving you the structure of the statement at a glance, it is an educational tool (especially for managers of the enterprise). The graph shows the reader the amount of profit in various sectors (such as gross profit, operating profit, recurring profit, profit for the current term, etc), thus showing where the emphasis of management is placed. This offers a much more effective means of assisting management's decision-making than traditional financial statements.

(1) Profit and Loss Graph

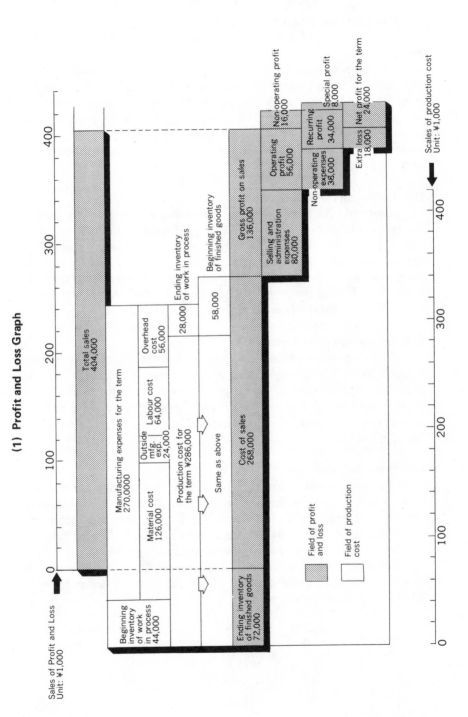

[CHART 1]

2. THE GRAPHIC BALANCE SHEET

Purpose

The purpose is similar to that of the previous graph of profit and loss. The only difference is that the profit and loss graph gives you the dynamic phase of an enterprise's accounting, while this graph presents a static phase in terms of credit and debt. This graph will clearly show you structural ratios of owned capital or of current assets and fixed assets, and you can obtain a general idea of the stability or healthiness of the financial condition of the business.

How to draw up the balance sheet

First make the highest reading of the ordinate of the graph the same as the figures at the bottom of your balance sheet, i.e., the totals of assets (debit) and capital (credit). Use either side of the centre line (parallel to the ordinate) for assets and capital, breaking down sections for detailed items as shown on the sample sheet. If, as in this case, the readings are made identical to those of the previous graph, you will be able to use both charts to establish the turnover ratios of capital and of various assets.

Relationship with other documents

This graph is a visible static analysis of a business accounting. If various turnover rates are studied by looking both at this graph and at the graph of profit and loss, activities of capital can be discerned. If the balance sheet graph is used alone, it is easy to evaluate various ratios showing stability such as structural ratios of various assets or liabilities, current ratios, quick ratios, or fixed ratios.

How to use this sheet

The sheet makes it possible to determine the cause of a low turnover ratio of gross capital. If the area for accounts receivable is comparatively large, it means the turnover rate is low. To raise it, strict accounts receivable control may be needed to shorten the period of credit. If the area for work in process is large, it means a low turnover rate for such goods.

To correct the situation, the manufacturing plan should be revised to shorten production time. With regard to the credit side, similar observations between different items may be made.

(2) Graphic Balance Sheet

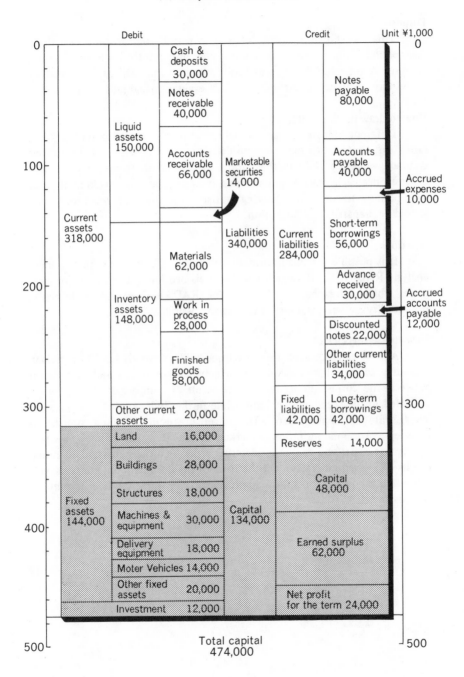

[CHART 2]

25

3. MANAGEMENT ANALYSIS CHART

Purpose

This is a statistical chart, designed to permit comparison over a three-year period of the various ratios which play important roles in management analysis. A total of 26 different ratios are given in a well adjusted, systematized way, to allow five different kinds of evaluation and judgement.

How to draw up this chart

Different kinds and sizes of industries may require different types of ratios, but those ratios that are considered most universal, or of the greatest common value are given in the sample. It is desirable to prepare this chart at least once each year. A blank form should be printed on the kind of paper that permits tracing after entering statistics or other information. Copies should be prepared for distribution.

Relations

It is possible for this information to be transferred to the management analysis RADAR Chart, which will be explained later. The five major categories which correspond to those in the RADAR Chart are productivity, profitability, activity, stability, and growth possibility.

How to use this chart

As has been indicated, there are three kinds of comparison: Comparison according to time factors, comparison between enterprises and comparison between the corresponding ratios. The result of comparing time factors is indicated in the 'Tendency' column while in the 'Index' column appears the average rate within an industry. The judgement resulting from a comparison between corresponding ratios is marked in the 'Remarks' column. By preparing this chart, you can easily determine the financial status and operating results of a given enterprise. On the basis of the information it contains, you can establish ratios for future improvement for three to five accounting periods ahead.

(3) Management Analysis Chart

	Business ratio	Term 17		Term 18		Term 19		Tendency	Index	Remarks
Formula for Judgement productivity	Sales per employee	$\frac{308,134,000}{118}$	2,610,000	$\frac{354,893,000}{127}$	2,780,000	$\frac{491,125,000}{180}$	2,730,000		10,090,000	30% up first
	Net added value per employee	$\frac{132,364,000}{118}$	1,122,000	$\frac{159,930,000}{127}$	1,250,000	$\frac{196,945,000}{180}$	1,094,000 91,000		2,159,000	Value added of material : Subcontracting expenses
	Labor equipment ratio	$\frac{120,733,000}{118}$	1,020,000	$\frac{100,516,000}{127}$	790,000	$\frac{193,792,000}{180}$	1,072,000		2,376,000	More investment than this is risky
	Wage distribution ratio	$\frac{550,684,000}{132,364,000}$	38	$\frac{58,122,000}{159,930,000}$	36.5	$\frac{84,717,000}{196,945,000}$	43%		31.3%	Because of low added value, the ratio is high, even if the labor costs are low
	Wage base	$\frac{50,684,000}{118}$	428,000 36,600	$\frac{58,122,000}{127}$	460,000 38,400	$\frac{84,717,000}{180}$	470,000 39,000		676,000	Too low in the non-ferrous industry
Formula for Judgement profitability	Total capital profit ratio	$\frac{\triangle 2,137,000}{395,805,000}$	△ 0.54%	$\frac{3,950,000}{384,537,000}$	1.024%	$\frac{79,000}{541,230,000}$	0.014%		5.91%	Extremely low
	Sales/gross profit ratio	$\frac{62,495,000}{308,134,000}$	21.3	$\frac{74,817,000}{354,893,000}$	19.4	$\frac{99,118,000}{491,125,000}$	20.1%		22%	Not good or bad, but admin. & selling expenses will be high
	Sales/operating profit ratio	$\frac{12,515,000}{308,134,000}$	3.97	$\frac{23,847,000}{354,893,000}$	6.71	$\frac{21,118,000}{491,125,000}$	4.3%		7%	Ditto
	Net profit/sales ratio	$\frac{\triangle 2,137,000}{308,134,000}$	△ 0.657	$\frac{3,950,000}{354,893,000}$	1.11	$\frac{79,000}{491,125,000}$	0.0161%		5.27	Interest, ¥20 million effected
	Owned capital net profit ratio	$\frac{\triangle 2,137,000}{23,002,000}$	△ 8.73	$\frac{3,950,000}{29,816,000}$	13.2	$\frac{79,000}{23,048,000}$	0.034%		20%	In addition to the low ratio of owned capital, this profit ratio is too low
	Sales adm. expenses & selling exp. ratio	$\frac{49,978,000}{308,134,000}$	16.2	$\frac{50,969,000}{354,893,000}$	14.7	$\frac{77,999,000}{491,125,000}$	15.8%		13%	This item should be thoroughly reviewed
Formula for judgement activity	Total capital turnover ratio	$\frac{308,134,000}{395,805,000}$	77%	$\frac{354,893,000}{384,537,000}$	92	$\frac{491,125,000}{541,230,000}$	90.5%		95%	This ratio too low in comparison with the low labour equipment ratio. Preferably 150%
	Current assets turnover ratio	$\frac{308,134,000}{275,071,000}$	120	$\frac{354,893,000}{284,020,000}$	115	$\frac{491,125,000}{347,437,000}$	141%			This resulted from the low o/a receivable turnover ratio
	Inventory assets turnover ratio	$\frac{308,134,000}{56,558,000}$	5.45	$\frac{354,893,000}{42,240,000}$	9.72	$\frac{491,125,000}{73,236,000}$	6.7			Should maintain the level of previous terms
	a/c receivable turnover ratio	$\frac{308,134,000}{115,624,000}$	2.67	$\frac{354,893,000}{117,289,000}$	2.95	$\frac{491,125,000}{169,656,000}$	2.9			Low. Raise a/c receivable turnover ratio
	Fixed assets turnover ratio	$\frac{308,134,000}{120,733,000}$	2.53	$\frac{354,893,000}{100,516,000}$	3.54	$\frac{491,125,000}{193,792,000}$	2.55			Sales relatively low
Formula for judgement stability	Interest expense ratio	$\frac{19,333,000}{308,134,000}$	6.25	$\frac{22,408,000}{354,893,000}$	6.31	$\frac{20,775,000}{491,125,000}$	4.1%		Under 3%	Short-term borrowing and notes payable too high
	Current ratio	$\frac{275,071,000}{336,448,000}$	81.6	$\frac{284,020,000}{311,829,000}$	93.9	$\frac{347,437,000}{432,396,000}$	80%		130%	Danger
	Quick ratio	$\frac{197,726,000}{336,448,000}$	58.5	$\frac{226,042,000}{311,829,000}$	72.7	$\frac{253,380,000}{432,396,000}$	58.5%		Under 80%	Ditto
	Owned capital ratio	$\frac{23,002,000}{395,805,000}$	5.8	$\frac{29,816,000}{384,537,000}$	7.75	$\frac{23,048,000}{541,230,000}$	4.25%		25	Too rapid growth was expected
	Ratio of fixed assets to long-term capital	$\frac{120,733,000}{55,775,000}$	281	$\frac{100,020,000}{68,925,000}$	146	$\frac{193,792,980}{103,899,000}$	187%		Under 100	Switching short to long resulted in this good ratio. Another pause is expected.
Formula for judgement growth possibility	Sales growth rate	$\frac{308,134,000}{257,004,000}$	120	$\frac{354,893,000}{308,134,000}$	114	$\frac{491,125,487}{354,893,000}$	139%		115	Current equipment is in full operation this year
	Added value growth rate	$\frac{132,364,000}{106,770,000}$		$\frac{159,930,000}{132,364,000}$	121	$\frac{196,945,000}{159,930,000}$	123.5%		120	High rate is normal because of personnel increase
	Labour strength increase rate	$\frac{118}{108}$		$\frac{127}{118}$	108	$\frac{180}{127}$	142%		110	Rapid personnel expansion
	Total capital increase rate	$\frac{395,805,000}{277,806,000}$	70	$\frac{384,537,000}{395,805,000}$	97	$\frac{541,230,000}{384,537,000}$	142%		115	Danger
	Net profit increase rate	$\frac{\triangle 2,137,000}{19,542,000}$		$\frac{\triangle 3,950,000}{2,137,000}$		$\frac{3,579,000}{3,950,000}$	90.5%		110	Net profit gradually decreasing

[CHART 3]

4. BAR GRAPH FOR COST STRUCTURE BY PRODUCT

Purpose

An ordinary statement of the cost of products is a report showing the gross cost of all the products of an enterprise. It does not give you any idea of a detailed cost breakdown by product. Therefore, it is hard to discover where cost reduction is possible and it is impossible to use the Product Mix Strategy (which will be explained later) to increase profits. This graph aims at presenting cost structure ratios in percentages, by product, and at giving suggestions for cost reduction at a glance.

How to draw up this graph

Based on the product-wise production cost table, let the sales amount be 100 per cent. Break down its content into detailed items and plot them on section paper. For that purpose, we shall have to compute the percentage of every item of production cost.

The one shown by each product in the bar graph is a product-wise production cost structure bar graph (4).

The vertical axis indicates the percentages of production cost structure and the horizontal axis can be used for showing the scales of sales volume. The different width of each bar indicates the different volume of sales. Though we can't make out the exact amount of each item of production cost, the scale of each cost component is shown by the dimension, and we can compare it relatively with others.

Relations

This chart shows the cost structure on the basis of gross sales and also reveals the relationship between the manufacturing, administrative and selling costs for each product. Therefore, it can be the basis for a cost reduction plan for all of these costs. Profit is shown as operating profit, except when interest rates or other special costs cannot be disregarded.

How to use this graph

With this graph you can pinpoint where to take action for cost or expenditure reduction. If the percentage of material costs is high, you can take cost reduction action such as VA for material. If labour cost is high, positive action should be taken employing techniques such as IE or work study.

If interest rates are high, some alternate ways of obtaining capital should be devised and the amount of money borrowed from banking facilities should be cut down. In other words, you can pinpoint where best to cut costs.

Further, by drawing the graph product by product, you should be able to identify profitable and unprofitable products.

(4) Bar Graph for Cost Structure by Product

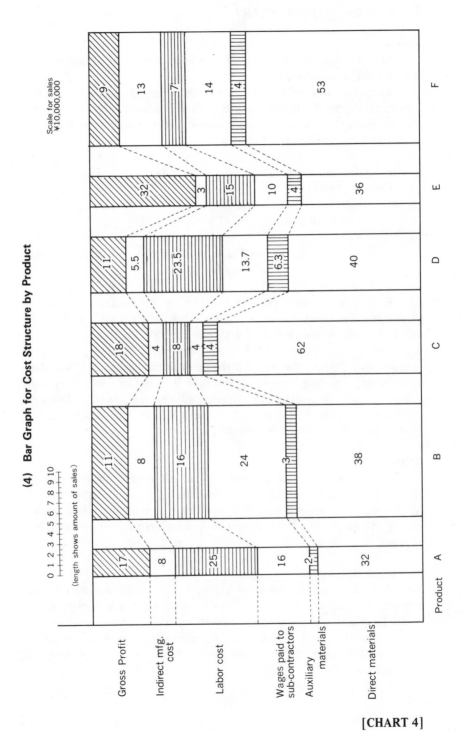

Scale for sales
¥10,000,000

0 1 2 3 4 5 6 7 8 9 10
(length shows amount of sales)

Product	A	B	C	D	E	F
Gross Profit	17	11	18	11	32	9
Indirect mfg. cost	8	8	4	5.5	3	13
Labor cost	25	16	8	23.5	15	7
Wages paid to sub-contractors	16	24	4	13.7	10	14
Auxiliary materials	2	3	4	6.3	4	4
Direct materials	32	38	62	40	36	53

[CHART 4]

29

5.   BREAK-EVEN POINT CHART

Purpose
The total capital-profit ratio is the product of the total capital turnover ratio and sales-net profit rate.

To analyze and evaluate the sales profit rate and to draw up a plan (i.e. a profit plan), this B.E.P. Chart is used. The B.E.P. means the point of total sales at which there is neither profit nor loss. Fewer sales mean losses and greater sales mean profit, as the chart shows.

How to draw up this chart
Refer to chart (5).

Sales	23,900 yen
Fixed costs	8,241 yen
Variable costs	10,985 yen
	(Ratio of Variable cost = variable costs/sales = 46%)

First take the fixed costs, 8,241 yen, on the ordinate and draw a parallel line (AF) to the axis of abscissa. Then take the sales, 23,900 yen, on the axis of abscissa and draw a vertical line BV. On this line, from the point (x), its intersection with line AF, mark off a distance equal to the variable costs, 10,985 yen and call the point reached point V. If you draw a line from A, passing through V, you have the total cost line. Next, draw a line OS from the origin at 45 degrees, this being the sales line. The point of intersection between OS and AV is the B.E.P. The sales amount here is 15,260 yen, where neither loss nor profit is incurred.

Relations
This chart shows relations between current sales, costs, expenses and profits. It is used to evaluate the profitability of an enterprise as a whole. Also, it makes it possible to estimate the sales amount needed to reach a given profit target. The B.E.P. is used to draw up a profit plan (to be explained later).

How to use this chart
With this chart you can see which cost item contributes most to total expenditure, how much reduction can be made in it, which expenses are controllable and which are not. Furthermore, you can decide what method to use, depending on the type of B.E.P., and the pattern of the company's profit position (bankruptcy, chronic deficit, highly profitable or stabilized) may be discerned.

(5) Break-Even Point Chart

Variable expenses	
Material costs	6,114
Wages paid to subcontractors	4,131
Manufacturing expenses	740
	10,985

Gross expenses 19,226
Sales 23,900

This is shown in the following formula

$$8,241 \div (1 - \frac{10,985}{23,900}) = 15,260$$

Fixed expenses	
Personnel expenses	5,193
Plant expenses	561
Gen. adm. & selling expenses	1,349
Depreciation expenses	500
Interest	323
Borrowings repayable within the current term	315
	8,241

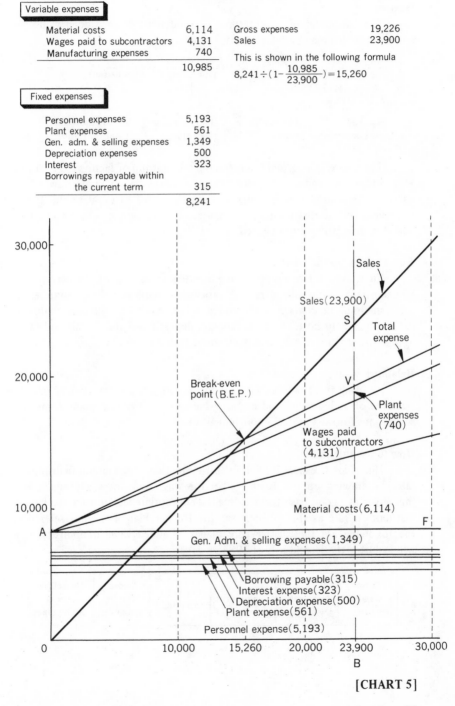

[CHART 5]

6. ADDED VALUE ANALYSIS PIE CHART

Purpose

The barometer of an enterprise's productivity is the added value per employee which may be calculated as follows:

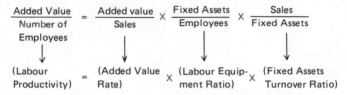

The above is a formula showing the relationship of factors contributing to added value productivity. However, it is necessary to know how added value is distributed among costs and expenses and to evaluate the appropriateness of the distribution. To analytically evaluate it, the pie chart of added value distribution is needed.

How to draw up the chart

First, draw a circle representing the sales amount. Mark the percentages of material cost and subcontractors' processing charges on the circumference. The remaining percentage is the added value. Work out the percentages of net profit, labour cost, financial expense, depreciation and rentals and taxes against the amount of sales and make another distribution of the pie.

Relations

By using these two pie charts at the same time, you can analyze relative contents of added value and added value rates and obtain many hints and suggestions for the physical improvement of an enterprise.

How to use this chart

This chart is especially helpful for evaluation of the labour distribution rate. In drawing up the Rucker Plan for wage and salary administration, this serves as a good basis for deciding the appropriateness of using the labour distribution rate as the constant for the Rucker Plan. For your reference, the following are the relative percentages of added value of industry as a whole during the second half of 1984, in Japan.

Total added value	Net Profit	Labour cost	Financial expenses	Depreciation expenses	Rental and tax & public taxes

(6)　Added Value Analysis Pie Chart (For One Term)

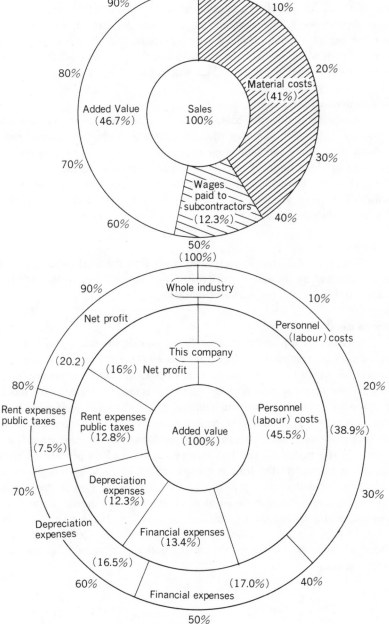

[CHART 6]

33

7. TURNOVER PERIOD OF CAPITAL ASSETS CHART

Purpose

Since the (total capital) turnover ratio has a big influence on the profit rate of (total capital), it is a barometer of the management effectiveness of an enterprise. We have to consider improvement, or ways of shortening the turnover period of total capital. For this purpose, this chart is of great help. In fact, by dividing 365 days by the turnover rate, you can get the turnover period of each individual asset, and see whether it is long or short.

How to draw up the chart

On the debit side of a balance sheet you have total assets with a break-down. By dividing the amount of sales by these assets, the turnover ratios of both total assets and individual assets are calculated. Again, by dividing 365 days by these turnover rates, you can find turnover periods for each of the asset items. Developing these periods on a chart, where the ordinate is graduated in days, you will be able to determine relative turnover periods of assets as shown in chart (7).

Relations

Since the total capital profit ratio is equal to the total capital turnover ratio multiplied by the sales — net profit ratio, raising either of the latter two ratios — or both — will improve profitability.

How to use this chart

Raising the turnover ratio depends on making the numerator larger, or the denominator smaller. If the current assets turnover period is long, try to establish which factor of the assets has the longer turnover period. If, for instance, the turnover period of a/c receivable is longer, greater effort should be made to collect accounts outstanding. If the turnover period for notes receivable is longer, it means the period of credit is relatively long and therefore negotiations should be carried out with your accounting department to shorten the period. If the turnover period of work in process is longer, this means manufacturing time is comparatively long and efforts should be made to shorten it either by IE, or by improved production control. If the turnover period for raw material in stock is long, this indicates too much inventory and measures should be taken to reduce it. If the turnover period of fixed assets is long, it indicates a high modernization level as shown in labour equipment rate. To shorten it, nothing is more effective than increasing sales.

(7)   Turnover Period of Capital Assets Chart

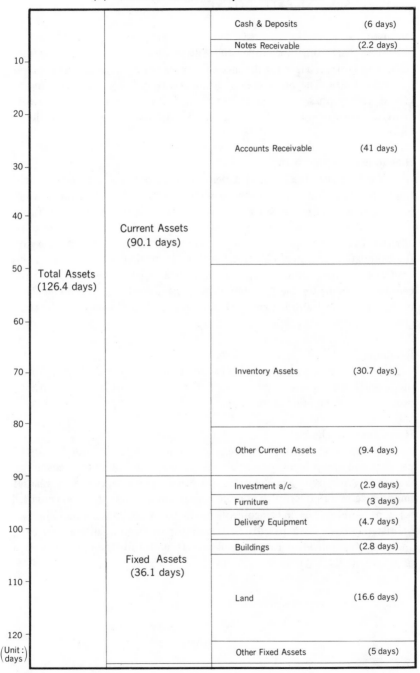

[CHART 7]

8. PARETO ANALYSIS OF PRODUCTION COST, MANUFACTURING EXPENSES, AND EXPENDITURES

Purpose

The chart, sometimes called the ABC analysis chart, shows all expenses (including business costs, for the sake of completeness) in bar graphs arranged in order of size. The purpose is to group relatively larger cost items and to give special emphasis to their management and control. The idea is to concentrate management efforts on significant cost items, leaving minor items untouched.

How to draw up the chart

First, arrange the larger cost items in order of size and draw bar graphs for them. Next, draw a line showing the cumulative total from the first bar to the last, so that gross expenditure is obtained. Then make the gross figure 100 per cent and draw a line at the 80 per cent level, parallel to the axis of abscissa. Draw a vertical line from the point of intersection of this line with the cumulative total line. Call group A those items that fall to the left of this vertical line. In the same way, another vertical line is drawn on the 95 per cent point. Items on the left side of this line are called group B and those on the right side are called group C. All items are thus divided into the three groups —A, B and C.

Relations

This is a cost graph according to each product as previously mentioned, modified to meet strategic purposes. If this kind of chart includes individual products, it will be more useful.

How to use this chart

Group A accounts for 80 per cent of total expenses, group B for 15 per cent and group C for only 5 per cent. However, the number of cost items is generally reversed. Knowing this, we can make management by relative importance more effective. It is more convenient if different colours are used for controllable items and uncontrollable items. When considering reduction of material costs, if a pareto chart is prepared covering all material costs and costs for individual parts, it will be very useful for the implementation of value analysis (VA).

(8) Pareto Analysis of Production Cost, Manufacturing Expenses and Expenditures

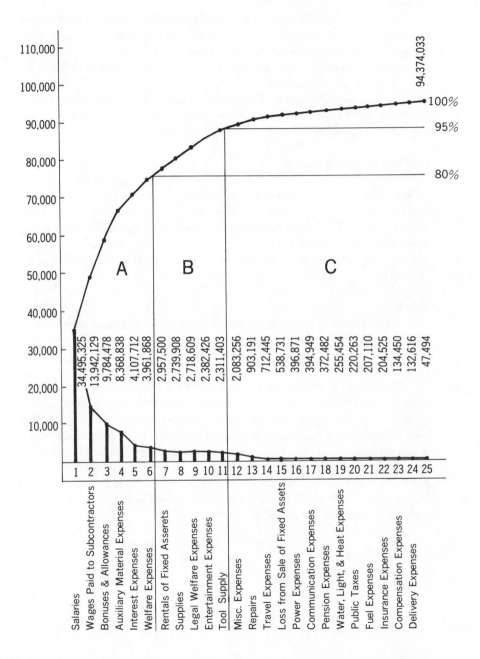

[CHART 8]

9. THE CAUSE AND EFFECT DIAGRAM FOR REDUCTION OF COSTS AND OTHER EXPENSES (ISSUE TREE)

Purpose

The cause and effect diagram systematically shows various factors contributing to an intermediate or a final effect. Furthermore, it indicates mutual relationships between factors similar to the relationships between the trunk, the branches, and the twigs of a tree. The cause and effect diagram may be drawn up for rejected products, delayed delivery, etc. The diagram here aims at cost reduction. Though this diagram lists active methods to achieve final cost reduction, it may be used to show the causes of cost increase which can lead to alternative, corrective action.

How to draw up the diagram

There are two methods of listing factors (causes and effects). One is to write down all the factors you can think of. Then, using a number classification method, group them into larger factors, medium size factors and smaller factors. The other method is to list all major factors first and then group these into medium size factors and the medium size factors into smaller factors. With either of these methods you can easily draw up a diagram like chart (9).

Relations

This diagram enables one to plan a feasible cost reduction programme which can be integrated into a regular operational system.

How to use this chart

By looking at this diagram you can establish what costs can be reduced easily and effectively. It may be convenient to establish the structural ratios of each major factor (in this case the largest classification items of costs).

Priorities and responsibilities should be decided for each of the cost reduction items. If, at this time, a cost reduction programme is developed, cost reduction becomes more effective than if each item is administered independently. It is always important for a plan not to fail midstream simply because the five W's and one H (why, what, where, when, who and how) have not been clearly prescribed.

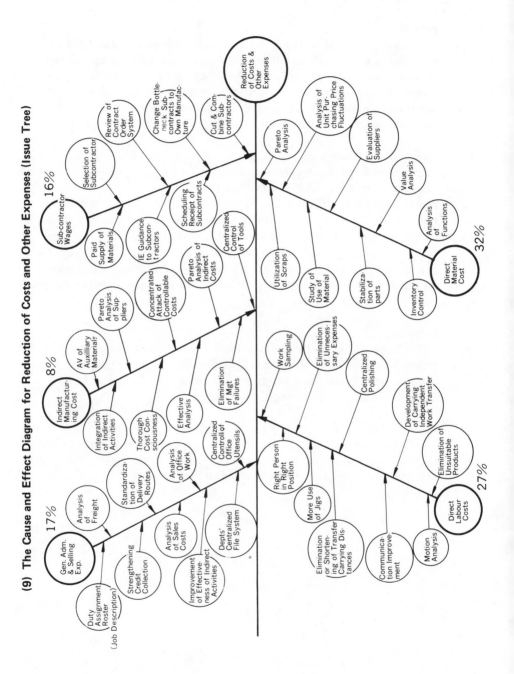

(9) The Cause and Effect Diagram for Reduction of Costs and Other Expenses (Issue Tree)

[CHART 9]

39

10.   COST REDUCTION TARGET CHART

Purpose

Essentially, cost reduction should be an overall concern of all employees. Workers can and should have their cost consciousness raised. Targets for cost reduction need to be specified. Further, they ought to be allocated on an individual basis. Unless these targets are specifically assigned in detail, they will never progress beyond the verbal stage because everyone will vainly hope that someone else will take care of it.

How to draw up this table

The table of cost reduction targets aims at clarifying who must reduce what, when, where and by how much. The cost reduction target chart (10), is only an example. Different companies will develop different charts to suit their needs. On the basis of a chart like the one shown, each department should be able to make its own detailed format. The 30 per cent increase from the previous year, indicated in the second column, is arbitrary. Of course, there is no reason for every item to show a 30 per cent increase since variable costs, like sales costs, increase while fixed expenses do not change in proportion to sales increases.

Relations

Unless you know by how much costs will go down when the profit plan is drawn up, based on the B.E.P. for the year, the profit plan itself is on shaky ground. Later, when the target system structural chart is drawn up, the value of this chart will be again recognized.

How to use this table

When the target system chart is ready, this chart and the cost reduction causes and effect diagram are issued to all members of the organization. The first stage of the cost reduction programme is now underway.

(10) Cost Reduction Target Chart

		130% of previous performance		Objectives for the term		Amount of reduction		In charge of reduction	
			%		%		%	Position	Name
Gross sales		150,000	100	150,000	100	—	—	Manager, Business Operations	Watabe
Direct Material Cost	Principal material cost	57,000	38	54,000	36	3,000	2	Manager, Manufacturing	Yuasa
	Auxiliary material cost	3,000	2	2,250	1.5	750	0.5	Chief, Manufacturing Section	Kitayama
	Supplementary material cost	2,250	1.5	2,250	1.5	—	—	Chief, Purchasing Section	Taguchi
Direct labour expenses		45,000	30	45,000	30	—	—	Manager, Manufacturing	Yuasa
	Wages paid to sub-contractors	9,000	6	8,250	5.5	750	0.5	Chief, Subcontract Branch	Koizumi
	Expendable tools & supplies	1,050	0.7	750	0.5	300	0.2	Chief, Manufacturing Section	Kitayama
Direct Expenses	Power expenses	1,800	1.2	2,250	1.5	(+)450	(+)0.3	Chief, Manufacturing Section	Kitayama
	Repair expenses	450	0.3	300	0.2	150	0.1	Repair Branch	Todata
	Other direct expenses	450	0.3	300	0.2	150	0.1	Chief, Manufacturing Section	Kitayama
Indirect Manufacturing Expenses	Indirect labour expenses	3,000	2	2,250	1.5	750	0.5	Manager, Manufacturing	Yuasa
	Cost of parttime workers	1,500	1	1,200	0.8	300	0.2	Chief, Manufacturing Section	Kitayama
	Other indirect expenses	1,500	1	1,200	0.8	300	0.2	Chief, Manufacturing Section	Kitayama
Gross profit		24,000	16	30,000	20	6,000	(+)4	Manager, Manufacturing	Yuasa
General Admin. & Selling Expenses	Research & trial production expenses	6,300	4.2	6,000	4	300	0.2	Chief, Engineering Section	Takagi
	Salaries for researchers	2,550	1.7	2,550	1.7	—	—	Chief, Engineering Section	Takagi
	Personnel expenses of indirect department	3,000	2	2,400	1.6	600	0.4	Chief, General Affairs	Nakada
	Freight	4,500	3	3,000	2	1,500	1	Chief, Business Operations	Okaba
	Advertising & promotional expenses	1,200	0.8	1,200	0.8	—	—	Chief, Administration Section	Seki
	Other gen. admin. & sales expenses	1,500	1	900	0.6	600	0.4	Chief, General Affairs	Nakada
Operating profit		7,500	5	16,500	11	(+)9,000	(+)6	Manager, Business Operations	Watabe
Non-Operating Expenses	Interest expenses	3,000	2	3,000	2	—	—	Chief, Accounting Section	Ishii
	Discount expenses	3,000	2	2,250	1.5	750	0.5	Chief, Business Operations Section	Shimamoto
Recurring Profit		1,500	1	11,250	7.5	(+)9,750	(+)6.5	President	Yokoi

[CHART 10]

11.   PRODUCT WISE MARGINAL PROFIT CHART

Purpose

To calculate profit ordinarily, we subtract total cost from sales for a given period, i.e., total sales — total cost = profit. With the new type of cost accounting system, known as "direct costing", what is to be subtracted from total sales is not total cost but variable cost, i.e., total sales — variable cost = profit. This profit is called the marginal income. The marginal income is fixed cost plus profit. For example, suppose the price of a product is 100 yen and 80 yen is its variable cost. The remaining 20 yen is what you have to collect as fixed costs; when the fixed costs have been collected, the balance is profit. In other words, the fixed costs and profit are one and the same. This means that when the amount of sales reaches the B.E.P. the fixed costs are recovered completely with this marginal income, and actual profits start.

How to draw up the chart

First, plot the total amount of fixed costs on the ordinate downward from the zero origin and draw a line parallel to the axis of abscissa. Next, plot on the axis the sales of each product, in the order of magnitude of their rate of marginal income, which is determined separately. Draw vertical lines through these points. Then draw a fixed costs collection line from the origin on the base line up toward the upper right corner. The angle of this line is to be ascertained as the tangent of sales against marginal income. When the line is connected through the last product, your chart is complete. Where this line of collection intersects with the original axis of fixed costs is the B.E.P. When sales increase beyond this point, profits also increase, as chart (11) shows.

Relations

Later, this will be the basis for the Products Mix Programme Chart.

How to use this chart

The previous B.E.P. Chart was prepared on the basis of gross products and is useful only for general evaluation. This chart, however, will show graphically the profitability of each item. Furthermore, because the products are arranged in the order of their marginal income rate, you can obtain a rough idea of what would result from using a scale, if you extend sales of the items indicated on the left side of the chart.

(11) Product-wise Marginal Profit Chart

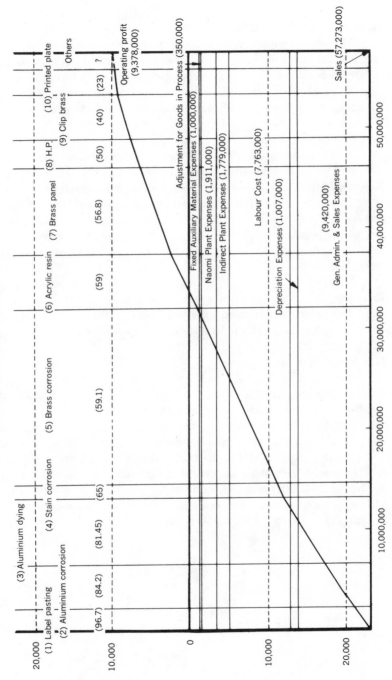

[CHART 11]

43

12. MANAGEMENT ANALYSIS RADAR CHART

Purpose

This chart analyzes management to permit one to ascertain at a glance the financial status of an enterprise. It shows the reader both the strengths and the weaknesses of the enterprise and provides top management with clear-cut guidance on how to improve their business. It also establishes a very strong motive for implementing management improvement.

How to draw up the chart

As is shown in chart (12), to make a judgment from five points of view each point includes five or six major management ratios. Each ratio is evaluated in five grades: Very good, good, normal, bad, and very bad.

There are three methods of evaluating factors: (1) comparison of time periods, (2) comparison with the same types of industries and (3) comparison with a suitable or standard rate. The "Management Guide for Small Industries", prepared by the Small Business Agency, every year, is useful for the second method.

Relations

This radar chart is based on a judgement of the excellence or deficiencies of each of the ratios on the management analysis chart (3).

How to use this chart

The circles for 'normal', 'bad', and 'very bad' grades are shaded in red to emphasise the critical area and the need for improvement. The area produced by the lines outside the 'normal' circle are shaded green and indicate the strengths of the enterprise and may be used as the basis for establishing plans to further strengthen such favourable conditions.

As an analogy, RADAR charts play the role of radar on a ship called the "Enterprise" and show the course of her sailing. It is desirable to draw up this RADAR chart over the period of the past three fiscal terms. The rise and fall of each rate will be shown clearly at a glance by comparing the rate of each period covered by the RADAR chart.

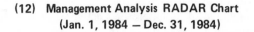

(12) Management Analysis RADAR Chart
(Jan. 1, 1984 — Dec. 31, 1984)

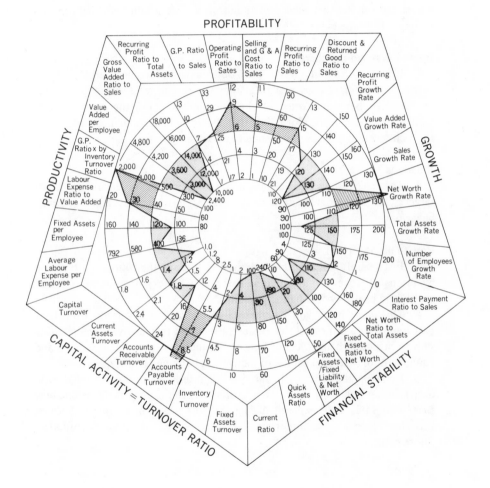

[CHART 12]

13.   CAPITAL AND PROFITS CHART

Purpose
The sum of owned capital and borrowed capital is known as total capital, the lifeblood of an enterprise's activities. It is, therefore, important for an entrepreneur to know historically how the capital funds invested were collected and how profitably they are being used. This chart shows at a glance the relation between capital and profit and it will be of help in estimating profit targets for the future.

How to draw up the chart
Plot total capital on the horizontal axis and earned surplus on the vertical. Then draw lines radiating from the origin, representing percentage relationships between earned surplus and capital. From the balance sheets of the last several years, plot points that show total capital and earned surplus for each term on the chart and connect these points.

Relations
This chart shows basic data and trends for use in calculating profit targets. Also, it provides a basis for evaluating and analyzing past profit behaviour.

How to use this chart
Just as useful information is derived to forecast the course of a typhoon by means of a weather chart, it is helpful to forecast the future status of capital and profit by finding the past trend.

This chart helps you to estimate future capital and profit from their past trends. You can establish past aberrations and then analyze their relationship to business changes, conditions of the industry, investment in plant and equipment, or increased capital or loans from banking facilities.

Knowing that the total capital profit rate is the result of capital turnover rate multiplied by sales — net profit rate, you can try to determine how these two rates have behaved during the past years. In summary, because this chart tracks these important rates chronologically, it helps formulate future plans.

(13) **Capital and Profits Chart (After Tax)**

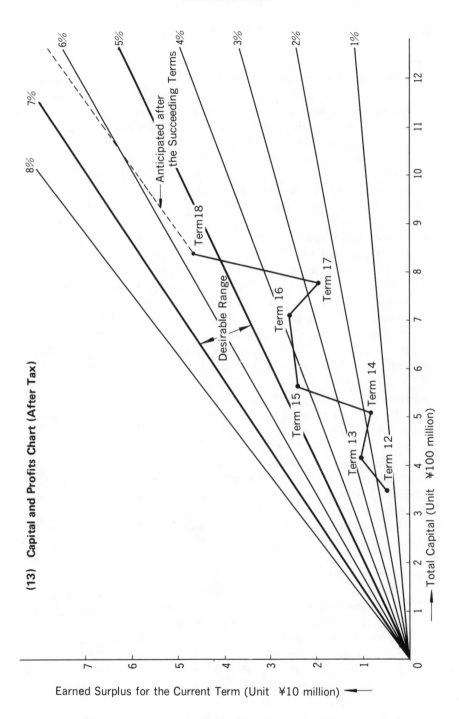

Earned Surplus for the Current Term (Unit ¥10 million) ◄—

— Total Capital (Unit ¥100 million)

8%

7%

6%

5%

Anticipated after
the Succeeding Terms

4%

3%

2%

1%

Term18

Desirable Range

Term 16

Term 17

Term 15

Term 14

Term 13

Term 12

[CHART 13]

47

14. TABLE FOR ESTABLISHING PROFIT GOALS

Purpose
You should not decide the profit goals in your profit plan arbitrarily. They should be reasonable and objective from the viewpoint of conditions and circumstances both inside and outside the business. For estimating profit targets there are three methods: the deductive method, the inductive method and the semi-inductive method.

Apply these methods separately, then determine the amounts and rates of profit that are most appropriate according to the conditions determined by these three methods. This chart is arranged to facilitate such computation, comparison and decision making.

How to draw up the table
It is sufficient to fill in the sample chart with appropriate figures provided you understand the purposes and principles of each method beforehand. The deductive method here means chronological comparison within the enterprise, with other firms in the industry and with the whole industry. The inductive method means analyzing profits logically and the semi-inductive method aims at meeting the practical needs of the enterprise for its survival. On the basis of these computations, plus a measure of intuitive judgement, you should be able to establish a profit target for the year.

Relations
The contents of the capital and profits chart (13) and the management ratios improvement plan, i.e., the management analysis chart (3) and the management analysis RADAR chart (12), should be considered for inclusion when making profit estimates. A marginal profit table by product (14B) and a marginal profit graph by product (14C) will be useful in helping to determine profit goals. These are prepared utilizing the same principles as the marginal profit chart (11).

Upon completion of the profit goals table, a profit plan is to be drawn up by using the B.E.P. chart. (See next section.)

How to use this table
The three factors in the inductive method are the following:
(1) Interest on owned capital
   The capital invested in most businesses consists of owned capital plus borrowed capital. Interest is paid directly on the borrowed capital. The foregone interest on owned capital should also be taken into account as a cost factor. If this capital were not invested in your own business, it would earn interest elsewhere.
(2) Reserves for enterprise risks
   Risks are incurred in any business. Some of them are covered by

(14A) Table for Establishing Profit Goals

Method	No.	Remarks		Amount	%	Total	%
Deductive Method	(1)	Actual total capital profit rate a. Previous year		29,837,000	3.1	/////	/////
		b. Two years ago		79,020,000	6.95	/////	/////
		c. Three years ago		70,494,000	6.2	/////	/////
	(2)	Total capital profit rate of the industry (Management indexes of small businesses)		64,010,000	5.63	/////	/////
	(3)	Total capital profit rate of the industry (Management indexes of small businesses)		86,412,000	7.6	/////	/////
	(4)	Reasonable total capital profit rate and amount obtained through deductive method		/////	/////	79,590,000	7
Inductive Method	(1)	Own capital interest		29,760,000	15	/////	/////
	(2)	Risks of enterprise		18,940,000	2	/////	/////
	(3)	Efforts of enterprise		18,940,000	2	/////	/////
	(4)	Reasonable total capital profit rate and amount obtained through inductive method		/////	/////	67,640,000	
	(5)	Profit before tax=(4)÷(1−Tax Rate)		/////	/////	15,300,000	13.21
Semi-inductive Method	(1)	Corporate Tax=Net profit × tax rate		78,300,000		/////	/////
	(2)	Outside Distribution	Divided	3,600,000	12	/////	/////
			Staff's Bonuses	500,000		/////	/////
	(3)	Company Internal Reserves	Revenue Reserve	30,000,000		/////	/////
			Voluntary Reserve	30,000,000		/////	/////
			Others	0		/////	/////
	(4)	Reasonable total capital profit rate and amount obtained through semi-inductive method		/////	/////	142,400,000	12.52

Note 1: Total capital for the term =   1,137,000,000   3: Capital 30,000,000
     2: Owned capital for the term =   198,400,000

Profit goal amount for the term: 150,300,000 yen (13.21 %)

Reference:
Corporation tax

Tax rates on ordinary income in every business year	Public interest corporations. Cooperative societies		23%
	Ordinary corporations, nonjuridical organizations whose capital		
	amounts to ¥100 million or less	Annual income under ¥3 million	28%
		Annual income over ¥3 million	35%
	Ordinary corporations of capital over ¥100 million		35%
Reduced tax rates on ordinary income distributed as dividends	Cooperative societies & others		19%
	Ordinary corporations		
		Annual income under ¥3 million	22%
		Annual income over ¥3 million	26%
Tax rate on undistributed profit of family corporation	Annual undistributed profit under ¥30 million		10%
	Annual undistributed profit over ¥30 million & under ¥100 million		15%
	Annual undistributed profit over ¥100 million		20%
Tax rate on approved pension funds			10%

Note: Taxation ratios tend to differ year by year, country to country and ratios should be
       amended accordingly.

[CHART 14A]

(14B) Marginal Profit Table by Product

	Product Name / Item	'A'	'B'	'C'	'D'	'E'	Total
Sales		173,500	100,700	97,500	168,900	92,400	633,000
Variable cost	Direct material cost	78,780	23,000	40,690	39,320	42,340	224,130
	Subsidiary material cost	10,150	4,120	8,400	16,970	6,230	45,870
	Direct labour cost	28,200	9,360	30,120	21,480	10,140	99,300
	Power cost	5,400	1,050	3,310	5,800	2,250	17,810
	Subcontractor costs	1,420	9,800	4,770	7,320	2,170	25,480
	Packing expenses	5,800	720	2,150	4,910	3,140	16,720
	Freight	7,350	950	5,280	2,200	2,980	18,760
Subtotal		137,100	49,000	94,720	98,000	69,250	448,070
Variable cost ratio		79.02%	48.6%	97.14%	58.02%	74.94%	70.78%
Marginal income		36,400	51,700	2,780	70,900	23,150	184,930
Marginal income ratio		20.98%	51.4%	2.86%	41.98%	25.06%	29.22%
Marginal income rank		(5)	(1)	(6)	(2)	(4)	(3)
Fixed cost				122,530			

[CHART 14B]

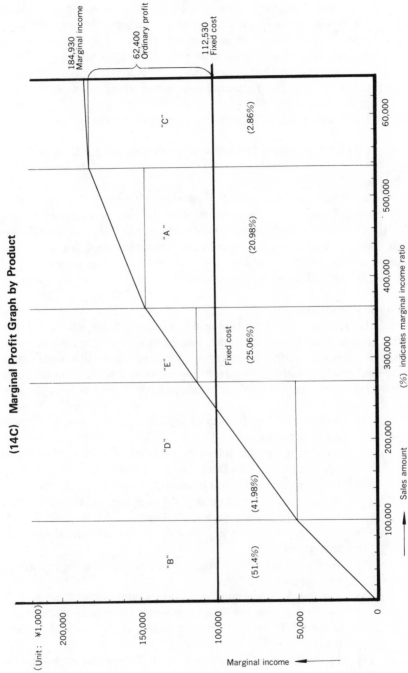

(14C) Marginal Profit Graph by Product

(Unit: ¥1,000)

(%) indicates marginal income ratio

Sales amount

Marginal income

184,930 Marginal income

62,400 Ordinary profit

112,530 Fixed cost

"C" (2.86%)

"A" (20.98%)

"E" Fixed cost (25.06%)

"D" (41.98%)

"B" (51.4%)

200,000 · 150,000 · 100,000 · 50,000 · 0

60,000 · 500,000 · 400,000 · 300,000 · 200,000 · 100,000

traditional, budgetary methods such as insurance premiums, reserves for bad debts or reserves for price fluctuations. However, there are other dangers for which no approved funds are authorized, such as dangers from economic, social or political changes. An enterprise must have reserves to withstand or service such potential costs.

(3)   Others, such as profit resulting from the efforts of the corporate enterprise.

This is pure profit in the universal meaning of the word.

15.   CHART FOR PROFIT PLAN BASED ON THE B.E.P. CHART

Purpose

This chart utilizes the B.E.P. methodology to develop the profit plan. In the B.E.P. chart, profit was evaluated on the basis of the formula: Sales − (fixed costs + variable costs) = profits. Reversing the equation shifts the emphasis to: Profit = sales − (fixed costs + variable costs). The idea is that profit is to be planned in advance and that the two costs are to be controlled within the limit of the amount remaining after deducting profit from sales.

How to draw up the chart

To develop a profit plan using the B.E.P. chart, we must first decide the amount of profit the enterprise requires, then determine the amount of possible sales and thirdly plan to control the fixed and variable costs within the limit of the remainder after deducting the desired profit from sales. The following are the steps involved in preparing a profit chart to serve this purpose:

(1)   Draw a graph with ordinate and abscissa as shown. Both scales are in monetary units.

(2)   Both right and left sides are graduated to show the amount of sales (or production). Draw sales line 1 at 45 degrees.

(3)   Find the maximum possible amount of sales.

(4)   Decide point 2 for planned profit as required in the budget. Plot 1 on the abscissa and draw vertical line 2.

(5)   Draw line 3 after scaling variable cost at the vertical sales line from the bottom.

(6)   Decide the amount of fixed costs and fix it on the left side as axis point 4.

(7)   For line 4, connect the axis point 4 with the profit point 2 on the vertical sales line. The point where line 1 and line 4 intersect is the B.E.P. Above this point there is a profit and below there is a loss.

(8)   The area created by points 0, 4, 2, 3 shows the allowable area for fixed costs.

Relations

For preparation of this chart, the computation of the profit target on the previous page should have been made as accurately as possible.

How to use this chart

The most important factors in planning profit goals are (1) estimated profit, (2) fixed costs, and (3) B.E.P. These are the basic problems of the management policies of an enterprise and comprise the total profit plan itself.

(15)   Chart for Profit Plan

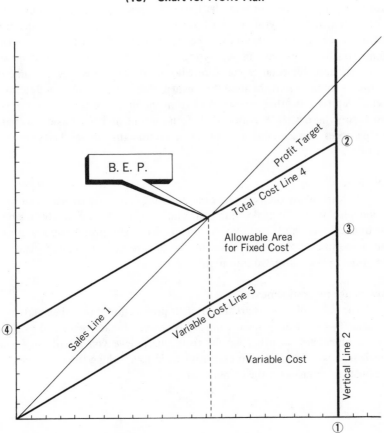

[CHART 15]

53

16. ESTIMATED PROFIT AND LOSS STATEMENT AND BALANCE SHEET FOR 3 YEARS

Purpose

After management ratios are worked out and analyzed, a plan for their improvement should be drawn up. Management ratios should not be merely acknowledged but an aggressive attitude to improve them in the future should be adopted. To achieve desirable management ratios, it is necessary to make at least a three-year estimate of profit and loss and draw up a balance sheet to base future activities on. These three-year projections should contain improvement plans for management ratios. These charts are designed to meet such requirements.

How to make these statements

Forms, as abbreviated as possible, must be prepared in advance of the profit and loss statement and the balance sheet. The starting point is the profit target for each year. If you trace back to sales, gross profit, operating profit, or recurring profit, you will be able to derive the cost of sales, general administrative expenses, nonoperating expenses and nonrecurring losses. From the desirable total capital profit ratio, you can determine the amount of total capital: From the desirable owned capital ratio, you can determine owned capital and other capital: And from the desirable turnover ratio, you can figure the desirable amounts of both current and fixed assets. It is for the purposes of ascertaining these major factors that these charts are summarized.

Relations

This is one of the two phases of the long term management plans i.e., period plan itself. To make this plan you have to prepare in advance both the dynamic and static ratio improvement plans. This plan is also a summary and a shadow of the other phase of the long-term management plan, i.e., the project plan, converted into monetary values.

How to use these statements

The value of these charts lies in their preparation. From their statement of major factors, management can readily discern broad trends and establish general objectives. In other words, these charts give you a bird's eye view, which is very helpful for top management in establishing the objectives and the financial policies for the coming years.

(16A) Estimated Profit & Loss
(From April 1, 1982 to March 31, 1983)

Debit			Credit		
Cost of sales	1,383,300,000	Material cost 1,227,800,000	Net sales	1,530,000,000	Product sales 820,000,000
		Wood freight 60,000,000			Wood sales 485,000,000
		Labour cost 25,500,000			By-products sales 157,000,000
		Wages for sawing 30,000,000			Other sales 68,000,000
		Depreciation expenses 15,000,000			
		Other sales costs 25,000,000			
Gross profit on sales	146,700,000		Gross profit on sales	146,700,000	
Gen. Admin. & selling expenses	47,000,000				
Operating profit	99,700,000		Operating profit	99,700,000	
Non-operating expenses	30,000,000		Non-operating income	7,000,000	
Recurring profit	76,700,000		Recurring profit	76,700,000	
Non-recurring loss	—		Non-recurring profit	—	
Profit before tax	76,700,000				
Corporate tax	36,900,000				
Profit after tax	39,800,000				

[CHART 16A]

(16B) Estimated Balance Sheet
(As of March 31, 1983)

Debit			Credit		
Current assets	635,453,000	Quick assets (Cash & deposits) 286,850,000	Current liabilities	573,700,000	Reserve for refining 133,700,000
		a/c receivable 35,000,000			a/c payable 20,000,000
		Inventory assets 228,509,000			Short-term borrowing 300,000,000
		Other current assets 85,094,000			Other current liabilities 120,000,000
Fixed assets	131,547,000	Buildings (incl. structure) 13,733,000	Reserves	27,000,000	Reserve for uncollectable a/c 6,000,000
		Machines (delivery equipment) 24,703,000			Reserve for price fluctuations 16,000,000
		Land 30,068,000			Reserve for retirement allowance 5,000,000
		Forest 32,951,000	Net worth		Reserve for refining allowances 30,000,000
		Others 10,322,000			Capital 7,500,000
		Intangible fixed assets 9,500			Legal reserve 47,000,000
		Investments 19,770,000			Voluntary reserve 42,000,000
					Profit brought forward 39,800,000
Total	767,000,000		Profit for the term	767,000,000	

[CHART 16B]

17.   GRAPH OF LONG-TERM MANAGEMENT PLAN

Purpose

Because the future has promising possibilities, people not only feel attached to their jobs, but concentrate their abilities and energies on improving them. If the promise is obscured by abstract words or combinations of incomprehensible figures, it won't be very stimulating. For example, chart (17A) may show a fine goal for the five-year management plan. But you need to explain it from all angles, using pictures and graphs to enhance its impact. Chart (17B) is a picture designed to show the future by means of such methods.

How to construct the graph

This is simply a graph which shows the five-year management plan. It should be noted that the graph is not only for top management, but also for all employees to gain a thorough understanding. No difficult charts, tables or words should be used here. Several colours should be used to make the chart attractive.

Relations

This is a visible extension of charts (16A) and (16B). Its basis is the long-term estimated profit and loss statement and balance sheet. On the basis of this, the objectives structure organization chart for each year can easily be prepared.

How to use this chart

This is also a long-term management plan for management and a means of achieving a better relationship with the work force. For this latter purpose, it is preferable to hold an orientation meeting for all employees. A detailed, easy-to-understand explanation should be given on such matters as the relation between the amount of sales and added values, the meaning and composition of the source of wages, using pie charts and other aids. A long-term plan is not a prophecy. It is an objective which all members of the company should cooperatively strive to achieve.

(17A) Five Year Plan Pay Sources,
Size of Personnel & Average Pay

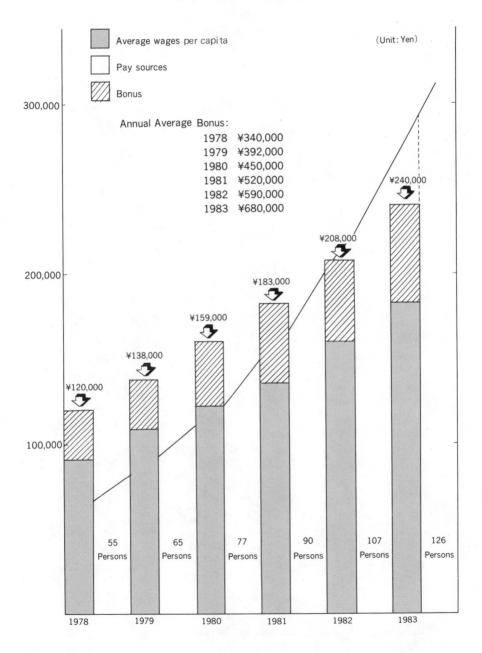

Average wages per capita   (Unit: Yen)

Pay sources

Bonus

Annual Average Bonus:
   1978   ¥340,000
   1979   ¥392,000
   1980   ¥450,000
   1981   ¥520,000
   1982   ¥590,000
   1983   ¥680,000

¥240,000

¥208,000

¥183,000

¥159,000

¥138,000

¥120,000

300,000

200,000

100,000

55 Persons   65 Persons   77 Persons   90 Persons   107 Persons   126 Persons

1978   1979   1980   1981   1982   1983

[CHART 17A]

(17B) Graph of Long-Term Plan
(5 Years)

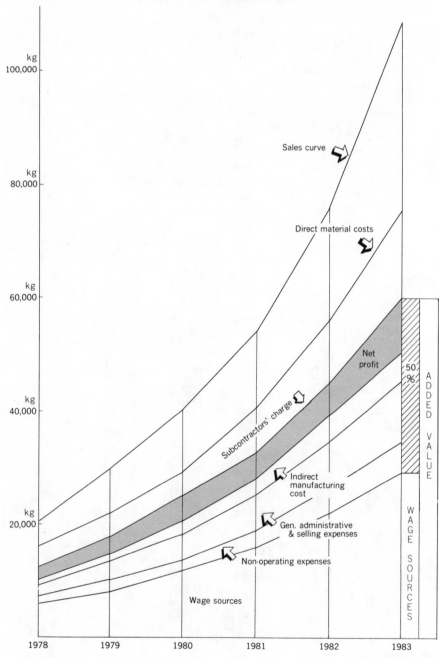

[CHART 17B]

18. CAPITAL TURNOVER ANALYSIS CHART

Purpose

There are some companies which are in the black, but yet are bankrupted while issuing dishonoured bills. This 'bankruptcy in the black' is difficult to comprehend. However, the rule of a capitalistic economy is that when the flow of operating funds stops, the enterprise itself must also stop. Drastic measures may be necessary to prevent such a mishap. When a company is headed toward bankruptcy due to shortage of operating funds, it is common for only the person in charge of operating funds to experience acute concern. Managers of other functional divisions frequently are unaware, ambivalent, or do not feel responsible to initiate corrective action.

Bankruptcy sometimes happens abruptly, to the surprise of everybody. To avoid such sudden death, it is important to check charts continuously to monitor capital turnover.

How to draw up the chart

You can easily see the flow or turnover process of capital in chart (18A). The sample chart shows a one-time flow of funds for ease of understanding. However, the turnover of each item differs, depending on time. If, for example, actual figures of B/S and P/L of the last term were fitted into this chart, you would be able to group the actual flow situation visually.

How to use this chart

In the management of an industrial enterprise, business results (or profitability) and financial status (or security) are the two most critical barometers.

Many managers are indifferent to the analysis of company security, while very enthusiastic in their analysis of data pertaining to sales volume. Of course, as profits rise, security also increases. However, the management of a business is a more complex and integrated operation. Chart (18B) shows 14 barriers to the flow of funds. What countermeasures should be taken to make the flow go smoothly? The answer is to check business management in terms of the items listed on the lower left chart and to make sure nothing necessary is left disregarded concerning the security of the enterprise.

(18A) Capital Turnover Analysis Chart

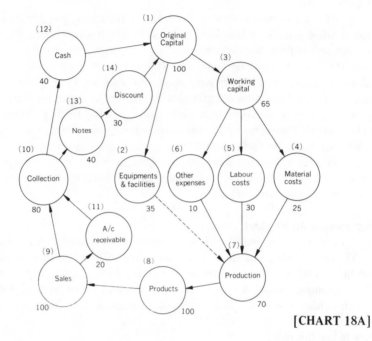

[CHART 18A]

(18B) Fourteen Disruptive Barriers to Smooth Capital Turnover

	Item	Internal factors	External factors
1	Original capital	Small amount of working capital/difficulty in increasing capital	Investment in outside enterprises
2	Equipment investment	Sudden expansion/deviation from adequate size of business operation	Use of short-term funds for equipment
3	Operating funds	Wrong forecasting of demand	Increase short-term borrowing/Rise of burden of interest
4	Materials	Bad design, wasteful materials/poor stock control	Rise of the prices of raw materials/lack of raw materials
5	Labour	Cut in personnel expenses/mass exodus from jobs. Labour dispute.	Rise of personnel expenses/pressure from upper organization
6	Operating expenses	No contribution to the increase of sales/increased operating expenses. (Spenders on office account)	Fixing trend of variable operating expenses/price raising mood
7	Production	No improvement of product design. Poor production techniques	Shortening production time/increasing cost price
8	Products	Reduced prices/poor condition of inventories	Production of new products/competition with imported goods
9	Sales	Ambiguous accounting/concentration on one account	Price-cutting competition
10	Collection	Lack of collection techniques/laziness or dishonesty on the part of collectors	Business depression/government's retrenchment policy
11	a/c receivable	Incomplete a/c ledger/increased amount of a/c receivable	Lengthened credit for a/c receivable and bad debts
12	Cash	Low cash collection rate/selling and poor collection	High interest rates
13	Notes	Lack of techniques for checking credit-worthiness	Long-term notes/receipt of dishonored notes
14	Discount	Illegal loans, accommodation notes	Increased interest rates

[CHART 18B]

19. FUND OPERATION DIAGRAM

Purpose

As mentioned previously, a lack of operating funds may not provoke alarm, but it certainly constitutes a danger signal for business and can also threaten the very existence of an enterprise. In order to avoid this situation and to stabilize the security of business finance, the flow of funds and their sufficiency or insufficiency should be constantly reviewed. To avoid the shock of imminent bankruptcy, you should not only utilize the financing table which every company prepares, but also go a step further by forecasting your finances. A diagram method will help to determine them concretely and thoroughly. The following operating fund diagram not only ensures the safety of business finance, but also the economic efficiency of the use of funds. In short, it will tell you how to get the maximum utility out of the minimum possible sum.

How to make the diagram

First of all, make a table as shown in (19A). This means making estimates of operating income and expenditure for a period of one year in advance.

It is desirable to make the estimates as scientifically as possible by employing secular trend fluctuation analyses, or seasonal sales fluctuation analyses, based on past results. In this case you should forecast the ratios to each other of cash, credit and bills receivable in your collections, which are the source of your income. In the case of purchasing, you must forecast the ratio to each other of cash, credit and bills payable in your payments after fully studying the matter.

Complete the fund operation table estimates including monthly salaries and various operating expenses, omitting nothing, as in (19A). The result of this is to be plotted in the fund operation diagram of (19B). Operating income and expenditure are plotted in the lower half. This is the form in which lines (8) and (18) of table (19A) are transferred.

Next, draw the balance line of cumulative operating expenditures subtracted from cumulative operating income in the upper half, and have the horizontal axis indicate zero. Sufficiency and insufficiency of funds fall above and below the horizontal axis. The plot below the horizontal axis visually shows the extent of lack of funds. If you read the scale on the vertical axis, you can easily determine how short you are of funds.

Relations

Here, the actual state of the turnover of funds, especially the flow of current funds, which we understood conceptually in (18A) and (18B), has been made apparent. The profit and loss budget and the fund budget are two major pillars of business administration and management. If you have no knowledge of the state of funds, you are not qualified to perform strategic management.

How to read them

What information can be derived from a fund operation diagram like this? What measures should be taken? What you can determine from this diagram is that funds will be short from April to September, except during July. You need ¥30,000,000 during the three months April, May and June and ¥60,000,000 during September. In brief, a short-term loan is needed for these six months. As you know your financial requirements about a year in advance and have already arranged to pay back the loan by October, you can negotiate with financial establishments with composure and confidence. The details of the measures to be taken and the actual financial situation can be obtained by tracing back from this diagram to lines (19) − (26) of the tentative fund operation table.

(19A) Prospective Fund Operation Table

Unit: ¥1,000

Item		Month	Calculation formula	Jan	Feb	Mar	Apr	May	Jun	Jul	Aug	Sept	Oct	Nov	Dec
Income	Sales	1 Cash sales		96,200	71,400	102,300	64,900	87,300	89,400	101,300	52,400	128,200	125,300	100,500	133,900
		2 Credit sales, collection		23,990	34,260	19,440	30,380	38,490	13,340	44,520	33,850	21,930	63,040	71,360	68,460
		3 Bills payable on due date		41,200	46,200	33,500	31,800	24,300	39,200	31,300	26,300	53,800	29,500	57,300	61,400
		4		–	–	–	–	–	–	–	–	–	–	–	–
		5 Other cash income		–	–	–	360	–	410	300	50	70	–	540	160
	6 Payment in advance			1,200	240	–	1,600	210	–	–	–	4,300	7,160	–	–
	7 Miscellaneous income			410	200	480	160	700	150	80	400	200	700	1,300	280
8 Total income			(1) · (7)	163,000	152,300	155,700	129,200	149,000	142,500	177,500	113,000	208,500	225,700	231,000	264,200
Outgoings	Purchases for stock	9 Cash purchases		64,000	43,670	75,100	88,400	47,300	43,200	37,500	43,900	73,380	43,500	59,900	82,400
		10 Purchases on credit		21,300	31,000	41,600	23,900	41,200	23,400	31,300	50,300	44,900	24,300	40,200	28,300
		11 Settlement by bills		17,900	10,300	13,200	32,300	19,600	19,600	24,200	18,900	41,700	14,500	54,300	52,420
	12 Wages, salaries			10,700	11,300	9,980	11,400	10,700	23,500	11,100	12,100	39,700	10,400	12,100	32,300
	13 Cash			–	–	3,280	3,280	–	3,280	–	–	–	3,280	–	–
	14 Miscellaneous expenses			21,000	19,000	24,000	22,500	21,600	20,900	19,300	23,200	21,800	22,500	20,700	22,500
	15 Payment for equipment funds			350	350	350	350	350	350	350	350	22,350	350	350	350
	16 Bank deposits, installment funds, reserve funds			70	80	70	70	80	70	70	680	70	70	80	70
	17 Payment in advance			8,080	–	3,400	–	3,670	4,350	3,580	6,070	–	7,800	11,870	2,360
18 Total outgoings			(9) · (17)	143,400	115,700	167,700	182,200	155,800	138,700	127,400	155,500	243,900	126,800	199,500	220,700
19 Redeemed amount of loans				2,300	2,300	2,300	2,100	2,100	2,100	2,100	2,100	2,100	61,900	1,900	1,900
20 Cash carried over from previous month				4,300	21,600	55,900	41,600	16,500	7,600	9,300	57,300	12,700	5,200	42,200	71,800
21 Balance, positive or negative				21,600	55,900	41,600	−13,500	7,600	9,300	57,300	12,700	−24,800	42,200	71,800	113,400
Sum appropriated	22 New loans			–	–	–	–	–	–	–	–	–	–	–	–
	23 Loans to be renewed			–	–	–	–	–	–	–	–	–	–	–	–
	24 Amount discounted on bills			–	–	–	30,000	–	–	–	–	30,000	–	–	–
25 Total sum appropriated			(22) · (24)	–	–	–	30,000	–	–	–	–	30,000	–	–	–
26 Cash sum to be carried over to the following month				21,600	55,900	41,600	16,500	7,600	9,300	57,300	12,700	5,200	42,200	71,800	113,400
Estimates	27 Sales (cash & sales on credit)			160,700	135,000	156,000	142,000	167,600	123,000	199,400	140,200	163,000	173,000	223,600	286,000
	28 Sum for stock purchases (cash & purchases on credit)			115,300	100,900	121,600	95,000	112,000	79,300	140,900	88,300	122,700	134,000	148,300	224,000
	29 Balance of sales on credit			43,200	39,300	37,300	35,400	45,100	33,200	48,600	49,100	44,200	47,300	54,600	61,800
	30 Balance of purchases on credit			34,700	29,400	23,600	40,800	25,900	30,600	39,920	43,420	22,600	36,300	31,420	53,700
	31 Balance of bills receivable			71,300	64,900	80,600	69,400	71,100	70,600	72,300	70,900	68,500	91,400	83,100	110,200
	32 Balance of bills payable			60,100	39,400	41,300	50,100	41,780	43,400	23,600	48,790	24,100	46,770	40,320	41,600
	33 Balance of bills discounted			34,200	38,400	41,300	42,900	37,300	39,300	40,300	44,440	45,630	39,490	38,200	73,400

[CHART 19A]

63

(19B) Fund Operation Diagram

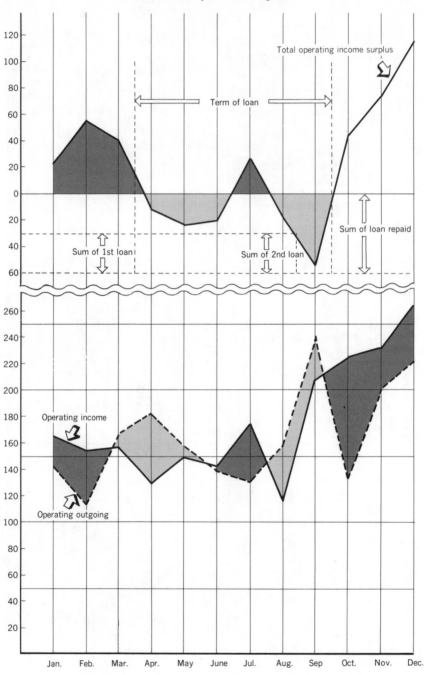

[CHART 19B]

20. STRUCTURE ORGANIZATION CHART

Purpose

The essence of Mr. E.C. Schleh's theory of management is defined in his words: "What management by objectives aims at is to establish relationships between the overall objective of an organization and the individual objectives of each employee and to make the accomplishment of such objectives satisfy their human interest and desires." These objectives should not be abstract but should be clearly defined goals. At one time, each employee's duties were strictly defined and shown in the functional structure chart. These, however, seem now to have become classic, as this structure is interpreted as a divided system of general objectives. The objectives structure organization chart has replaced the classic functional organization chart for use as an effective motive for activating organizational cells as well as individuals' objectives.

How to draw up the chart

First, establish the objective of the company as shown. This is the objective for which the whole company must unite its efforts to accomplish for the year. This objective is broken down into individual assignments for the president, staff, department heads and chiefs of sections and branches. Thus, objectives are mutually connected like a chain, both vertically and horizontally. Quantitative allocation of objectives is expanded qualitatively and interpreted by each position. They then act as the guide for the company's efforts toward accomplishment of the objective. Because each member of the organization clearly understands his own objective in relation to the overall objective of the business, he becomes able to manage his duties himself and at the same time acquires strong motivation. This chart should be prepared to meet such requirements.

Relations

This is the plan which can really be used in all management planning processes and it plays the role of an overall guideline. With this type of a format for everyone to operate from, no one should have any doubt about his or her own objective.

How to use this chart

A copy of chart (20) is distributed to all those in responsible positions. Each staff member should mark off his own block and place where easily visible. As it is deemed necessary, each staff member must plan his own course of action to accomplish the particular objective.

(20) Objective Structure

Item	%	Amount
Sales	100	280,000,000
Direct costs	67.4	188,730,000
Subcontracting exp.	8.32	23,300,000
(Added value)	24.2	67,910,000
Direct labour exp.	4.99	13,987,000
(Total pers. exp.)	9.5	26,550,000
Mfg. expenses	0.6	1,670,000
Mfg. Ind. Costs	6.62	18,520,000
Gross profit	12.0	33,713,000
Research exp.	0.4	1,000,000
Adm. selling exp.	4.2	11,813,000
Interest & others	0.4	1,300,000
Operating profit	7.0	19,600,000

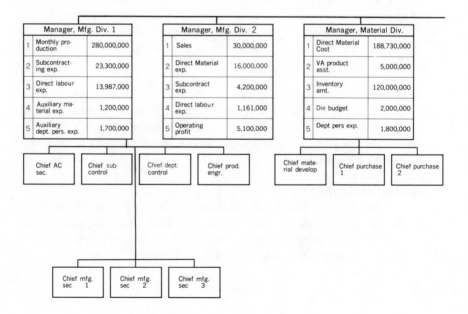

Chief Production Control	
1 Arg. lead time	120d
2 Delivery delay rate	5%
3 Line arg. work-working rate	90%

Manager, Mfg. Div. 1	
1 Monthly production	280,000,000
2 Subcontracting exp.	23,300,000
3 Direct labour exp.	13,987,000
4 Auxiliary material exp.	1,200,000
5 Auxiliary dept. pers. exp.	1,700,000

Manager, Mfg. Div. 2	
1 Sales	30,000,000
2 Direct Material exp.	16,000,000
3 Subcontract exp.	4,200,000
4 Direct labour exp.	1,161,000
5 Operating profit	5,100,000

Manager, Material Div.	
1 Direct Material Cost	188,730,000
2 VA product asst.	5,000,000
3 Inventory amt.	120,000,000
4 Die budget	2,000,000
5 Dept pers exp.	1,800,000

Chief AC sec. Chief sub-control Chief dept. control Chief prod. engr.

Chief material develop Chief purchase 1 Chief purchase 2

Chief mfg. sec 1 Chief mfg. sec 2 Chief mfg. sec 3

Organization Chart

President		
1	Export sales	70%
2	Domestic sales	30%
3	New product project	(month) 1
4	Net profit for the term	240,000,000
5	Total capital profit rate	10%

Exec. Vice President		
1	Recurring profit (Yr)	20,000,000
2	Operating profit (Mo)	19,600,000
3	Gross profit (Mo)	33,713,000
4	Own capital ratio	10%
5	Current ratio	120%

Managing Director		
1	Added value	67,910,000
2	Added value ratio	36%
3	Labour equipment ratio	512,000
4	Added value for employee	113,000
5	Labour distribution rate	40,000

Manager, Enginnering		
1	Direct material costs	188,730,000
2	Design schedule (days)	30d
3	Research exp.	1,570,000
4	Projects per employee	4,000,000
5	Dept. pers. exp.	1,150,000

Manager, Business Operations		
1	Monthly sales	280,000,000
2	Lead time	130d
3	Entertainment exp.	500,000
4	Pack material exp.	4,000,000
5	Dept. pers. exp.	1,700,000

Controller		
1	Adm. loss	0
2	Adm. selling exp.	11,813,000
3	Mfg. Ind. exp.	18,520,000
4	Total pers. exp.	26,550,000
5	Dept. pers. exp.	577,000

Chief engr. sec. 1

Chief engr. sec. 2

Chief business opn.

Chief business adm.

Chief accounting

Chief General Affairs		
1	Welfare exp.	2,800,000
2	Turnover ratio	18%
3	Office supplies	550,000
4	Travel exp.	950,000
5	Sec. pers. exp	600,000

Chief comput. br.

[CHART 20]

21. SALES AND GROSS PROFIT ESTIMATE AND PERFORMANCE GRAPH

Purpose

Sales and gross profit are the most important objectives in the management by objectives system. To an enterprise, sales are the lifeblood and gross profit is the energy carried by the blood. The two objectives, then, should be watched every day on a special graph as a basis for guidance and supervision of operating departments. The type of graph used is a triangular graph and is easy to draw and also convenient to use.

How to construct the graph

First, to accommodate both sales and gross profit on a single chart, graduations are made on both sides of the chart. (We can make one graduation system on either side. However, if the gross profit rate is 20 to 30 per cent, the line remains at the lower part of the chart and this reduces its visual effect.) Draw a vertical line through the 31st point of the axis and plot the sales objective on the line as indicated by the scale on the left side. Next, draw a line from the original point to this objective. This is the sales objective line. Next, plot the gross profit objective point on the 31st sales line using the gross profit scale on the right side. The line to this from the original point is the gross profit objective line. If you plot actual daily results on the chart, you can easily compare them with estimated amounts.

Relations

This is a chart to be used for daily monitoring after plans have been put into effect. The establishment of company objectives should precede the use of this chart.

How to use the chart

To exercise daily control over daily results by no means involves subjecting managers to daily bouts of joy or sorrow. The idea is to allow them to play a part in accomplishing the objective of the month by watching the situation over the course of the month. This chart should not to be kept privately by managers, but should be open to all members of the department (business operations).

(21) Sales and Gross Profit Estimate and Performance Graph

(Term Ending October 1982)

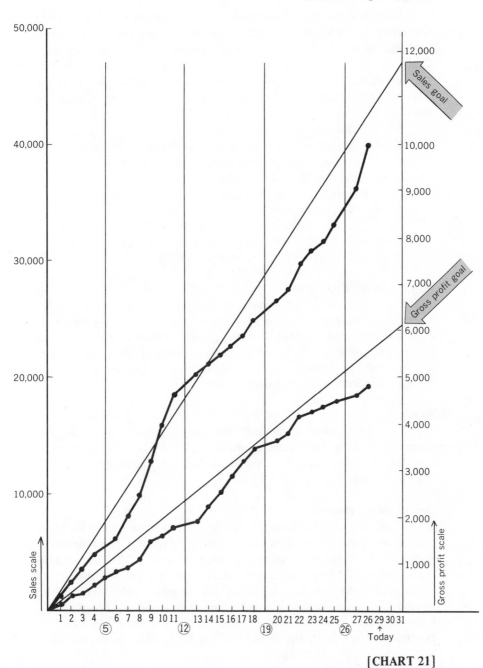

[CHART 21]

22. CURVES OF CURRENT PURCHASES, STOCKS, PRODUCTION AND SALES

Purpose

In showing results of purchases, stock, production and sales of an enterprise, the status of material in stock, work in process and products in stock can be indicated as an organic relationship with the curves shown in chart (22). Each curve is the cumulative total of individual items. The chart will furnish managers with ample information and hints for their daily performance of management. For example, if you look at the curves vertically, you will find:

A – B   Quantity of material on hand
B – C   Amount of casting production in process
C – D   Amount of machined products in process
D – E   Amount of finished products in stock

If you look at them horizontally, i.e., over time, you will find:

A – B   Material turnover period
B – C   Casting products in process turnover period
C – D   Machined products in process turnover period
D – E   Finished products turnover period

How to construct the curves

First, plot a cumulative curve of product shipments, starting at the origin. Next, starting from the point on the ordinate that represents the amount of finished products in storage, plot cumulative curves for cast products and for finished products. Construct similar curves for stock issued and purchases. This graph should, of course, be maintained on a daily basis by making additions to each of the cumulative lines.

Relations

The chart shows synthetically from the standpoint of quantitative management all the purchasing, production and sales activities of an enterprise. You can determine from one chart their movement both organically and synthetically.

How to use the curves

From the chart, the amount of finished products in stock at the beginning of the month clearly indicates that they are excessive. From the middle of the month to the end (actually, the middle period is 10th-20th and the end period is 21st-30th) the amount of products in process increases. This shows poor production control, especially at the peak on the 21st. It signals the need to take immediate remedial measures to improve production techniques and process control. On the other hand, at the end of the month an extreme shortage is shown of material on hand. This means that quick countermeasures are needed. The gap between line C and line D indicates the poor yield rate of the casting shop. As shown here, this movement curve chart is a management tool which not only shows actual conditions, but also indicates actions necessary to cope with such conditions.

(22) Curves of Current Purchases, Stocks, Production & Sales

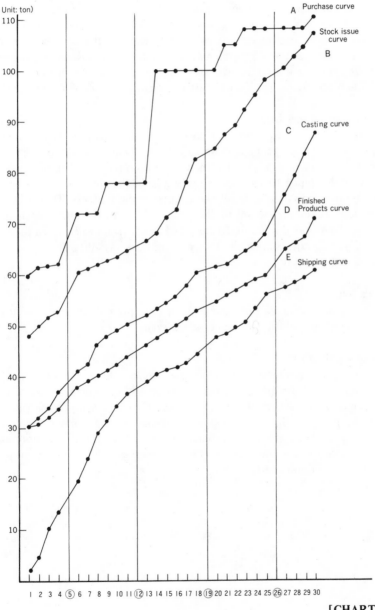

[CHART 22]

23. MANAGEMENT IMPROVEMENT PROGRAMME GANTT CHART

Purpose

It is said that top management should decide 'what', while middle management should decide 'how'. Up to now we have tried to analyze a business, using management data for guidelines, to establish objectives based on results and to decide how to use the results to achieve the objectives of 'what' to do, using the common terminology of data. Now even when we know 'what' to do, if we do not have knowledge if 'how' to carry it out, we shall not be able to achieve the planned effectiveness. It is, therefore, mandatory to have a series of programmes for combining necessary management methods into the most effective and efficient practices to finally achieve established objectives. The Gantt chart is prepared to meet this requirement.

How to draw up the chart

It is necessary to conduct a complete management diagnosis prior to preparation of the programme. Preferably, the programme should be drawn up with the assistance of a qualified management consultant. The programme should be developed to enhance the strengths of the enterprise, correct the shortcomings and consolidate all the efforts of the business. The chart has to be designed to correspond to the kind and size of the business. Double lines on the month blocks designate schedules that are to be filled in with red ink as they are completed. This will contrast any differences between the plan and the results.

Regulations

This is a synthetic programme for a year, prescribing what should be improved and how objectives should be achieved.

How to use the chart

Management improvement techniques are not to be monopolized by a handful of staff or specialists. It requires an all out reform system within the company. To accomplish this, the abilities of as many employees as possible must be utilized and employees must be given opportunities to participate in the improvement programme itself. It is, therefore, important and desirable to have the names of the persons responsible for each project included in the Gantt chart.

(23) Management Improvement Programme Gantt Chart

#	Contents of management improvement plan	Procedures and techniques for improvement	1st mo	2nd mo	3rd mo	4th mo	5th mo	6th mo	7th mo	8th mo	9th mo	10th mo	11th mo	12th mo
I	**Management Plan:** Establish a profit plan & concentrate total company work force on it. Plan not for short-term profit, but for long-term stabilized profit													
1	Basic management policy: long term management plan	Examine management principles: protective of industry concerned; long-term estimate	█											
2	Profit plan: product mix plan	Computation of managerial income; line or programming; product mix		█								█	█	
3	Management ratios improvement plan	Analysis of financial statements; point for ratio improvement; cost reduction objectives			█	█								
4	Three-year estimated profit & loss: estimated B/S	Convert individual plans to time plans; compilation policy of total budget				█								
5	Design of standard management strategies	Seven charts three tables; management data book report control								█				
II	**Organization & Training:** Build up a highly efficient management system. Plan to have managers who are low in number but high in ability; increase management ability and establishment of management by objectives													
6	Basic plans of organization and structure	Examine present organization; reasonable number and organization staff			█									
7	Improvement of duty assignment	Task list, duty chart; duty assignment chart; reassignment of duties			█						█			
8	Table of assigned duties & authorities	Job analysis; duty assignment chart; functional structure chart			█									
9	MTP & workmanship training	MTP for TWI; workmanship; orientation												
III	**Labour Management:** Give employees sense of stability and "motivation". Let them work up to their capacity by scientific ability evaluating system and by assigning them jobs which suit their talent and ability													
10	Labour management plan based on attitude survey	NAK type morale survey, shop meetings						█						
11	Right man in right job through aptitude tests	Emotional stability test by Uchida; Cleplin's polygraph						█						
12	Rationalization of wage system	New CPI position classification system; promotion standard line; allowance system							█					
13	Performance appraisal for methods, bonus, assignment & training purposes	CIP performance appraisal system rating training					█			█				
14	Improvement of communication effectiveness	Suggestion programme; grievance & appeals examining committee; employee counsel system									█			
IV	**Marketing:** Effective combination of sales strategy & sales techniques will strengthen competitive power of an enterprise, prepare salesmen, and construct its future													
15	Set up sales objectives; draw up sales plan	Demand estimation; evaluation of product life; sales allocation			█									
16	Marketing strategy	Marketing survey, product development; management analysis; sales promotion plan			█									
17	Plan & control sales activity	Marketing map; analysis of competitors; basic points of sales activity; home visits plan							█					
18	Sales training courses	Aptitude test for salesmen; sales courses; role playing							█					
V	**IE:** This is the clue to improvement of productivity of added value. Through this, cost reduction can be most dramatically achieved by eliminating from factory wasteful work, labour, material and costs													
19	Organization of reasonable processing system; establishment of standard process times	Chart of products process analysis; handling analysis; layout				█	█							
20	Smooth flow of materials	Route analysis; congestion analysis; handling analysis; layout						█						
21	Motion improvement; improvement of multiple work	Therblig; analysis; design of jigs & tools; analysis chart of multiple work							█					
22	Improvement of rate of operation	Work sampling, staggering plan; determination of rate of allowance								█				
VI	**Process Control:** Here are methods for effectively eliminating losses in manpower, lowered working rate, delayed and handling, resulting from changes of plan													
23	Consolidation & control of business, engineering, material, subcontracts, & production activity	Critical path (PERT); control organization & system												
24	Prevention of delay in delivery	Cause & effect diagram of delayed delivery; delayed delivery & histogram									█			
25	Production plan & control procedures	Plan & control for procedures, materials, manpower, schedules of work and their implementation									█			
26	Rational machine loading; surplus control	Gantt chart; brick laying chart (chart for planning manpower)										█		
27	Various methods of process control	Process control board; signs; design of slips for control purposes												
VII	**Material Control:** Here consolidate the best methods and key points for cost reduction, meeting delivery dates & efficient storage control; introduction of new material management methods													
28	Cost reduction of priority materials	ABC analysis by pareto line chart (by item and by supplier)					█							
29	Effectuation of purchases & expediting procedures	Come-up system; control chart									█			
30	Establishment of rational control system of sub-contractors	Evaluation, guidance & development of subcontractors; co-operation with VA									█			
31	Introduction & establishment of value analysis system	Principle & practice of value analysis									█			
32	Rationalization of inventory control	Locator card system; control of regularly stored items; unit stocks												█

[CHART 23]

73

Chapter 3
CHARTS ON MARKETING AND SALES

POINTS AT ISSUE

First, objectively answer the 33 questions concerning the current business activities of your company, listed on the following page. It is necessary to think beyond a sales point of view and try a marketing approach with a broader perspective. If more than 5 of the answers are "yes", begin at once to try to isolate the problems.

OUTLINE OF MARKETING

Marketing can be defined as 'the performance of business activities directed toward, and related to, the flow of goods or services from producer to consumer or user'. It is a broad way of thinking which evolves from conventional concepts of sales. It puts less emphasis on each sale involving physical transfer among resalers intervening in trade channels, and more emphasis on determining all the integrated resalers having to do with this flow of goods, i.e. those between producer and consumers.

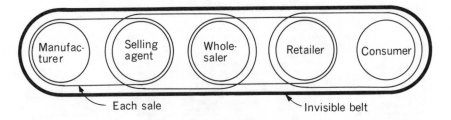

According to the above chart, it is necessary to think of sales in terms of the invisible belt which sets the whole in motion, instead of solely focusing on each sale between manufacturer and selling agent, selling agent and wholesaler, wholesaler and retailer, retailer and consumer.

Charts on Marketing and Sales

Name of Company : _____   Date : _____

Check List to Identify Marketing Problems

Item	No.	Questions	Yes	No	Remarks
I. Market not understood	1	Is it difficult for you to determine the size and share of the market for your products and to forecast demand?			
	2	Is there unpredictable seasonal variation in demand for your products and is your product planning prone to disorder?			
	3	Do you resort only to high-pressure selling, for you can not determine the actual condition of the market ?			
	4	Are you repeating failure in sales without analyzing causes of it?			
II. Sales target mistakes	5	Have you set unreasonable sales targets and assigned unrealistic sales quotas?			
	6	Are your salesmen lacking motivation for achieving their sales targets?			
	7	Have you made low profit ; or have losses increased with sales?			
	8	Are the fluctuations in your monthly sales too big?			
III. Sales strategy not effective	9	Is the growth of sales top-heavy and is poor business chronic?			
	10	Have you a costly but ineffective sales promotion programme ?			
	11	Are you worried about lack of ideas to promote sales?			
	12	Are you undecided about choosing trade channels for promoting the flow of goods and services with the lowest distribution costs?			
	13	Are you making an expensive outlay for advertisement to no effect?			
IV. Lack of personal selling ability	14	Are the selling points of each product unclarified and are salesmen at a loss as to what prospective customers to visit?			
	15	Are you managing without any technique of arguments to meet sales resistance?			
	16	Do you have many salesmen lacking sales closing ability?			
	17	Are you disregarding customers' interests?			
	18	Are you very busy with claims and complaints handling?			
	19	Is the salesmen's ability to close a deal making poor progress?			
V. Lack of salemen's combative spirit	20	Has the fighting spirit in your sales team been reduced and has the salesmen's will to work been lost?			
	21	Is your salesmen's turnover ratio very high?			
	22	Is there any question about salesmen's aptitude? Are there many cases of a square peg in a round hole in your staffing?			
	23	Are you in doubt about what wage structure to choose? Is the current policy the cause of demoralization?			
	24	Do you have any salesmen underachieving owing to poor human relations or other reasons?			
VI. Wrong management of sales activity	25	Have communications between the sales division and the production division been retarded ? Are you spending too much time in conference?			
	26	Are you in trouble with your salesmen because of your poor management? Are you getting along without any sales reports of and close touch with your visiting salesmen?			
	27	Are both senior officials and subordinates checking each other, with the former wishing to educate the latter and the latter wishing to change the way of thinking of the former?			
	28	Are sales affairs tremendously complicated and is the flow of reports and information delayed?			
	29	Are cliques and sectionalism rampant in your organization? Hence, no trustworthy qualities or cheerful attitude can be found?			
VII. Management of accounts	30	Are you having trouble in collecting bills and are your accounts unpaid for long periods?			
	31	Are you controlling your accounts and money without adequate documentation?			
	32	Are you neglecting periodic evaluations of sales efficiency of each salesman?			
	33	Do you usually forget to compare actual achievements with predetermined estimates and targets?			

Marketing Cycle Plan

(1) Marketing research
(2) Product planning
(3) Demand forecast
(4) Profit plan
(5) Main sales target
(6) Basic sales plan
(7) Adjustment and coordination of all enterprise divisions
(8) Final sales plan
(9) Regional sales plan
(10) Distribution plan
(11) Retailers plan

ORGANIC CHART OF MARKETING AND SALES TOOLS

Up to now, we have had a general view of the actual conditions of the market, i.e. the cyclic sales around the consumer. Now, changing the angle, we would like to look at the cycle between marketing and sales within an enterprise. In other words, what are the activities of an enterprise with respect to the market? In other words, look at the marketing process of all sales divisions of which the marketing manager is the centre.

Now, let us here think about the system of marketing and sales. First, look at the organic chart of marketing and sales management techniques. The marketing process is divided into four large areas.

The first area is the area of 'research and evaluation of present situations'. It is divided into 'analysis of external data', involving large scale economic surveys, 'market research' into products of the enterprise and 'analysis of internal data', which clarifies past and present marketing conditions.

Organic Chart of Marketing and Sales Tools

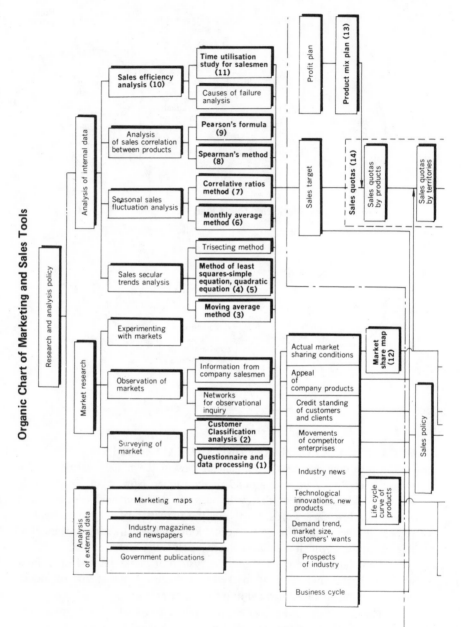

Resarch and evaluation present situations

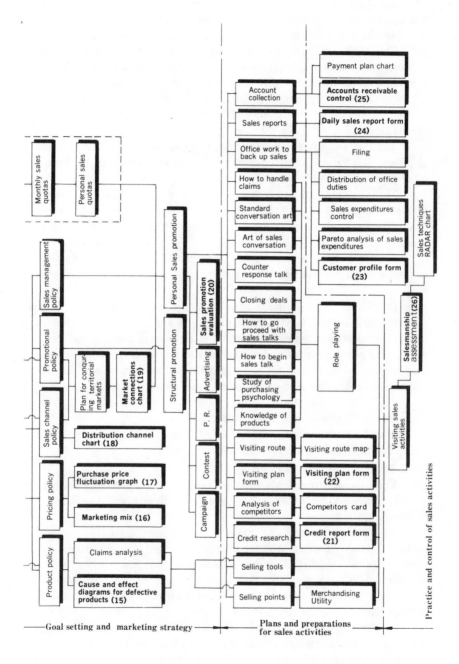

The second area is 'goal setting and planning of marketing strategy', based on research and evaluation of present conditions. This is a dynamic marketing plan, the core of which is strategy.

The sales objective here must be based on scientific analysis and appraisal.

The third area embraces the operating plans for marketing, which support the dynamic strategic plan, i.e., 'plans and preparations of sales activities'. These depend largely on the sales manager's ability to supervise salesmen. They are static, routine and tactical plans (as opposed to strategic in the second area), and compared with marketing and practices in the second area.

The last and fourth area is primarily the exercise and control of sales activities. This organic chart reveals the developing sequence of the management process – see, plan and do.

The first area, research and evaluation of the present situation, is divided into three large parts under a definite policy of research and analysis. The parts are 'analysis of external data', 'market research' and 'analysis of internal data'.

'External data' is coordinated through analysis and interpretation, examples being government publications, industry magazines, newspapers, etc.

Data from related organizations may be suitable for your market research purposes and very useful if practically applied. Also, each industry has its own statistics with their special industrial standpoint. It can be productive to make inquires of each company, association, society and federation. You may be able to use, for your direct mail communications, addresses taken from new telephone directories and other classified directories.

'Market research' consists of four stages:

Step 1, Clarification of the problem,

Step 2, Constructing the model,

Step 3, Gathering information and data, and

Step 4, Interpretation of the above.

Your special attention should be devoted to Step 1. It is useless to collect enormous amounts of data without defining and clarifying the problems involved.

No matter how carefully data may be collected, data not serving the actual purpose is useless, whilst consuming colossal amounts of time and labour. In other words, the first process is to determine what sort of data is to be collected to suit a particular purpose, i.e. choose an alternative approach or decide a policy. In short, it is necessary to make clear the relationship between decision making and researching.

A questionnaire for surveying the market is incorporated in this flow chart. The particular market, in this case, is for car accessories. (1)

Customer classification study (2) is valuable for small scale retailers and for business conditions where selling is performed over the counter.

For analyzing existing internal data, *secular trends analysis of sales* is first necessary. For this analysis there are three methods:

(3) *Moving average method*

(4) *Method of least squares with simple equation*

(5) *Method of least squares with quadratic equation*

Besides these methods, there is a chart technique called the trisection method, which is not covered here.

Next, for *seasonal sales fluctuation analysis, the monthly average method* (6) is shown. The *correlative ratios method* (7) is also useful when there is a possibility that seasonal characteristics will be eliminated by large fluctuations of the business cycle or economic growth rate. This enables the seasonal characteristics to be assessed more effectively by investigating the influence of a high economic growth rate, or a pronounced business cycle.

In correlation analysis, the technique for finding a factor, plus how and in what degree it has influenced sales of a certain production can be investigated. Spearman's method (8) and Pearson's formula (9) are shown and explained.

Next comes the analysis of efficiency of salesmen's activity. This means a *sales efficiency analysis chart* (10) to determine sales target achievement rates and cash collection rates.

To find the efficiency in actual conditions with which a salesman uses his time in his daily activities, a *time utilization study graph for salesmen* (11) becomes useful.

After completing internal research, let us turn our attention again to the actual share of the market occupied by our company and its products.

A *market share map* (12) should now be drawn up. This technique developed and named by me, as the Lanchester Map, involves dividing the market into small segments and determining the market sharing conditions in these segments. This is the first step toward conquering a territorial market according to Lanchester's principle.

Now we enter the second area, i.e. the planning of marketing strategy. First, when a profit plan is developed for a product mix, a *product mix plan by linear programming* (13) can be made. For this, a suitable method for L.P. is presented on a simple chart.

When the preparations are finished, the sales target will be set. But the sales target will not be practical until it is transformed into a sales quota. A product mix should include a product wise *sales quota chart* (14).

When the market share map is analyzed, it will show territorial sales quotas and further, monthly sales quotas will be determined on the basis of the seasonal sales fluctuation index. Next, personal sales quotas will be fixed, based on the results of personal sales efficiency analysis. We include as much information as possible as links in the chain of better product strategy. A precondition for this purpose is the *cause and effect diagram for defective products* (15).

A pricing policy is an important part of marketing strategy and the *marketing mix chart* (16) is presented as a technique to be adopted completely from the viewpoint of marketing. A *purchase price fluctuation graph* (17) gives much data for determining sales prices.

Next, a *distribution channel chart* (18) is presented as a preliminary technique to build distribution channel policy. A *market connections chart* (19) is a preliminary technique for sales promotional strategy. Next, the various approaches, methods and ideas which relate to promotion are all integrated into the actual *sales promotion evaluation chart* (20).

With this, the second area of strategic planning is completed. The third area relates to plans and preparations for routine sales activities. Points of sale and other selling factors are coordinated with selling tools.

Whenever a salesman makes a business call, he must firmly grasp the credit standing of the customer. We have frequently heard of traders who endeavoured to sell more and more and were finally obliged to sell their own homes, mainly because of inadequate credit research.

It is helpful to have salesmen carry *credit report forms* (21) and to teach them to use the forms. When salesmen start to visit customers, it is desirable that their activities be efficient and effective.

For this purpose, it is necessary to make *visiting plan forms* (22). All daily visiting activities should be based on these forms. The third area, plans and preparations for sales activities, is now completed.

The fourth area involves implementing and controlling sales activities.

These activities are aimed at prospective customers. A *customer profile form* (23) should be completed to enable salesmen to give the smoothest, most effective sales talks possible. The customer profile forms can be remarkably effective, and it is vital that they be completed.

A *daily sales report form* (24) should be completed after every day's work. This daily sales report form differs from the conventional daily sales form, but can be quite effective.

An *accounts receivable control graph* (25) is useful for account collection. This is an extremely effective control technique based on a dynamic curve graph. Finally, a *salesmanship assessment chart* (26) and a RADAR chart are shown to complete the salesmen's sales activities. (In this case, an example of over-the-counter service is shown.)

The fourth area is thus completed. Because of space considerations, many other effective charts have been omitted. As there are more than 100 charts which relate to marketing alone, it is unavoidable. Concerning the object correlation, function and effect of the charts, explanations appear later, together with the explanations of the charts themselves. Here, with this one chart, please try to comprehend the interrelation between planning, execution and control of marketing and sales.

Interrelation Between Planning, Executing & Controlling of Marketing & Sales

	I — Assessing the market	II — Sales development plan	III — Strategic planning	IV — Developing salesmen's ability	V — Generating combative spirit in salesmen	VI — Managing sales activities	VII — Profit plan and managing finance
(1)	Demand forecast	Sales policy	Originality of strategy	Knowledge of products	Test of qualifications	Suitable size of sales organization	Setting profit goal
(2)	Sales efficiency analysis	Sales target	How to use causes of failure analysis	Study of purchasing psychology	Placing qualified persons	Duty analysis	Setting cost reduction goal
(3)	Secular trends analysis	Sales quotas	How to develop territories	How to proceed with a sales talk	Allotting time	Internal communications	Profit plan
(4)	Seasonal fluctuations analysis	Product mix plan	How to expand market share	How to begin sales conversations	Assessing ability	Managing indirect personnel	Fund operation table
(5)	Correlation analysis	Visits plan	How to handle prospective customers	Test closing	Evaluating performance	Office work to back up sales	Business analysis ratios
(6)	Market share research	Fixing visiting routes	Imagery	Point of sale conversation	Remuneration	Sales statistics	Budget control
(7)	Purchasing motivation analysis	Marketing map	Project team	Closing sales	Leadership qualities of management	Reduction of sales costs	Analysis of budget difference
(8)	Cause of failure analysis	Merchandising utility	Sales campaign	How to handle claims	Training camp	Sales literature design	Credit research
(9)	Analysis of competitors	Selling points	Direct mail	Diversification of customers	Sales contests	Allotting duties	Controlling accounts receivable
(10)	Information sources	Selling tools (i.e., Approach Book)	Power to implement ideas	Role playing	Perfecting salesmanship	Measuring volume of office work	Control of collecting activities

Increased Marketability and Competitiveness

Approach	No.	Action	Measures which the sales manager must study	Measures which salesmen must study	Consultation (Agency business to expand the scope of the enterprise)
			Check mark on the item the company must execute and apply		
I Assessing the market	1	Demand forecast	How to improve	–	◎
	2	Sales efficiency analysis	How to do	How to do	◎
	3	Seculiar trends analysis	How to do	–	◎
	4	Seasonal fluctuations analysis	How to do	–	◎
	5	Correlation analysis	How to do	–	◎
	6	Market share research	How to do	How to use	○
	7	Purchasing motivation analysis	How to do	How to use	○
	8	Cause of failure analysis	How to do	How to use	○
	9	Analysis of competitors	How to do	How to use	○
	10	Information sources	How to organise	How to use	○
II Sales development plan	1	Sales policy	How to set up	Retaining	○
	2	Sales target	How to set up	Execution	○
	3	Sales quotas	How to do	Execution	○
	4	Product mix plan	How to do	Understanding	◎
	5	Visits plan	How to do	How to do	○
	6	Fixing visiting routes	How to do	How to do	○
	7	Marketing map	How to organise	How to use	◎
	8	Merchandising utility	Development	Understanding	○
	9	Selling points	Development	Execution	○
	10	Selling tools	How to make	How to use	○
III Planning strategy	1	Originality of strategy	Developing creative talents	Developing creative talents	○
	2	How to use causes of failure	How to make	How to use	○
	3	How to develop territories	How to plan	Execution	◎
	4	How to expand market share	How to plan	Execution	◎
	5	How to handle prospective customers	How to do	How to use	◎
	6	Imagery	Development	Understanding	○
	7	Project team	Development	–	—
	8	Sales campaign	Development	–	—
	9	Direct mail	How to do	–	—
	10	Power to implement ideas	How to train subordinates	Acquiring	○
IV Developing salesmen's ability	1	Knowledge of products	How to teach	How to learn	○
	2	Study of purchasing psychology	How to teach	Understanding	○
	3	How to proceed with a sales talk	Acquiring	Acquiring	—
	4	How to begin sales conversations	Acquiring	Acquiring	—
	5	Testclosing	Acquiring	Acquiring	—
	6	Counter response talk	Standardization	Acquiring	—
	7	Closing deals	Acquiring	Acquiring	—
	8	How to handle claims	How to teach	Acquiring	—
	9	Diversification of customers	Understanding	Understanding	—
	10	Role playing	How to improve	Execution	○

Approach	No.	Action	Check mark on the item the company must execute and apply		Consultation (Agency business to expand the scope of the enterprise)
			Measures which the sales manager must study	Measures which salesmen must study	
V Generating combative spirit in salesmen	1	Test of qualifications	Taking	Taking	◎
	2	Placing qualified persons	How to do	–	–
	3	Allotting time	How to do	How to do	–
	4	Assessing ability	How to do	Understanding	◎
	5	Evaluating performance	How to do	Understanding	◎
	6	Remuneration	How to do	–	○
	7	Leadership qualities of management	Acquiring	–	–
	8	Training camp	How to improve	–	◎
	9	Sales contests	How to improve	Execution	◎
	10	Perfecting salesmanship	How to teach	Acquiring	–
VI Managing sales activities	1	Suitable size of sales organization	Development	–	○
	2	Duty analysis	Development	How to make	○
	3	Internal communications	Development	–	–
	4	Managing indirect personnel	Development	–	○
	5	Office work to back up sales	Improvement	–	◎
	6	Sales stastics	Coordination	–	◎
	7	Reduction of sales costs	How to improve	Execution	○
	8	Form designing	How to do	–	◎
	9	Allotting duties	Development	–	◎
	10	Measuring volume of office work	How to do	–	○
VII Profit plan and managing finance	1	Setting profit goal	Development	–	◎
	2	Setting cost reduction goal	Development	–	◎
	3	Profit plan	Development	–	◎
	4	Fund operation table	Development	–	◎
	5	Business analysis ratios	How to read	–	◎
	6	Budget control	How to improve	–	○
	7	Analysis of budget difference	How to improve	–	◎
	8	Credit research	Development	Execution	○
	9	Controlling accounts receivable	Execution	Execution	○
	10	Control of collecting activities	Execution	Execution	–

○ Cooperation ◎ Able to be executed by consulting agency

MARKETING AND SALES TACTICS

Performance is more important than theory. The theories and techniques of marketing are of value for strengthening and enhancing the company's power to compete in the market.

The next chart is designed for the practical purpose of strengthening competitive power and increasing ability to contest the market. Effective and profitable marketing and sales are achieved by scientifically thought-out plans. It is most profitable to steadily apply, one by one, the techniques which are systematized in this chart.

Now, use this chart to try to solve the problems of the business department of your company. In order to do this, you must carry out self-diagnosis, and must not reject the idea saying: "I already know these things". (Also, write your diagnostic results in the blanks provided.)

1. QUESTIONNAIRE FOR SURVEYING THE MARKET

Purpose

This questionnaire is for researching the actual status of the market. It is ridiculous to design and market a product without knowing the likes and dislikes, tastes and wants of the customer. After determining these factors, you must aim at a distinct target. Marketing is also said to be a technique for penetrating the masses of consumers. Complacency on the part of enterprises often has disastrous consequences. Marketing research may also be called 'looking before one leaps' in order to avoid risks.

It is to be filled in for both actual and potential customers of a product which is either about to be, or has already been put onto the market. It can also be filled in by a trained interviewer when interviewing the customer. The design of the questionnaire card must, of course, vary according to whether it concerns industrial or consumer goods. The chart shown here is only an example. The interviewees should be selected on the basis of sampling methods. The number of interviewees is determined by the percentage of desired results, confidence limits and accuracy.

$$N = \frac{t^2(1 - P)}{S^2 P}$$

Relations

Market surveys should never consist of vague, ambiguous probings. It is important to make the purpose clear before beginning a survey and to calculate beforehand what approach or tactics are to be used when the survey results are collated. Surveying a market is expensive, whether it is done by the company itself or by a professional institution. It is necessary to pay close attention to the cost of the survey and research.

Evaluations

The same survey data, depending on how it is utlized, can be either worthless or invaluable. In addition, the same data is analyzed from many viewpoints and can be utilized for many purposes.

This example is a chart of survey data for the car accessories trade and is designed as a Pareto line table. It is interesting that we can determine different trends for goods in hand and for goods to be produced in the future. Such data would be useful for traders and retailers in car accessories thinking about their future merchandising requirements.

(1A) Questionnaire for Surveying the Car Accessories Market

Name:	Sex: Age:	Occupation:	Address:	Type of car uses:

1. Which of the following commodities have you bought? Where did you buy them? Will you please circle the relevant choices.

			Department store	Car accessory specialty store	Service station	Car dealer	Automobile repair shop	Auto parts specialty shop	Wholesaler of parts and accessories	Others	Unknown	Future buying intention
Room Accessories	101	Cushions										
	102	Backrest										
	103	Headrest										
	104	Body cover										
	105	Seat cover										
	106	Curtain										
	107	Cigar lighter										
	108	Cigar case										
	109	Auto compass										
Driving Equipment	201	Key case										
	202	Key holder										
	203	Handle cover										
	204	Sun glasses										
	205	Gloves										
	206	Leather vest										
	207	Safety belt										
	208	Sleeping bag										
	209	Car shoes										
Safety Equipment	301	Car lock										
	302	Cable lock										
	303	Burglar-proof chain										
	304	Master key										
	305	Crash helmet										
Others	401	Tapes and crests										
	402	Car TV										
	403	Puppet trafficator										

2. Which of the following were your motives for buying car accessories? Will you please check the relevant letter.

   A) Seen advertised in speciality magazine   B) Seen in other cars
   C) Seen exhibited in shops   D) Conversation with car-driving mate
   E) Other motives   F) Unknown

3. What car accessories do you intend to buy in the future? Please fill in the blanks in the column on the extreme right of the above chart with circles.

[CHART 24A]

(1B) Total Results of Questionnaire on Car Accessories
Table 1 Proportion of product sold by Occupation

No.	Names of products	Occupation				Total
		Business proprietor	Company employee	Student	Female	
1	Map	25.0	23.2	24.4	27.4	100
2	Sun glasses	23.6	19.8	29.4	27.2	100
3	Key holder	21.0	16.3	34.1	28.7	100
4	Cushions	19.8	29.0	29.8	21.5	100
5	Seat cover	16.5	16.5	34.7	32.3	100
6	Gloves	27.3	27.3	24.3	21.2	100
7	Mascot	26.3	19.2	26.3	28.3	100
8	Head backrest	30.0	17.5	22.5	30.0	100
9	Handle cover	29.7	18.9	25.7	25.7	100
10	Cigar lighter	11.0	12.3	45.2	31.5	100
11	Key case	21.7	11.0	36.0	31.3	100
12	Body cover	13.3	26.7	36.7	23.3	100
13	Auto clock	13.6	20.3	44.1	22.0	100
14	Backrest	30.9	21.8	30.9	16.4	100
15	Cigar case	31.3	10.4	16.7	14.6	100
16	Car shoes	14.4	16.4	22.6	47.0	100
17	Artificial flowers	21.4	11.9	50.0	16.7	100
18	Room spot	5.0	5.0	45.0	45.0	100
19	Clips	26.4	31.5	21.8	21.8	100
20	Thermometer	16.2	18.9	21.6	43.3	100

(Arranged in order of extent of ownership experience)

[CHART 24B]

Table 1C Accessories Purchases by Type of Store

Classification	Name of Products	Department store	Car acc. specialty store	Service station	Car dealer	Automobile repair shop	Auto parts specialty shop	Wholesalers of parts and accessories	Others	Unknown
Room Accessories	Cushions, Artificial flowers, Backrest, Seat cover, Mascot	24.5	12.9	13.4	23.6	4.8	7.1	3.4	7.9	2.4
Driving Eqp't.	Key case, Car coat, Sun glasses, Map, Safety belt, Car shoes	35.7	11.3	12.0	9.3	1.5	7.3	2.9	18.6	1.3
Safety Eqp't.	Car lock, Back alarm, Burglar-proof chain, Fire extinguisher, Helmet, Red flag	15.7	8.5	11.1	27.6	9.8	16.3	1.3	10.5	5.2
Others	Tapes and crests, Car TV	19.6	9.8	11.8	27.5	—	9.8	5.9	11.8	3.9
Total		28.5	11.8	12.6	17.5	3.7	7.9	3.1	12.6	2.3

[CHART 24C]

Table 1D Car Accessories in Demand

Rank of % of total	Name of Products	% of total	Occupations (155)				Types of cars				
			Business proprietor	Company employee	Student	Female	Deluxe	Standard	Light car	Sports car	Imported sedan
1	Head Backrest	13.5	25.9	28.7	7.4	37.0	12.8	7.4	10.0	–	4.5
2	Safety belt	9.5	10.5	15.7	10.6	63.3	8.2	9.2	–	–	9.1
3	Cushion	5.0	50.0	10.0	20.0	20.0	3.7	9.2	–	25.0	–
4	Mascot	4.0	50.0	–	12.5	37.5	11.0	7.3	–	–	4.6
5	Umbrella stand	3.5	–	–	–	–	4.5	–	–	–	4.5
6	Auto compass	3.0	25.0	50.0	–	25.0	3.7	–	–	–	–
7	Calendar	3.0	–	–	–	–	0.9	–	–	–	–
8	Tapes and crests	3.0	–	–	–	–	3.7	–	7.0	–	–
9	Cigar lighter	2.5	–	–	–	–	2.8	–	–	–	4.5
10	Coat hanger	2.5	–	–	–	–	0.9	–	–	–	–

[CHART 24D]

91

Table 1E Motivation for Purchase of Car Accessories

Class \\ Motive	Business proprietor	Company employee	Student	Female	Whole
Seen advertised in speciality magazine	–	4.0	20.0	4.0	7.0
Seen in other cars	12.0	18.0	14.0	12.0	14.0
Seen exhibited in shops	54.0	54.0	38.0	60.0	51.5
Conversations with car-driving mate	–	2.0	30.0	10.0	10.5
Other motives	30.0	22.0	10.0	26.0	22.0
Unknown	4.0	–	–	–	2.0

[CHART 24E]

Table 1F Purchasing Market Segment by Location

Place \\ Class	Depart-ment store	Car accesso-ries speciality store	Service station	Car dealer	Auto-mobile repair shop	Auto parts speciality shop	Wholesalers of parts and accesso-ries	Others	Un-known
Business proprietor	23.1	13.7	27.1	9.0	3.4	3.4	4.3	15.5	0.7
Company employee	26.6	6.5	25.6	10.3	2.0	4.5	6.5	16.6	1.3
Student	25.6	19.6	1.2	21.3	3.2	16.4	1.9	7.5	3.3
Female	37.3	4.7	6.8	24.1	5.7	3.3	1.3	14.0	2.8
Whole	28.5	11.8	12.6	17.5	3.7	7.9	3.1	12.6	2.3

[CHART 24F]

92

Table 1G   Level of Consumer Demand Corresponding to the Percentage of Ownership Experience

Goods demanded by potential customers (%)	Code	Pareto tabulation, Name of products		Goods in stock held by present customers
14 12 10 8 6 4 2				10 20 30 40 50 60 70 80 90
32	215	Map	(1)	
25	204	Sun glasses	(2)	
	202	Key holder	(3)	
3	101	Cushions	(4)	
6	105	Seat cover	(5)	
20	205	Gloves	(6)	
4	121	Mascots	(7)	
	103	Head backrest	(8)	
1	203	Handle cover	(9)	
9	107	Cigar lighter	(10)	
	201	Key case	(11)	
16	104	Body cover	(12)	
24	111	Auto clock	(13)	
27	102	Backrest	(14)	
29	108	Cigar case	(15)	
12	209	Car shoes	(16)	
23	123	Artificial flowers	(17)	
	119	Room spot	(18)	
	115	Clips	(19)	
19	110	Thermometer	(20)	
2	207	Safety belt	(21)	
21	206	Leather vest	(22)	
34	211	Drive seat	(23)	
8	401	Tapes and crests	(24)	
	124	Others	(25)	
28	106	Curtain	(26)	
10	118	Coat hanger	(27)	
	308	Red flag	(28)	
	301	Car lock	(29)	
6	109	Auto compass	(30)	
	210	Car bottle	(31)	
30	114	Dash tray	(32)	
35	214	Drive seat	(33)	
	120	Baskets	(34)	
33	122	Vases	(35)	
13	213	Portable refrigerator	(36)	
	302	Cable lock	(37)	
31	118	Magazine rack	(38)	
36	304	Super key	(39)	
37	305	Helmet	(40)	
22	306	Back alarm	(41)	
	218	Other driving equipment	(42)	
17	312	Signal light	(43)	
	217	Driving bag	(44)	
26	117	Safety chair	(45)	
14	307	Fire extinguisher	(46)	
	313	Other safety equipment	(47)	
7	112	Calender	(48)	
5	115	Umbrella stand	(49)	
	208	Sleeping bag	(50)	
	310	Warning light	(51)	
	216	Auto hanger	(52)	
	303	Burglar-proof chain	(53)	
	311	Three-colour signal light	(54)	
15	401	Car TV	(55)	
	212	Auto table	(56)	
38	309	Smoke candle	(—)	
18	404	Mascot indicator	(—)	

(Quoted from P.14 "Car accessories tommorrow", Yano Economic Research Institute).

[CHART 24G]

2. CUSTOMER CLASSIFICATION STUDY

Purpose

This is a technique for collecting and analyzing data on classification of customers who purchase over the counter. Determining the types of customers is an indispensable procedure for a retail shop which seeks to improve its merchandising. The distributed percentage for each classification of customers in each time division, if understood, tells much about the way to lay out shop front, showcases and display cards.

How to construct

I shall now explain an actual example of the chart. First, obtain five coloured marbles, clover-patterned and star-patterned. The clover-patterned marbles represent nondurable consumer goods and the star-shaped ones represent durable consumer goods.

In addition, by colour, the red marbles represent regular customers, blue ones represent regular cash customers, yellow represent salaried men, the green represent owners of small businesses and the orange represent students. Here we have ten (five colours x two) symbols of customer classification. Now, prepare the two boxes shown in the picture below, which have ten partitions and place them near your cash register.

Whenever a customer buys an item he is classified and a marble in the relevant upper box will be dropped into the partition of the lower box. Change the lower boxes every hour, counting the marbles in them in each time division. In this way you will get the desired result.

Hints

Assemble the data thus collected as you see in the charts. The data necessary for the customer classification chart and the customer time change chart can be compiled. If the data is further transformed into a bar chart, we shall be able to understand clearly the character of the shop.

How to read

As you can see how crowded the shop is from the *customer change by time chart,* you will be able to use your labour time efficiently by providing assistants preponderantly at the busiest time and by dividing them at quiet times (here 4.00 p.m. to 6.00 p.m.) into the group remaining on duty and the earlier-leaving group. In accordance with the data for *customer classification chart,* it will be known on which customer classification your energies should be centralized. This example suggests that most emphasis should be placed on regular cash customers and random salaried customers. It also suggests correcting for the inefficiency of using almost one third of effective space to display durable consumer goods which are requested by only 18 persons a week (or three a day).

Whenever a customer buys, in accordance with the relevant classification, one marble in the corresponding relevant upper partition must be dropped into the lower partition.

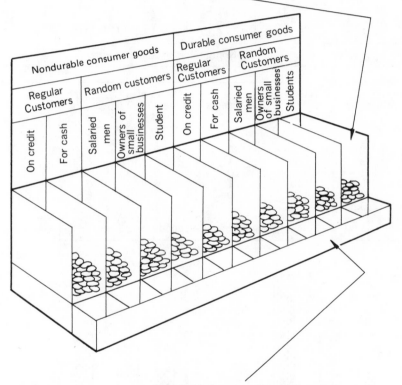

Change this box every hour and count the marbles by colour.

(2A) Customer Classification Study

	Salaried men	Owners of small business	Students	Purchase by nearby office	On credit
1st week	395	65	15	276	189
2nd week	433	75	14	335	208
3rd week	441	60	25	312	167
4th week	461	54	18	418	184
Total	1731	254	72	1341	748
Average	455	63.5	18	335	187
Index	411	60.7	17.1	318	17.8
Nondurable consumer goods					

On credit	Purchase by nearby office	Students	Owners of small business	Salaried men	
10	5	0	1	9	
2	3	0	0	8	
3	12	1	2	8	
1	5	0	3	1	
16	25	1	6	26	
4	6	0	1.5	6.5	1,054.5
3.8	5.6	0	1.2	6.2	
Durable consumer goods					

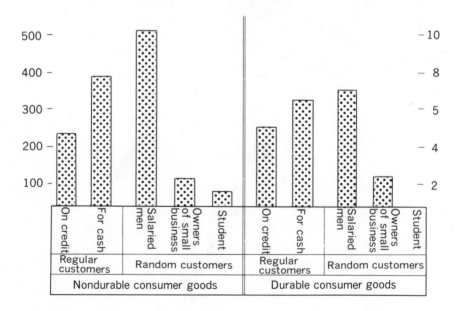

[CHART 25A]

(2B) Customer Change by Time Chart

	10 o'clock	11 o'clock	12 o'clock	1 o'clock	2 o'clock
1st week	87	170	114	115	122
2nd week	96	155	96	129	155
3rd week	93	149	137	127	136
4th week	116	155	138	130	192
Total	392	629	485	501	605
Average	98	157	121	125	151
Index	83	133.5	102	106	128

3 o'clock	4 o'clock	5 o'clock	6 'oclock		
148	131	78	29		
159	154	102	39		
144	142	65	37		
174	136	80	23		
625	562	325	128		
156	140	81	32	1061/9	118
133	118.5	68.6	27		

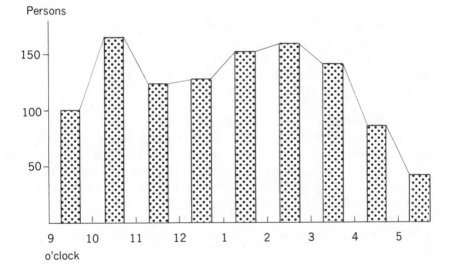

[CHART 25B]

97

3.   SECULAR TREND ANALYSIS (MOVING AVERAGE METHOD)

Purpose

The aim of *secular trend of sales analysis* is to determine scientifically whether the pattern of sales is tending upward or downward or remains unchanged — the ups and downs of sales over short periods receiving less emphasis.

This means finding the direction of sales and eliminating minor deviations from the main trend. The primary methods for this purpose are:

(1)   *Moving average method*

(2)   *Least squares method*

(3)   *Trisection method*

First, the *moving average method* will be explained.

How to construct

Prepare a monthly sales list (3A). Moving averages are obtained by dividing the months into groups at odd-numbered intervals, such as three months, five months, or seven months, then summing each group and dividing each total by the same odd number.

The chart shows an example of a three-month moving average. Plot the average sales of January, February and March at February and the average of February, March and April at March and so on. Five-month moving averages and seven-month moving averages can be obtained in the same way.

Hints

After you get a moving average, plot this on a graph (3B). Thus, the fluctuations of previous actual sales results will smoothed, and the degree of deviation caused by large monthly fluctuations will be reduced. The trend curve of moving averages will become gentler and it will be easier to assess the trend in sales rationally. As the time span for the moving average increases, the trend curve becomes smoother. For example, a seven-month average will be smoother than a five-month curve and a five-month curve will be smoother than a three-month curve, etc.

How to read and use

If you use this method separately for individual products, you will be able to assess the character of sales movements for each product. If you use it separately by region, the trend of sales in each region will be clarified. Although past performance does not always indicate the future, the trend will be extended into the future if other conditions remain the same. By estimating the future along a projected line, actual methods to increase sales separately both by product and by region will be easier to devise.

(3A) Moving Average Table

	Months	Sales turnover	Moving average (3 months)	Moving average (5 months)
	April 4	39,739,000		
	May 5	32,160,000	36,879,000	
	June 6	38,738,000	34,423,333.3̇	34,389,600
	July 7	32,372,000	33,349,666.6̇	34,886,000
1981	August 8	28,939,000	34,510,666.6̇	36,716,000
	September 9	42,221,000	37,491,000	39,835,000
	October 10	41,313,000	45,954,666.6̇	42,382,200
	November 11	54,330,000	46,917,000	44,548,400
	December 12	45,108,000	46,402,666.6̇	44,881,800
	January 1	39,770,000	42,922,000	44,831,800
	February 2	43,888,000	41,573,666.6̇	44,421,400
	March 3	41,063,000	45,743,000	41,538,600
	April 4	52,278,000	41,345,000	41,823,800
	May 5	30,694,000	41,389,333.3̇	43,606,800
	June 6	41,196,000	41,564,333.3̇	42,358,600
1982	July 7	52,803,000	42,940,333.3̇	46,659,200
	August 8	34,822,000	37,135,333.3̇	42,018,800
	September 9	23,781,000	38,698,333.3̇	41,579,200
	October 10	57,492,000	40,090,333.3̇	42,101,800
	November 11	38,998,000	50,635,333.3̇	43,417,400
	December 12	55,416,000	45,271,333.3̇	48,969,400
	January 1	41,400,000	49,452,333.3̇	46,133,400
1983	February 2	51,541,000	45,417,666.6̇	
	March 3	43,312,000		

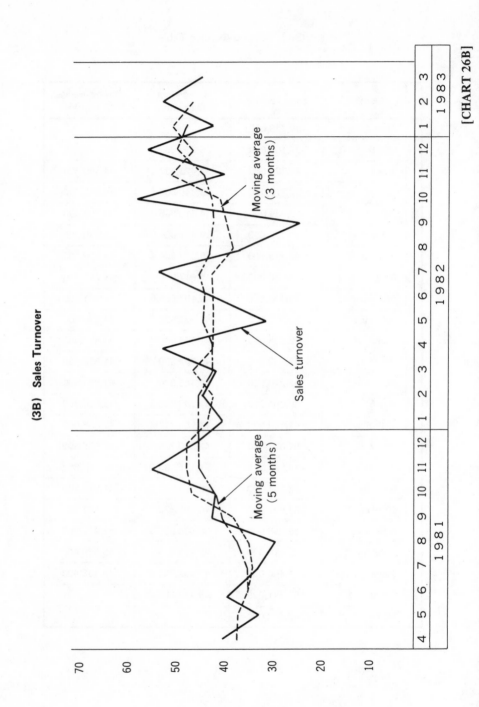

(3B) Sales Turnover

[CHART 26B]

4. SECULAR TREND ANALYSIS (METHOD OF LEAST SQUARES – SIMPLE EQUATION)

Purpose

The purpose of least squares trend analysis is the same as the foregoing, but the method of calculation is different. The *least squares method* is a more mathematically intensive derivation of the secular trend curve.

How to construct

The *least squares method* involves determining a curve or a straight line which minimizes the sum of the squares of the distances between the calculated trend curve or line and each point (or actual sales result) plotted on the graph. First, the simple equation method will be explained.

(1) Itemize the sales results for each period in column S.
(2) Assign a zero to the middle period in column X, in this case for 1975.
(3) Now write $-1, -2$ and -3 in each blank for every period upward, $+1, +2$ and $+3$ in each blank for every period downward in column X.
(4) Find the value X^2 in each case.
(5) Find the values for Sx. For example, for 1972 it is $3,500 \times (-3) = -10,500$. Successively, fill in each blank with the Sx value for each period.
(6) Now find the Σ values, these being the sums for each column.
(7) Now apply the formula (simple equation) from table 4A, and solve for the unknown quantities a and b.

In this case, we get a = 4,500, b = 500.

(8) Now find the value of S' for each period.

1972	$4,500 + (-3) \times 500 = 3,000$
1973	$4,500 + (-2) \times 500 = 3,500$
1974	$4,500 + (-1) \times 500 = 4,000$
1975	$4,500 + (0) \times 500 = 4,500$
1976	$4,500 + (+1) \times 500 = 5,000$
1977	$4,500 + (+2) \times 500 = 5,500$
1978	$4,500 + (+3) \times 500 = 6,000$

Hints

Plot each numerical value of S' on a graph and draw the trend line. In the case of the simple equation, the trend line is a straight line and in the case of the quadratic equation, it is a parabola.

How to read

The explanation is the same as the previous one, but the trend line is less erratic than that of the moving averages.

(4A) Trend Analysis By The Least Squares Method

Formulas

a	Simple equation (Straight line)		$y = a + bx$
b	Quadratic equation (Parabola)		$y = a + bx + cx^2$
c	Cubic equation (Curvilinear)		$y = a + bx + cx^2 + dx$

I Simple equation

$$\begin{cases} \Sigma S = na + \boxed{b\Sigma x} \\ \Sigma Sx = \boxed{a\Sigma x} + b\Sigma x^2 \end{cases}$$

II Quadratic equation

$$\begin{cases} \Sigma S = na + \boxed{b\Sigma x^2} + c\Sigma x^2 \\ \Sigma Sx = \boxed{a\Sigma x} + b\Sigma x^2 \boxed{+ c\Sigma x^3} \\ \Sigma Sx^2 = a\Sigma x^2 + \boxed{c\Sigma x^3} + c\Sigma x^4 \end{cases}$$

III Cubic equation

$$\begin{cases} \Sigma S = na \boxed{+ b\Sigma x} + c\Sigma x^2 \boxed{+ d\Sigma x^3} \\ \Sigma Sx = \boxed{a\Sigma x} + b\Sigma x^2 + \boxed{c\Sigma x^3} + d\Sigma x^4 \\ \Sigma Sx^2 = a\Sigma x^2 \boxed{+ b\Sigma x^3} + c\Sigma x^4 \boxed{+ d\Sigma x^5} \\ \Sigma Sx^3 = \boxed{a\Sigma x^3} + b\Sigma x^4 \boxed{+ c\Sigma x^5} + d\Sigma x^6 \end{cases}$$

Figures enclosed by $\boxed{}$ can be omitted.

In actual calculation

S' = Value of sales trend

S = Actual sales

x = Period

Σ = Total

n = The number of periods. In most cases it is convenient to use odd numbers.

a, b, c, d = Arbitrary coefficients.

[CHART 27A]

(4B)   Least Squares Method . . . Simple Equation

n	S	x	x^2	Sx	S' $y=a+bx$
Number of period	Actual sales result	Value of period		S multiplied by x	Calculated value
1972	3,500	−3	9	−10,500	3,000
1973	4,000	−2	4	−8,000	3,500
1974	2,500	−1	1	−2,500	4,000
1975	5,000	0	0	0	4,500
1976	4,500	+1	1	+4,500	5,000
1977	5,500	+2	4	+11,000	5,500
1978	6,500	+3	9	+19,500	6,000
n=7	31,500	0	28	14,000	

$$\begin{cases} \Sigma S = na = 31{,}500 \\ \Sigma Sx = b\Sigma x^2 = 14{,}500 \end{cases} \quad \begin{cases} a = 4{,}500 \\ b = 500 \end{cases}$$

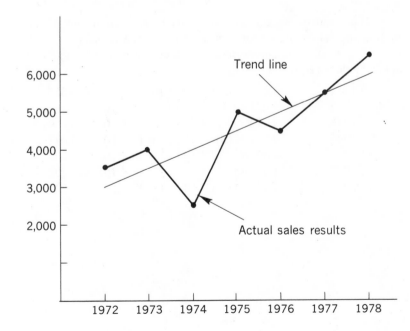

[CHART 27B]

103

5. SECULAR TREND ANALYSIS (METHOD OF LEAST SQUARES – QUADRATIC EQUATION)

Purpose

Here, a quadratic equation is used instead of a simple equation. The purpose of this *secular trend analysis* is the same as that already explained for the least squares method.

However, economic quantities are generally taken as growing by geometrical progression rather than by arithmetical progression. When we consider the fluctuations of sales results, the *least squares method by quadratic equation* can be used.

How to construct

As shown on the chart, fill in the blanks in the calculated value column of the quadratic equation successively after the other items are completed. The process is the same as that for the previous method. However, as the number of unknown quantities is now three, namely, a; b and c, the solution becomes a little more complicated. If you put the numerical values into the expression, you will get.

$$\Sigma S = na + c\Sigma x^2 \ldots \ldots \quad 31{,}500 = 7a + 28c \ldots \ldots (1)$$
$$\Sigma Sx = b\Sigma x^2 \ldots \ldots \ldots \quad 14{,}000 = 28b \ldots \ldots \ldots (2)$$
$$\Sigma Sx^2 = a\Sigma x^2 + c\Sigma x^4 \ldots \quad 135{,}000 = 28a + 196c \ldots (3)$$

This simultaneous equation, if solved by elimination and substitution to find the values of unknown quantities a, b and c, gives us a = 4,072, b = 500, c = 107. Now the expression to find S′ is handled in the same way as for the simple equation.

1972	$4{,}072 + (-3) \times 500 + (-3)^2 \times 107 = 3{,}535$
1973	$4{,}072 + (-2) \times 500 + (-2)^2 \times 107 = 3{,}508$
1974	$4{,}072 + (-1) \times 500 + (-1)^2 \times 107 = 3{,}679$
1975	$4{,}072 + (0) \times 500 + (0) \times 107 = 4{,}072$
1976	$4{,}072 + (31) \times 500 + (+1)^2 \times 107 = 4{,}679$
1977	$4{,}072 + (+2) \times 500 + (+2)^2 \times 107 = 5{,}508$
1978	$4{,}072 + (+3) \times 500 + (+3)^2 \times 107 = 6{,}535$

(5) Least Squares Method ... Quadratic Equation

n	S	x	x^2	Sx	x^4	Sx^2	S'
Number of period	Actual sales result			S multiplied by x		S multiplied by x^2	Calculated value
1972	3,500	−3	9	−10,500	81	31,500	3,535
1973	4,000	−2	4	−8,000	16	16,000	3,508
1974	2,500	−1	1	−2,500	1	2,500	3,679
1975	5,000	0	0	0	0	0	4,072
1976	4,500	+1	1	+4,500	1	4,500	4,679
1977	5,500	+2	4	+11,000	16	22,000	5,508
1978	6,500	+3	9	+19,000	81	58,500	6,535
n=7	31,500	0	28	14,000	196	135,000	

$$\begin{cases} \sum S = na + c\sum x^2 = 31,500 \\ \sum Sx = b\sum x^2 = 14,000 \\ \sum Sx^2 = a\sum x^2 + c\sum x^4 = 135,000 \end{cases} \qquad \begin{cases} a = 4,072 \\ b = 500 \\ c = 107 \end{cases}$$

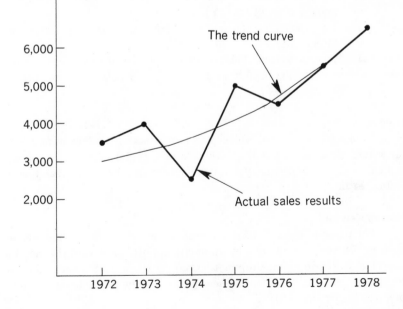

[CHART 28]

6. SEASONAL SALES FLUCTUATION ANALYSIS (MONTHLY AVERAGE METHOD)

Purpose

Sales of goods throughout the year, like the change of seasons are apt every year to show some periods when they increase and other periods when they usually decrease. The so-called 'February and August depression' is an example. This tendency is found with almost the same degree of increase and decrease in sales in reports in both boom years and depressed years. This phenomenon is called *seasonal fluctuation of sales*. There are two methods of seasonal sales fluctuation analysis, i.e., the *monthly average method* and the *correlative ratios method*. Here, the *monthly average method* is explained.

How to construct

First, make a list of actual monthly sales results for the past three years by product, as shown in the chart. The calculation process is as follows:

(1) Find the sum of sales for each month. On this chart, find the sum of sales for each month of the three years.

(2) Find the average of monthly sales for each month. (Divide each of the above sales sums by three.)

(3) Find the annual average of monthly sales (i.e. find the average of averages).

(4) Divide the average of sales for each month (X) by the average of annual average of sales (Y).

(5) The product of the quotient above multiplied by 100 is the seasonal index.

(6) Plot the seasonal indexes on a graph, and then you can analyze and examine them. Coordinate them in a polar coordinates graph like chart (6).

Note

Unlike trend analysis, which places emphasis on finding average long range tendencies instead of fluctuations in each period, *seasonal fluctuation analysis* is for isolating the typical or repetitive fluctuations of each month and/or season.

How to view and use

Fluctuations in sales exert a strong influence on the profitability of business. The profit made in a boom month are often lost with the dip in a dull month. Regarding the drop in sales, no matter how keen the endeavour to increase sales in that month, these efforts will be most effective only if prepared for well in advance.

So it is important to know the peculiarities of such fluctuations and

(6) Seasonal Sales Fluctuation Analysis
(Monthly Average Method)

Item \ Month	Jan.	Feb.	Mar.	Apr.	May	Jun.	Jul.	Aug.	Sep.	Oct.	Nov.	Dec.
1982	540	457	626	473	741	835	671	814	687	742	800	1,192
1983	682	741	880	837	651	1,351	949	1,062	858	1,121	1,252	1,376
1984	1,040	1,100	1,201	1,058	1,248	1,381	1,022	1,165	1,003	1,169	1,081	1,369
Σ	2,262	2,298	2,707	2,368	2,640	3,577	2,642	3,041	2,548	3,032	3,133	3,937
Average of sales for each month	754	766	902	789	880	1,189	881	1,013	849	1,011	1,044	1,312
Seasonal index	79.9	81	96	83.2	92.9	126	100.2	106.2	89.5	106	110	138

11,390
$\bar{x} = 949$

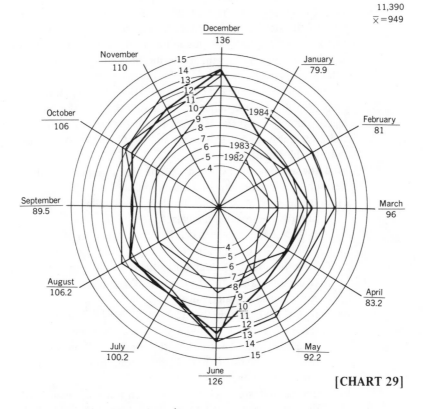

[CHART 29]

to find countermeasures against them.

For example, if sales drop in January and February in the cold winter and in July and August in the hot summer, it is necessary to find products which will sell well at those times and market them accordingly.

107

7. SEASONAL SALES FLUCTUATION ANALYSIS (CORRELATIVE RATIOS METHOD)

Purpose

The *monthly average method's* appealing characteristic is the simplicity of its compilation. This process cannot always yield good results if the fluctuation of sales is too large (for example, if rapid economic growth continues for several years), or when prices fluctuate wildly in a period of inflation or deflation. Therefore, in such circumstances, in spite of the relative complexity of the process, it is desirable to adopt the *correlative ratios method* presented here.

How to construct

First, collect actual monthly sales results for the past three years, and coordinate them as shown in the chart.

(1)   Find the correlative ratios of sales for each month. Regard the sales of the starting month (here it is January of the year 1976) as 100. Calculate (sales of this month) ÷ (sales of last month) on and after the second month, and write the quotients in the month column successively.

(2)   Find the mean value of the correlative ratios of each month.

(3)   Find the temporary index of each month. For this purpose, regard January always as 100, and regard the temporary index on and after February as (temporary index of last month) × (mean value of this month).

(4)   Find the seasonal index. First assume that (temporary index of December) × (mean value of January) = X

    a)   In the case of X = 100, the temporary indexes (3) are the same as the seasonal indexes.

    b)   If $X > 100$, assume that $(X - 100) \div 12 = Y$. Deduct the value of Y from the temporary index of each month on and after February. Deduct only the value of Y in February, twice the value of Y in March, three times the value in April and so on, successively.

    c)   If $X < 100$, assume that $(100 - X) \div 12 = Y$ and add the value of Y to the temporary index of each month on and after February. Add only the value of Y in February, twice the value of Y in March, three times the value in April, and so on, successively.

(5)   Find seasonal indexes, such that the mean point of them is 100.

    a)   Find the mean value of seasonal indexes (4), and regard it as Z.

    b)   Calculate (seasonal index of each month) ÷ Z × 100, and you will then get the seasonal fluctuation index by the correlative ratios method.

Note
The same as for the monthly average method.

How to view and use
The same as for the monthly average method.

(7) Seasonal Sales Fluctuation Analysis
(Correlative Ratios Method)

Item	Month	Jan.	Feb.	Mar.	Apr.	May	Jun.	Jul.	Aug.	Sep.	Oct.	Nov.	Dec.
Amount of sales	1982	521	382	513	414	627	445	781	536	675	432	765	791
	1983	561	613	687	458	446	689	841	635	640	462	681	878
	1984	699	713	689	548	742	935	1,037	1,001	792	860	1,120	1,362
Correlation of ratios	1982	100	73.0	134.2	80.5	151.5	71	176	68.2	126	64.0	23.0	103.8
	1983	71	109.2	122	67	97.5	154	122.3	75.4	101	72	147.5	104
	1984	79.5	102	96.5	79.5	103.6	126	110.2	96.2	78.8	108	130	121.8
Mean value		79.5	102	122	79.5	103.6	126	122.3	75.4	101	72	147.5	104
Temporary index		100	102	124.2	98.2	101	127.4	142	106.5	108	77.8	114.2	119.3
Seasonal index		100	102.43	125.06	99.5	108.2	129.55	144.8	109.5	111.4	81.6	118.5	124.1
Seasonal index		88.6	89.5	110.2	88	96	114.05	128	97	72.2	105	110	
Average index by month													

＊Note···· ·Temporary index 79.5×119.3＝948

Seasonal index $\dfrac{100-94.8}{12}=0.434$ $\quad\dfrac{1,354.64}{12}=112.88$

—— 1982
--- 1983
······ 1984
—— Seasonal index

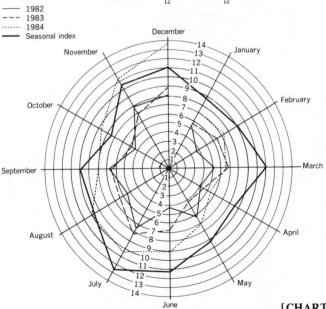

[CHART 30]

8. CORRELATION ANALYSIS (SPEARMAN'S METHOD)

Purpose

In the business world, two or more phenomena often have a causal relation between them. In economics, this is called a concurrent or supplemental relation. For example, if the consumption of rice decreases and that of bread increases, it is a concurrent relation and a 'negative correlation' A supplemental relation, such as if the number of cars registered increases, the consumption of gasoline increases also, is a 'positive correlation'. The purpose of *correlation analysis* is to evaluate the character and strength of such correlations. First, *Spearman's method* is explained.

How to construct

Collect and coordinate, beforehand, the monthly data on phenomena and factors which are thought to be correlated with each other. (Chart (8))

(1) Assign ordinal numbers according to the order or size of the data.

(2) Select the pairs of factors between which you want to know the correlation. Obtain the remainders when the monthly ordinal numbers of the pairs are deducted from each other and square them.

(3) Find the sum of the squares of the remainders of the ordinal numbers.

(4) Now apply the formula. n is the number of periods. ΣM^2 is the sum of squares of remainders of ordinal numbers.

(5) If $1 > \gamma > 0$, there is a positive correlation.
If $0 > \gamma > -1$, there is a negative correlation.
If $\gamma = 0$, no correlation.

$$\gamma = 1 - \frac{6\Sigma M^2}{n(n^2 - 1)}$$

Thus, you can determine the characteristics and strength of the correlations.

Note

Compare the calculated values with those obtained by *Pearson's formula* shown in the next section.

How to view and use

First, I suggest that you examine the correlations for your products according to this method of analysis. You can utilize it to find the correlation between the growth rate of sales of your product and that of your competitors' products, the correlation between the changes in your product sales and those of other related goods, etc. Thus you will be able to clarify various relations and obtain useful hints for your promotional tactics.

(8) Correlation Analysis
(Spearman's Method)

Formula $\boxed{\gamma = 1 - \dfrac{e\Sigma M^2}{n(n^2 - 1)}}$ ΣM^2 = the sum of squares of remainders of order numbers

If $1 > \gamma > 0$, there is a positive correlation

If $0 > \gamma > -1$, there is a negative correlation

If $\gamma = 0$, no correlation

n = 10	Sales costs		Average income of the consumers		Advertising cost		Dealers within a radius of 10 Km		Population within a radius of 10 Km	
	S	Rs	I	Ri	A	Rs	D	Rd	P	Rp
March	52,800,000	10	51,480	9	510,000	5	45	3	41,800	2.5
April	60,000,000	8	51,040	10	420,000	6	44	4	40,700	8
May	57,600,000	9	51,700	8	415,000	7	54	2	40,450	9
June	80,000,000	2	112,000	2	370,000	8	56	1	40,260	10
July	64,800,000	7	51,920	7	290,000	10	42	5	41,030	7
August	67,200,000	6	52,140	6	295,000	9	36	9	41,250	6
September	76,800,000	3	55,220	3	790,000	2	40	6	41,470	5
October	72,000,000	5	52,800	5	660,000	4	38	7	42,070	1
November	74,400,000	4	53,020	4	720,000	3	37	8	41,800	2.5
December	98,000,000	1	117,600	1	840,000	1	35	10	41,630	4

n = number of periods taken D = Dealer Ra = Rank of advertising cost

S = Sale P = Population Rd = Rank of number of dealers (in the same trade)

I = Income Rs = Rank of sale Rp = Population order number

A = Advertising Ri = Rank of income

Calculation Table for Spearman's Method

$(Rs - Ri)^2$		$(Rs - Ra)^2$		$(Rs - Rd)^2$		$(Rs - Rp)^2$	
$(10 - 9)^2$	1	$(10 - 5)^2$	25	$(10 - 3)^2$	49	$(10 - 2.5)^2$	56.25
$(8 - 10)^2$	4	$(8 - 6)^2$	4	$(8 - 4)^2$	16	$(8 - 8)^2$	0
$(9 - 8)^2$	1	$(9 - 7)^2$	4	$(9 - 2)^2$	49	$(9 - 9)^2$	0
$(2 - 2)^2$	0	$(2 - 8)^2$	36	$(2 - 1)^2$	1	$(2 - 10)^2$	64
$(7 - 7)^2$	0	$(7 - 10)^2$	9	$(7 - 5)^2$	4	$(7 - 7)^2$	0
$(6 - 6)^2$	0	$(6 - 9)^2$	9	$(6 - 9)^2$	9	$(6 - 6)^2$	0
$(3 - 5)^2$	0	$(3 - 1)^2$	1	$(3 - 6)^2$	9	$(3 - 5)^2$	4
$(5 - 5)^2$	0	$(5 - 4)^2$	1	$(5 - 7)^2$	4	$(5 - 1)^2$	16
$(4 - 4)^2$	0	$(4 - 3)^2$	1	$(4 - 8)^2$	16	$(4 - 2.5)^2$	2 25
$(1 - 1)^2$	0	$(1 - 1)^2$	0	$(1 - 10)^2$	81	$(1 - 4)^2$	9
$\Sigma M^2 = 6$		$\Sigma M^2 = 90$		$\Sigma M^2 = 238$		$\Sigma M^2 = 151.5$	

1. Correlation between S and I:

   $\gamma = 1 - \dfrac{36}{990} = \dfrac{954}{990} = 0.965$ a strong positive correlation

2. Correlation between S and A:

   $\gamma = 1 - \dfrac{540}{990} = \dfrac{450}{990} = 0.455$ a positive correlation

3. Correlation between S and D:

   $\gamma = 1 - \dfrac{1,428}{990} = \dfrac{438}{990} = -0.443$ a negative correlation

4. Correlation between S and P:

   $\gamma = 1 - \dfrac{909}{990} = \dfrac{81}{990} = 0.082$ no correlation

[CHART 31]

111

9. CORRELATION ANALYSIS (PEARSON'S FORMULA)

Purpose

The purpose of this *correlation analysis* is the same as that of *Spearman's method*, except that there a 'causal relation' is presumed. Here, the existence of direct causal relation is not always necessary. In other words, 'correlation' between A and B requires only a phenomenal relation for this application.

But we must be cautious with regard to meaningless pseudo-correlations, such as that assumed in the saying "A storm makes a cooper rich". Consider the following, cause A yields result A' and as a cause, A' yields result A''. If the chain of reactions is extended, the final result B is attained. (A storm (A) blows →○→○→○→ and finally "makes a cooper rich" (B)). But it would be erroneous to think of A as the direct cause of B.

How to construct

Coordinate the monthly data for each of the factors as shown in the chart. To determine correlations among your products, the data used must be actual sales results.

(1) Find the arithmetical average of each factor
(2) Calculate N − X = deviation (X) from the average
(3) Find the sum of the squares of each deviation
(4) Multiply by each other the deviation you want to compare, and find the sum of their products
(5) Apply the formula to them and calculate the results.

$$\gamma = \frac{\Sigma xy}{\sqrt{\Sigma x^2 \, \Sigma y^2}}$$

Note

If $1 > \gamma > 0$, there is a positive correlation. If $0 > \gamma > -1$, there is negative correlation. If $\gamma = 0$, there is no correlation. If the value is near to +1, the correlation is positive and high. If it is closer to zero, the correlation is slight.

How to view and use

What has a correlation with your products? It is important to always pay attention to statistical data in government publications and the publications of the industry or of your competitors. Also, you should always investigate what sort of correlations they are.

(9) Correlation Analysis
(Pearson's Formula)

Item / Month	A product	B product	C product	D product
March	4,460,000	1,230,000	360,000	1,480,000
April	4,230,000	980,000	290,000	1,920,000
May	4,640,000	1,110,000	460,000	1,600,000
June	6,020,000	860,000	580,000	1,520,000
July	5,170,000	920,000	480,000	1,730,000
August	4,890,000	1,280,000	440,000	1,790,000
September	4,920,000	1,180,000	470,000	2,000,000
October	5,680,000	1,040,000	570,000	1,930,000
November	5,730,000	960,000	540,000	1,960,000
December	6,110,000	1,070,000	620,000	1,730,000
Average	5,180,500	1,063,000	481,000	1,766,000

Month	a	b	c	d	a^2	b^2	c^2	d^2	ab	ac	ad
March	−73	17	−12	−29	5,329	289	144	841	−1,241	+876	+2,117
April	−95	−8	−19	15	9,025	64	361	225	+760	+1,805	−1,425
May	−55	5	−2	−17	3,025	25	4	289	−257	+110	+935
June	83	−20	10	−25	6,889	400	100	625	−1,660	+830	−2,075
July	−2	−14	0	−4	4	196	0	16	+28	0	+8
August	−30	22	−4	3	900	484	16	9	−660	+120	−90
September	−27	12	−1	23	729	144	1	529	−324	+27	−621
October	49	−2	9	16	2,401	4	81	256	−98	+441	+784
November	54	−10	6	19	2,916	100	36	361	−540	+324	+1,026
December	93	1	14	−4	8,649	1	196	16	+93	+1,302	−372
Sum	—	—	—	—	39,867	1,707	939	3,167	−3,915	5,835	287

Correlation	Formula	Result	Category
Correlation between A product and B product	$\dfrac{-3,915}{\sqrt{39,867 \times 1,707}} = \dfrac{-3,915}{8,249}$	−0.475	Negative correlation
Correlation between A product and C product	$\dfrac{5,835}{\sqrt{39,867 \times 939}} = \dfrac{5,835}{6,118}$	0.95	High positive correlation
Correlation between A product and D product	$\dfrac{287}{\sqrt{39,867 \times 3,167}} = \dfrac{287}{11,136}$	0.026	No correlation

[CHART 32]

113

10. SALES EFFICIENCY ANALYSIS CHART

Purpose

Salesmen leave the office and visit customers to sell their products. To maximize their sales efficiency and to eliminate waste or excess, we must numerically evaluate the facts and performance of their activity. For this purpose, a system must be arranged, beforehand, to log their performance in a table as completely as possible. Chart (10) is designed for this particular purpose. At the end of each month, find the sums of each column, apply the formula to them and work out the results. Then evaluate the results on the *RADAR chart*.

How to construct

Have the daily sales activity separately entered for each salesman in a table designed like chart (10-A). This record is obtained by entering the sum of the results of sales reports. Regarding the format of this table, you can design it in compliance with the type and conditions of your company.

Note

A separate chart is made for each salesman and is summed up every month. The results for each salesman are compared with the results of the other salesmen and ranking can thus be made. Assessing the strengths and weaknesses of each salesman, the sales manager will be able to determine the training needs of each.

If you compare the charts for each salesman, you will periodically be able to determine actual progress or retrogression and be able to train him more appropriately in the course of time.

How to view and use

The main point is to evaluate each ratio separately and independently, but it is also interesting to know the correlations among these ratios. For instance, what degree of positive correlation is there between the average number of customers visited daily and the ratio of sales performance? And,

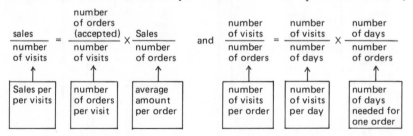

If you investigate these correlation ratios, the focal points for actual training will be clarified.

(10A) Sales Efficiency Analysis Chart

Name of salesman: Nagamasa Yamada Territory: Ward, Yokohama October, 1982 Sales goal 1,375,000 Gross profit goal 412,500

Month day (week)	Number of customers visited	Number of customers who ordered	QUOTA Amount ordered / Total amount ordered (1,375,000)	QUOTA Gross profit goal / Gross profit / Gross profit total (412,500)	Cash	Credit	Net aggregate of credit (Carryover 130,000)	Collected accounts	Expenses per visits	Details of accepted order	Details of collected accounts
1 Mon	7	2	55,000 60,000 5,000	16,500 20,000 3,500	20,000	40,000	130,000 40,000 170,000	0	740	Yamada Kogyo 20,000 Yoshimura Shoten 40,000	
2 Tue	4	0	55,000 △50,000	16,500 △13,000	0	0	170,000 0 100,000	70,000	140		
3 Wed	10	1	55,000 20,000 △40,000	16,500 7,500 △22,000	7,500	12,500	100,000 12,500 112,500	0	1,460	Toyama Press 7,500	Alus Koji 100,000 Kishi Kogyo 2,500
4 Thur	8	3	55,000 92,000 △3,000	7,500 42,000 △3,500	72,000	20,000	112,500 20,000 74,500	58,000	1,600	Masuda Mfg. 25,000 Yoshimura Shoten 47,000	Sumidaten 58,000
5 Fri	6	4	55,000 76,000 21,000	16,500 21,000 8,000	50,000	26,000	74,500 26,000 67,500	33,000	420	Towada Koji 27,000 Tateyama Kensetsu 23,000	Kitayama Kosaku 26,000
6 Sat	4	0	55,000 △37,000	16,500 0	0	0	67,500 0 67,500	0	560		
29 Thur	11	2	55,000 77,000 103,000	16,600 30,000 143,500	34,000	43,000	283,000 43,000 239,000	87,000	510	Russia Bread shop 34,000	Kitayama rubber 23,000 Tokyo Press 20,000
30 Fri	13	4	55,000 79,000 127,000	16,500 28,000 156,000	79,000	0	239,000 0 138,000	101,000	170	Yamakawa Tool 9,000 Kagami, Wood 70,000	Toyoko Super 101,000
31 Sat	6	4	55,000 93,000 165,000	16,500 32,500 172,000	90,000	3,000	138,000 3,000 129,000	12,000	460	Kishiwada Koji 43,000 Mitsukoshi 47,000	Tobita Sash 12,000
Σ	174	43	165,000 1,540,000	172,000 584,500	1,050,000	490,000	129,000	491,000	20,700		

[CHART 33A]

115

Sales Efficiency Ratios

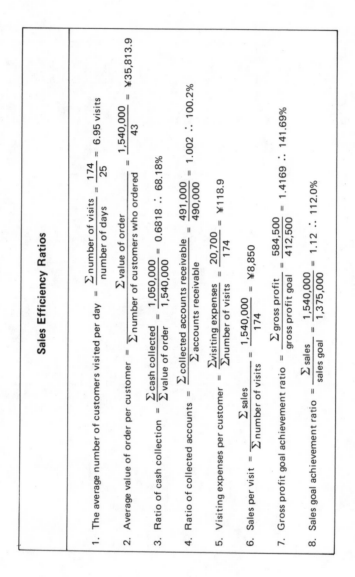

1. The average number of customers visited per day $= \dfrac{\sum \text{number of visits}}{\text{number of days}} = \dfrac{174}{25} = 6.95$ visits

2. Average value of order per customer $= \dfrac{\sum \text{value of order}}{\sum \text{number of customers who ordered}} = \dfrac{1,540,000}{43} = ¥35,813.9$

3. Ratio of cash collection $= \dfrac{\sum \text{cash collected}}{\sum \text{value of order}} = \dfrac{1,050,000}{1,540,000} = 0.6818 \therefore 68.18\%$

4. Ratio of collected accounts $= \dfrac{\sum \text{collected accounts receivable}}{\sum \text{accounts receivable}} = \dfrac{491,000}{490,000} = 1.002 \therefore 100.2\%$

5. Visiting expenses per customer $= \dfrac{\sum \text{visiting expenses}}{\sum \text{number of visits}} = \dfrac{20,700}{174} = ¥118.9$

6. Sales per visit $= \dfrac{\sum \text{sales}}{\sum \text{number of visits}} = \dfrac{1,540,000}{174} = ¥8,850$

7. Gross profit goal achievement ratio $= \dfrac{\sum \text{gross profit}}{\text{gross profit goal}} = \dfrac{584,500}{412,500} = 1.4169 \therefore 141.69\%$

8. Sales goal achievement ratio $= \dfrac{\sum \text{sales}}{\text{sales goal}} = \dfrac{1,540,000}{1,375,000} = 1.12 \therefore 112.0\%$

(10B) Sales Efficiency Analysis: RADAR Chart

Salesman:	Nagamasa Yamada	Sales Goal	¥1,375,000
Date:	October, 1982	Gross profit Goal	¥412,500

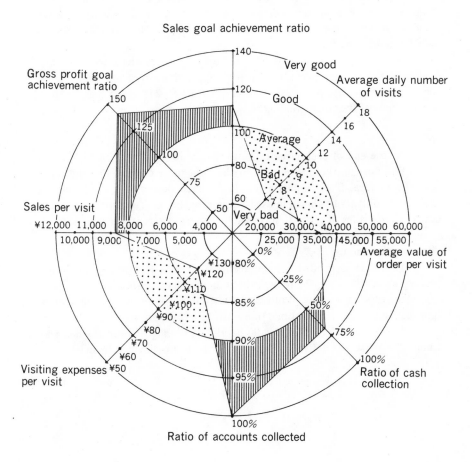

[CHART 33B]

117

11.   TIME UTILIZATION STUDY FOR SALESMEN

Purpose

The sales efficiency of a salesman depends largely on his making the most of his time. Hours spent for business talk is said to constitute the golden hours of salesmen, but it frequently happens that salesmen waste valuable time on incidental and ancillary work other than business talks. To maximize the productive use of time for sales negotiation, and collection, we must start by analyzing the actual conditions in which salesmen are spending their time.

How to construct

For this purpose, the sales report should be redesigned. The Daily Sales Report given on page 150 is an example of such a sales report. Its lower half is left blank to be filled in by the salesman, indicating his daily activities separately hour by hour.

Recording the results of his sales operations for the day, a salesman indicates the activity performed in each appropriate time slot. As all anticipated activities are previously written on the left side of the chart, he need only check off the corresponding cells.

Note

At the end of each week or month, sum up separately for each person the total hours on the bottom line of the right most column 152 and calculate the average. Show separate results for each person in a bar graph and show the contents of the time used allotted by hours. The time-usage habits and characteristics of each salesman will become obvious at a glance.

How to view and use

The time expended for demonstration, sales talk, presentation and closing shown here may be termed the golden hours for salesmen. To increase the more productive time, it must be studied how we can reduce the counter-productive factors (waiting time, transportation time, etc.).

A salesman of high sales volume also is usually efficient in using his time. It is most instructive for other salesmen to be shown such an example.

(11) Time Utilization Study Graph for Salesmen

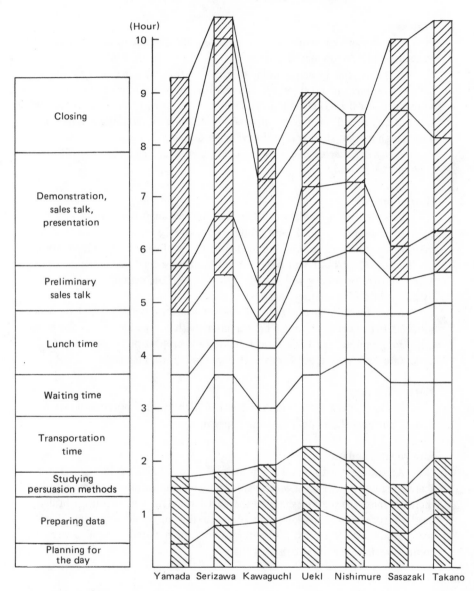

| Closing |
| Demonstration, sales talk, presentation |
| Preliminary sales talk |
| Lunch time |
| Waiting time |
| Transportation time |
| Studying persuasion methods |
| Preparing data |
| Planning for the day |

Yamada   Serizawa   Kawaguchl   Uekl   Nishimure   Sasazakl   Takano

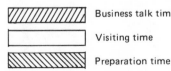

Business talk time

Visiting time

Preparation time

[CHART 34]

119

12. MARKET SHARE MAP

Purpose

Lanchester's principle is often used to cultivate territorial markets and to secure and develop market shares.

In short, this principle holds that by subdividing a market (geographically), grasping the ratio of market sharing by your product in the thus subdivided local market and utilizing a stronger sales force in high-sharing territories, you will be able to successively conquer all territories on the map with a high market sharing ratio for your products.

A *market sharing map* may be considered a strategic map to assess the ratio of market share.

How to prepare

First, obtain a blank map. If it is a coloured map, you can make a dry copy to obtain it in black and white. Next, plot your selling bases on the map with a coloured pencil. Subdivide territories of each base with partitioning lines into blocks. If you have not yet built up a territory, a supposed or administrative boundary will also do. Divide the whole map into small blocks by means of differentiating lines.

Now, investigate the ratio of market share of your product in each subdivided market. This must be coloured, with a separate colour for each ratio, for example, red for a ratio equal to or over 40%, orange for over 30%, yellow for over 20%, green for over 10% and blue for under 10%.

Note

In this map, a red colour represents a high level of potential customer appeal, but blue shows poor customer appeal.

How to view and use

According to Lanchester's principle, if a subdivided local market is shared higher, it will be more advantageous to concentrate your sales force there to raise the market share to the goal level. This will become a bridgehead of tomorrow's market. According to this principle, one should not try a frontal attack against a stronger competitor but first conquer a weaker competitor in order to raise market share.

(12) The Ratio of Market Share by Cities and Countries

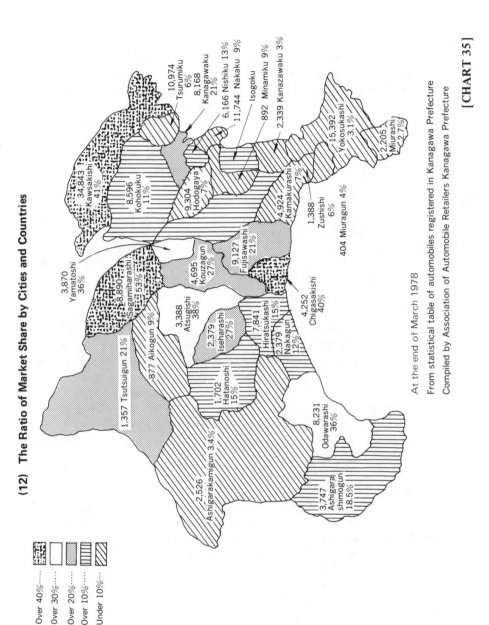

Over 40%......
Over 30%......
Over 20%......
Over 10%......
Under 10%......

34,843 Kawsakishi 41%

10,974 Tsurumiku 6%

8,168 Kanagawaku 21%

6,166 Nishiku 13%   11,744 Nakaku 9%

Isogoku
892 Minamiku 9%

2,339 Kanazawaku 3%

8,596 Kohokuku 11%

9,304 Hodogaya 7%

15,392 Yokosukashi 3.1%

2,205 Miurashi 2.7%

4,924 Kamakurashi 7%

3,870 Yamatoshi 36%

8,890 Sagamiharashi 53%

4,695 Kouzagun 27%

9,127 Fujisawashi 21%

1,388 Zushishi 6%

404 Miuragun 4%

1,357 Tsutsuigun 21%

877 Aikogun 9%

3,388 Atsugishi 38%

2,379 Iseharashi 27%

4,252 Chigasakishi 40%

7,841 Hiratsukashi 15%

2,379 Nakagun 12%

1,702 Hatanoshi 15%

2,526 Ashigarakamigun 3.4%

8,231 Odawarashi 36%

3,747 Ashigara shimogun 18.5%

At the end of March 1978

From statistical table of automobiles registered in Kanagawa Prefecture

Compiled by Association of Automobile Retailers Kanagawa Prefecture

[CHART 35]

13.   PRODUCT MIX PLAN BY LINEAR PROGRAMMING

Purpose

I have already explained the *marginal profit chart* under "management in general". The *product mix plan chart*, with some conditional limitations, is aimed at choosing the best mixes of products and revealing a method to yield the greatest profits. On the marginal profit chart, each product is ranked according to the marginal profits ratio and the sales of each product are plotted on the X axis. The fixed cost on the Y axis is recovered at an angle corresponding to the marginal profit ratio of each product. The point at which all fixed costs are recovered (break even point) is zero on Y. As we learned, profits are generated according to the increase in sales beyond this point.

We have developed a thorough understanding, through the marginal profits chart, of the fact that for increasing the profitability of an enterprise, it is effective to increase the sales of products of higher marginal profit ratio and to decrease the sales of products of lower marginal profit ratio proportionately. But this is not so easy in actual practice. In fact, it is often difficult to increase the sales of a product of higher marginal profit. (Customers permit a higher profit to compensate for their small amount of orders.)

Moreover, it frequently happens that the volume of resources to be put into the manufacturing of such goods is subject to limitations. Such limitations are, for example, the capacity of necessary equipment, the operating volume of works in process, the available capacity of contract or subcontract factories, total available volume of materials and parts, etc. How do you find the most realistic mixing of products to maximize profit production while allotting most suitably the limited resources to each product? In such circumstances, the *product mix plan by linear programming* is the only technique we can depend upon. Here I shall explain the most suitable product mix according to the technique of linear programming.

How to construct

I shall explain a solution reached by linear programming as an example. A certain manufacturer of transistor radios is making two kinds of products, A and B. The manufacture of one unit of product A requires:

I	Pre-processing of parts	20 minutes
	Assembling	40 minutes
	Mount processing (subcontracted)	35 minutes

The manufacture of a unit of product B requires

II	Pre-processing of parts	35 minutes
	Assembling	60 minutes
	Mount processing	20 minutes

The total monthly capacity of the manufacturer using his own workers and subcontracts is:

  III Preprocessing of parts 2,500 man hours = 150,000 minutes
      Assembling   4,000 man hours = 240,000 minutes
      Mount processing   2,333 man hours = 140,000 minutes

The gross sales profit is increased by ¥450 by production of a unit of product A, ¥550 by production of a unit of product B. The foregoing are the given conditions. How many units of each product should the manufacturer make to maximize his profit?

To solve this question, we have to begin by formulating the above conditions I, II and III as follows. If we regard product A as x and product B as y, the conditions become

$$20x + 35y \leqq 150,000 \ \ldots \ (1)$$
$$40x + 60y \leqq 240,000 \ \ldots \ (2)$$
$$35x + 20y \leqq 140,000 \ \ldots \ (3)$$

The required function is f(x, y) = 450x + 550y and we must find how to maximize it.

The solution of this function, which has two unknown quantities, can be obtained from the graph shown on the following chart. On this chart, the horizontal axis x represents production of A, the vertical axis y represents production of B. If we represent equation (1) on the graph, the triangle enclosed by straight line (1) and the vertical and horizontal axes represents parts preprocessing capacity. Then, regarding equation (2) above, the triangle enclosed by straight line (2) and the two axes represents assembling capacity. With equation (3), the triangle enclosed by line (3) and two axes represents mount processing capacity. Therefore, we can see that the area which satisfies equations (1), (2) and (3) at the same time is the diamond-shaped, crosshatched area (with oblique lines).

If we represent function f(x, y) = 450x + 550y on the graph, we draw a line parallel to this and find M by shifting on a parallel so that M reaches its largest value in the area. M is thus the production level required. Draw two perpendicular lines from M to axes A and B, and find each foot. You will now get A = 2,770 (units), B = 2,130 (units).

As point M is the intersecting point of line (2) and line (3), we can easily see that the consumption of both assembling and mount processing capacities are maximized. We can also see that the total gross sales profit is (2,770 sets × ¥550) + (2,130 sets × ¥450) = ¥2,481,000.

Note

Product mix by linear programming will be employed again, as it provides the strongest supporting data for sales quotas according to products.

How to view and use

Solution by linear programming on a graph is possible only when there are two unknown quantities. (Here there are two products, A and B). If there are more than two unknowns, it will be necessary to use a *Simplex chart*. Please study Simplex charts, using special works on linear programming.

(13) Solution of Linear Programming by Graph

If $20x + 40y \lesseqgtr 150{,}000$
$40x + 60y \lesseqgtr 240{,}000$
$35x + 20y \lesseqgtr 140{,}000$
let $f(x, y) = 450x + 550y$ the largest. Of course $x \lesseqgtr o$, $y \lesseqgtr o$.

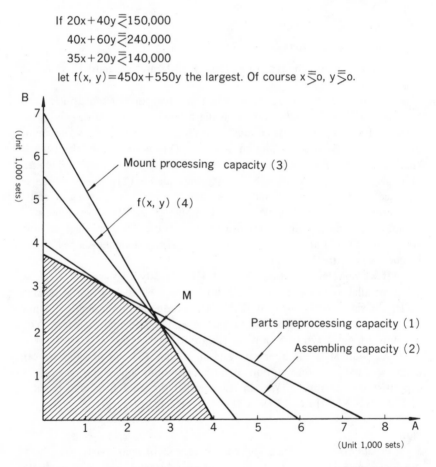

[CHART 36]

124

14. SALES QUOTA CHART

Purpose

There are standard times for manufacture which are used as control bases in factories and likewise, *sales quotas* can be used for control of salesmen in selling operations. If a sales quota is allotted to each salesman, it means that he must practice self-control. Optimum control of objectives is thus attained. With sales quotas, each person becomes aware of the connection between the objective of the organization as a whole and that of the individual. The salesforce can thus be strongly motivated to achieve desired objectives.

How to construct

A sales target is an accounting concept which is developed from a profit plan and is then divided and subdivided, as shown below, until individual personal quotas are reached.

(1) First, make *sales quotas* according to products, taking into account the life cycle curves of products, the *product mix* and the *marketing mix.*

(2) Build up monthly sales targets, based on *seasonal fluctuation analysis*, according to products. Monthly sales targets, according to products, are thereby established.

(3) Now, after dividing the market regionally and determining the characteristics of the share ratios for each territory, set the sales targets for territories, taking into account territorial development tactics. The sales target by products, by months and by territories is now set.

(4) Now, after determining the actual performance and ability of each salesman according to *sales efficiency analysis*, allot quotas for salesmen, taking into account future growth potential and the training policy to be adopted for individuals. Thus, the *sales quotas* by products, by months, by territories and by individual salesmen's characteristics is decided.

Note

For the purpose of motivating one's employees to an objective, it is important for each of them to understand clearly the mutual relation between the overall objective and his own personal objective. In addition, the whole and the part must be explained so that the connection can be understood theoretically.

How to use

When a target is set, it is not the only task of a sales manager to stimulate his people to achieve it, but it is also important for a sales manager to clearly show salesmen the difference between the target and the actual results, i.e. the difference by products, by months, by territories and by individual salesmen. The sales manager should also identify individual short-falls and help salesmen to increase their efficiency by giving guidance and leadership.

(14) Sales Quota, August, 1982 M Trading Co., Ltd.

By products	Quotas according to territories		Quotas according to salesman				
			Omura	Higashimura	Nishimura	Minamimure	Kitamura
Samson 9,780,000	Yokohama	2,830,000	1,200,000				1,630,000
	Kawasaki	4,050,000		2,700,000	1,350,000		
	Yokosuka	2,700,000				2,700,000	
	Kamakura	200,000	200,000				
Delilah 17,080,000	Yokohama	4,120,000	3,350,000				770,000
	Kawasaki	6,850,000		4,350,000	2,500,000		
	Shonan	6,110,000	1,950,000			4,160,000	
Romeo 3,750,000	Yokohama	1,520,000	980,000				540,000
	Kawasaki	1,110,000		760,000	350,000		
	Yokosuka	150,000				150,000	
	Kamakura	300,000	300,000				
	Zushi	670,000	670,000				
Juliet 3,890,000	Yokohama	1,980,000	600,000				1,380,000
	Kawasaki	1,530,000		480,000	1,050,000		
	Shonan	380,000				380,000	
		34,500,000	9,250,000	8,290,000	5,250,000	7,390,000	4,320,000

34,500,000

[CHART 37]

15. CAUSE AND EFFECT DIAGRAMS FOR DEFECTIVE PRODUCTS

Purpose

A claim for a defect, in a sense, is important information about a product for sales and marketing activity. It is necessary to endeavour to acquire such information instead of avoiding it.

It is just as important to understand exactly the reasons causing the defects for which claims are made. For this purpose, it is necessary to have up-to-date *cause and effect diagrams* for defective products. A *cause and effect diagram* is a chart which shows systematically the cause of defects in products, and it is most effective for helping to eliminate defects.

How to draw up

First, enumerate every factor thought to be a cause of defects in a product. Then group those factors which either are related to each other or have something in common. In these circumstances, a systematic grouping is useful. Represent the relationship between fundamentals and derivatives by groups on a tree-like figure with the branches indicating relationships. When all interrelated factors are thus represented, you will have a cause and effect diagram as shown in the following chart (15). As you can see on the chart, the diagrams are systematic flows which involve chains of first, second and third, etc. degree of causality.

Note

If you cannot carry out efficient grouping and systematizing of classification, there is a danger that the chart may develop a fishbone structure. In such a case, all causes are connected directly with defects, and this makes it impossible to eradicate causes of defects systematically. The structures must resemble trees rather than fishbones.

How to read and use

Whenever a claim is made against a product, analyze the causes according to the *cause and effect diagrams* for defective products and collect and record the number of occurrences of each claim factor for a certain period. Note the number of times for all such occasions for each factor, on *cause and effect diagrams*. Then represent each item by the order of frequency of claim factors on a bar graph.

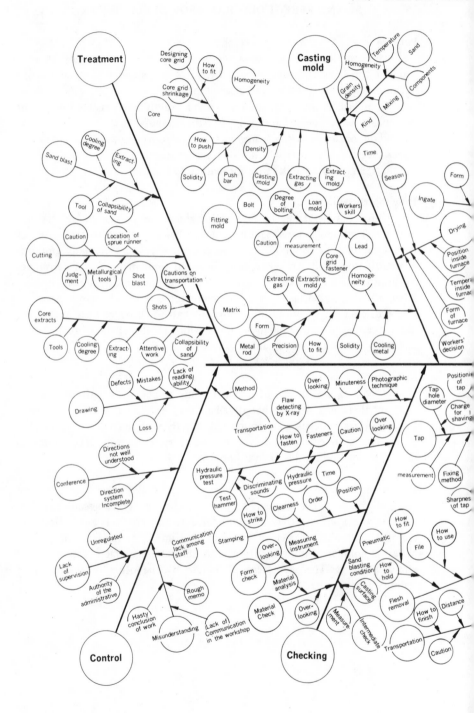

Diagram for Defective Products

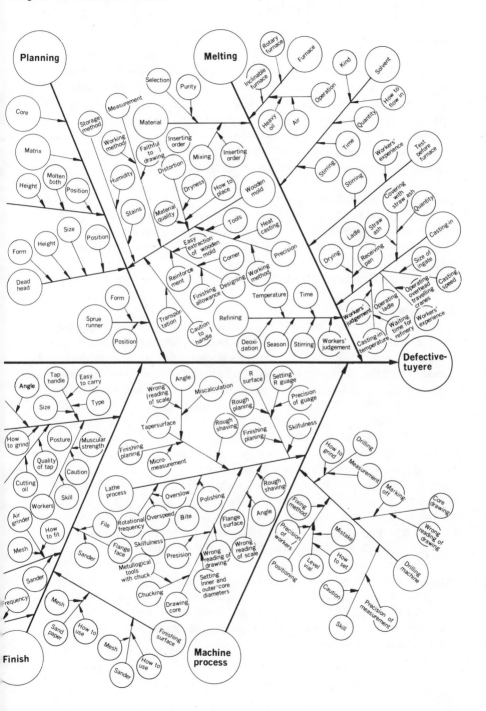

[CHART 38]

16.   MARKETING MIX CHART

Purpose

For a growing and developing company, management needs a dynamic way of thinking. Above all, it is important for all the personnel of the company to make every effort to develop and improve a marketing system. A management policy, oriented to marketing, must be employed. To begin with, the president, sales manager, accounting manager and production manager should participate in the decision to implement a positive marketing programme representing their own departments. As a technique for such occasions, a *marketing mix chart* is recommended.

How to draw up this chart

First, look at Chart (16). When sales prices and the number of products change, a chart in which gross gains, total expenses and profit have been calculated in advance is used. The design and format should be the responsibility of the accounting manager. The important point here is to use it effectively. This chart can be easily developed with a personal computer.

How to use this chart

As an example. Chart (16) is related to a new product, a multipurpose desk for schoolchildren made by a certain furniture manufacturing company. To discuss this, all the managers in charge of various departments are called. Let the business manager determine the price range which customers require. For example, let us fix the zone between ¥15,900 and ¥16,800. As in the chart, vertical lines (1) are drawn and those areas outside the lines will be rejected. Next, we ask the production manager to set the daily operation rate at the beginning of production of the new product. Delineate a zone between 5,000 and 6,500 units: two horizontal lines are (2) drawn on the chart. Those areas outside the line will be rejected.

Furthermore, we will narrow down the remaining areas by estimating the phases of profit and operating funds through guesswork and let the accounting manager choose one. For example, eliminate those above the total of ¥95 million as unsuitable. Then, as in (3) of the chart, horizontal lines will be drawn with areas below these lines eliminated.

Now, choosing one of the remaining five plans is the duty of the president. Here, from consideration of the learning ability of workers (as the products are new) and profitability, the safest plan (4), namely, sales price ¥15,900, number 5,000 units, profit ¥7.5 million, is finally adopted. In this draft project, all the managers in charge participated to determine the most reasonable *marketing mix*.

(16) Multipurpose Desk for School Children: Marketing Mix Chart

(Unit: ¥1 million)

Sales price / Number of units	¥15,000			¥15,900			¥16,800			¥18,000		
Remarks	Gross profit	Total expenses	Profit	Gross profit	Total expenses	Profit	Gross profit	Total expenses	Profit	Gross profit	Total expenses	Profit
2,500 sets	37.5	36	1.5	39.75	44.25	4.5	42	46.5	(−)4.5	45	51	(−) 6
3,000 sets	45	40.5	4.5	47.7	49.2	(−)1.5	50.4	53.4	(−)3	54	57	(−)3
3,500 sets	52.5	45	7.5	55.65	54.15	1.5	58.8	60.3	(−)1.5	63	63	0
4,000 sets	60	51	9	63.6	59.1	4.5	67.2	67.2	0	72	70.5	1.5
4,500 sets	67.5	55	12.5	71.55	65.55	6	75.6	74.1	1.5	81	78	3
5,000 sets	75	66	9	79.5	72	7.5	85.5	82.5	3	90	85.5	4.5
5,500 sets	82.5	75	7.5	87.45	79.95	7.5	93.9	89.4	4.5	99	93	6
6,000 sets	90	85.5	4.5	95.4	86.4	9.0	102.3	96.3	36	108	100.5	7.5
6,500 sets	97.5	96	1.5	103.35	95.85	7.5	110.7	103.2	7.5	117	106	11
7,000 sets	105	106.5	(−)1.5	117.3	116.8	0.5	119.1	113.1	6	126	115.5	1 10.5
7,500 sets	112.5	117	(−)4.5	109.25	102.25	0	127.5	126.0	1.5	135	127.5	7.5
8,000 sets	120	127.5	7.5	127.0	141	(−)14	134.4	136.0	(−)1.6	144	141	3

[CHART 39]

131

17.   PURCHASE PRICE FLUCTUATION GRAPH

Purpose
In the case of market commodities, to firmly grasp the daily fluctuation of purchasing prices is an important key to control the profitability of an enterprise. To operate cleverly in the market, wait until prices go up and then sell your goods. This is common sense for a merchant who depends on a special sixth sense and his experience. However, one should grasp the market trend as rationally and scientifically as possible, so as not to chance any fatal errors.

For that purpose, we should accurately grasp the real pattern of price fluctuation in the past and prepare to take the safest possible route in purchasing activity in future.

How to draw up this graph
First, we plot the actual state of purchasing price fluctuation, month by month, on the graph. Next, following the minimum involution mentioned previously, a price fluctuation trend line is drawn. The extension lines in each term into the future of this straight line (primary formula) or the curve line (secondary formula) are also their own expectation lines.

It is important for us to know the degree of 'straggling' around the trend line. For that purpose, it is desirable to keep within the standard deviation with regard to the 'straggling' of the monthly price fluctuation. The calculation formula for the standard deviation is:

$$\sigma = \sqrt{\frac{1}{N}\ (x_1 - \mu)^2 + (x_2 - \mu)^2 + \ldots \ldots (x_n - \mu)^2}$$

On this occasion, the dependability $--$ or confidence $--$ limit of the data is 2 sigmas for 95% and 3 sigmas for 99.7%. Let this be 2 sigmas. If ¥1,256 above this trend line and ¥1,256 below this trend line are the upper lower limits respectively, these will be the control limits $--$ in the case of imported American timber product unit prices.

Relations
As in the control limit forecasting of the course of a typhoon, the pattern of price fluctuation seems to be roughly a trend line, and we can assume that the 'straggling' in each month will not be out of this band, unless something unusual happens.

How to view and use the graph
If we have the record of monthly price fluctuations for the past three years, we can make a graph from it. What we must not forget here is the fact that the past record cannot always be the guarantee for the future. We must study constantly how different business fluctuations, political, economic and social factors, good and bad dealings will affect price fluctuations.

(17A) Unit Price Fluctuation Graph: Imported American
Timber per 10 Cubic Feet

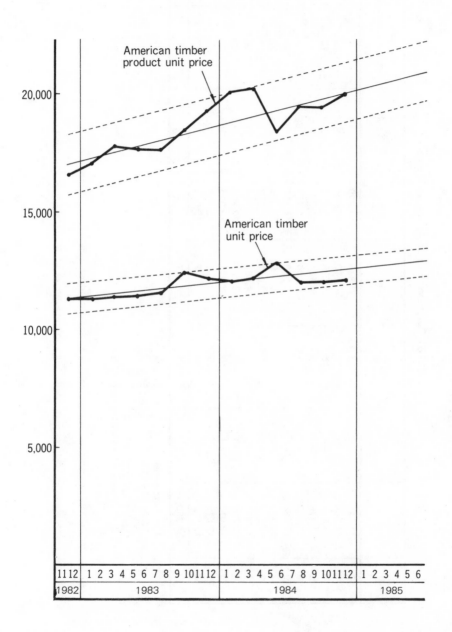

[CHART 40A]

(17B) Purchase Price of American Timber

Month	s	x	x^2	Sx	S'	(S − S')	Variable transformation d	d^2
12	11,306	−6	36	−67,836	11,325	19	2	4
2	11,306	−5	25	−56,530	11,424	118	12	144
4	11,394	−4	16	−45,576	11,523	129	13	169
6	11,476	−3	9	−34,428	11,622	146	15	255
8	11,652	−2	4	−23,304	11,721	69	7	49
10	12,366	−1	1	−12,366	11,820	546	55	3,025
12	12,143	0	0	0	11,919	224	22	484
2	12,012	+1	1	+12,012	12,018	4	1	1
4	12,277	+2	4	+24,554	12,117	160	16	256
6	12,807	+3	9	+38,421	12,216	591	59	3,481
8	12,012	+4	16	+48,048	12,315	303	30	900
10	12,012	+5	25	+60,060	12,414	402	40	1,600
12	12,187	+6	36	+73,122	12,513	326	33	1,089
	154,950		164	+16,177				11,457

$$\begin{cases} \Sigma S = 13a = 154.950 \\ \Sigma Sx = 164b = 16.177 \end{cases} \quad \begin{cases} a = 11.919 \\ b = 98.6 \end{cases}$$

$$\sigma = \sqrt{\frac{11,457}{13}} = \sqrt{881} = 29.7$$

Variable-transformed by $\frac{1}{10}$, 29.7 is multiplied by 10 and a standard deviation of 297 is obtained.

Take two sigmas above and below the trend line and add and subtract ¥594 to make the control limit line.

[CHART 40B]

(17C) American Timber Products Sales Price

Month	S	x	x^2	Sx	S'	(S − S')	Variable transformation d	d^2
12	16,571	−6	36	−99,426	17,031	460	46	2,146
2	17,075	−5	25	−85,355	17,295	220	22	484
4	17,780	−4	16	−71,120	17,559	221	22	484
6	17,681	−3	9	−53,043	17,823	142	14	196
8	17,615	−2	4	−35,230	18,087	472	47	2,209
10	18,474	−1	1	−18,474	18,351	123	12	144
12	19,289	0	0	0	18,615	674	67	4,489
2	20,103	+1	1	20,103	18,879	1,224	122	14,884
4	20,223	+2	4	40,446	19,143	1,080	108	11,664
6	18,336	+3	9	55,008	19,407	1,071	107	11,449
8	19,416	+4	16	77,664	19,671	255	25	625
10	19,416	+5	25	97,080	19,935	519	51	2,601
12	20,009	+6	36	12,005	20,199	190	19	361
	241,998		164	42,737	42,737			51,375

$$\begin{cases} \Sigma S = \zeta a = 13a = 241.998 \qquad a = 18.615 \\ \Sigma Sx = b\Sigma x^2 = 162b = 42.737 \qquad b = 264 \end{cases}$$

$$\sigma = \sqrt{\frac{51.375}{13}} = \sqrt{3,952} = 62.8$$

Variable-transformed by $\frac{1}{10}$, 62.8 is multiplied by 10 and the standard deviation of 628 is obtained.

Take two sigmas above and below the trend line, and add and subtract ¥1,256 to make the control limit line.

[CHART 40C]

135

18. DISTRIBUTION CHANNEL CHART

Purpose

Before proceeding with sales strategies, we must be sure of the present state of distribution channels. As a method of comprehending the present state of distribution channels, it may be useful to draw a channel-wise table, but as there are crossing and branchings within the flow, it is best to represent this on a chart. All the channels will be shown so, in the course of progress of the distribution revolution and of structural change of industry, we can mold a desired distribution channel policy.

How to draw up the chart

This is a *distribution channel chart* for textiles with woven goods as the central factor in Japan. Its methods can be applied to your company, however. In this case, by ignoring individual middlemen and taking them as a distribution organ in each distribution channel, we can check what percentage of products (or what amount of money) flows into each organ and put in in the chart. Here we can grasp the direction and size of the flow at a glance.

Relations

When the chart is prepared, it is important not only to utilize it as data for study or analysis, but also to convert it into a 'distribution channel reorganization chart', based on the new project.

Employing the information from this chart we proceed with a distribution channel policy as well as other projects.

How to view and use this chart

This will help us to observe what directions the distribution organization will take in the course of its transition, by looking carefully at the actual state of present-day distribution channels. We can also conveniently study what kind of help from dealers should be extended to each existing distribution channel.

Taking a long stride with a new concept, we can find a new distribution channel, adding it to the conventional one. Thus, the flow of the products of the company will be enlarged and deepened. Similar utilization of this chart is encouraged to enhance the movement of materials and products.

(18) Distribution Channel Chart of Fiber Goods in Japan with Textiles as Central Factor

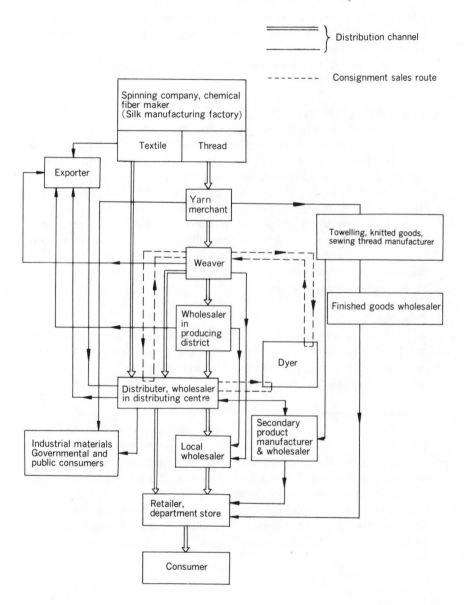

[CHART 41]

19. MARKET CONNECTIONS CHART

Purpose

An area market conquest plan views an area market in a macro fashion. When starting actual sales activity, however, we must move toward objectives in a micro way. For this, it is necessary to know what we should aim at and when and how we should approach our target. We must make clear these points in a *market connection chart*. It is, so to speak, a plan for exploitation of prospective customers.

How to draw up the chart

The methods of contacting prospective customers are:

1. A casual visit. 2. Finding them through relatives and friends. 3. Endless chain method. 4. Making use of VIPs. 5. Turn-key method. 6. Making use of parties. 7. Utilizing name and address books. 8. Utilizing publications. 9. Tie-up method. 10. Group utilization tactics. Whichever method you adopt, it is desirable that the connections 'from whom to whom' be drawn as exactly as possible in the chart. It is difficult to completely cover a useful visiting schedule even though we have the addresses of our prospective customers and a visiting schedule. This chart will serve as the means of utilizing the relations between visiting targets and their connection with us to the greatest advantage.

Relations

The chart will serve as a reference when we plot a practical sales promotion plan for salesmen later. It is desirable that this chart be drawn jointly by sales managers and salesmen. By using this chart, sales managers can study every action of salesmen very effectively.

How to use the chart

The names of each target prospective customer should be written in the circles, the size of which is determined by purchase order size. Record the appointment dates for visits to prospective customers. Following each meeting, fill in the circle using the colour red. If a sales agreement is not reached at the meeting, note the reason.

After a definite period (usually every month) renew the chart and at the same time analyze the reasons for failures during the previous period. Consider these points before embarking on the next target project to avoid similar errors.

(19) Market Connections Chart

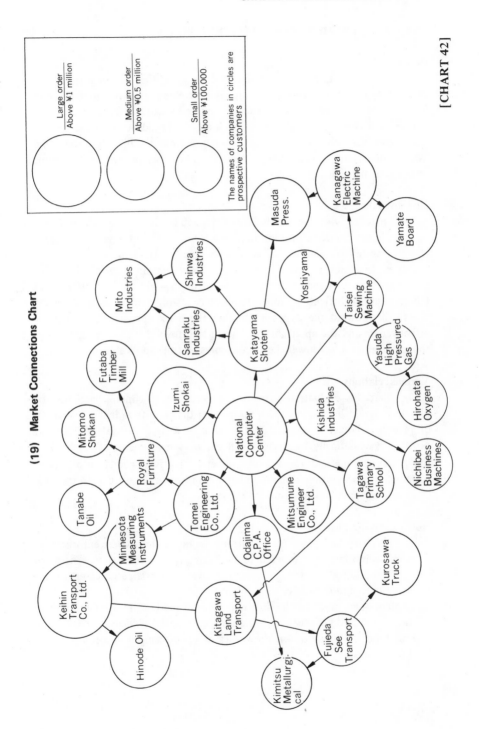

Large order
Above ¥1 million

Medium order
Above ¥0.5 million

Small order
Above ¥100,000

The names of companies in circles are prospective customers

[CHART 42]

20. SALES PROMOTION EVALUATION CHART

Purpose

Sales promotion is one of the fields in marketing to which the key is creative ideas; it brings about harmony and increased efficiency in the various activities of functional and personal selling and should be programmed as a course of action. For this purpose, each action should be evaluated synthetically and relatively. The *sales promotion evaluation chart* is introduced here. The planning, in which sales promotion policy has priority, is of prime importance here.

How to make

A meeting with completely free expression of ideas is the most effective environment when sales promotion policy is planned. All the sales promotion ideas suggested should be evaluated individually. The squares shown near each item in the chart comprise a column for evaluation purposes. The mark shown in the chart indicates the degree of applicability, from left to right (three stages — difficult to apply, applicable, readily applicable) accordingly, the further toward the upper left corner the mark appears, the higher the effectiveness and the applicability. The further toward the lower right corner the mark appears, the lower the effectiveness and the applicability.

Various relations

When this evaluation chart is completed, more concrete activities of planning should be possible. This means that the priority order for each item of planning should be decided in the form of a time schedule and should proceed systematically by deciding on the person in charge of application, the place and method for application, etc. This is all-round enforcement planning for sales promotion in which a coordinator, charged with the task of expediting procedures, should be chosen.

How to view and use

This chart is prepared for an automobile repair shop where enforcement of sales promotion is considered to be difficult. This chart shows there are many methods for attracting customers, even if no large-scale repairs are needed due to nonoccurrence of accidents.

Mentioned here are the direct promotion method, indirect promotion method, promotion of customers relations, and special services for customers. The method of classification, however, may be changed according to the kind of business.

(20) Repairs, Sales and Positive Measures Evaluation Chart (sample: an automobile repair shop)

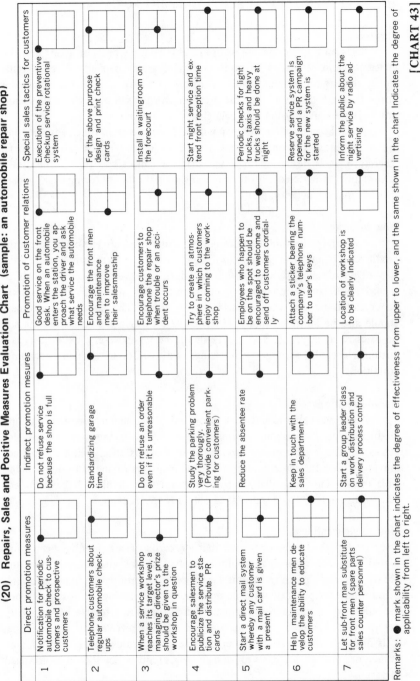

	Direct promotion measures	Indirect promotion mesures	Promotion of customer relations	Special sales tactics for customers
1	Notification for periodic automobile check to customers and prospective customers	Do not refuse service because the shop is full	Good service on the front desk. When an automobile enters the station, you approach the driver and ask what service the automobile needs	Execution of the preventive checkup service rotational system
2	Telephone customers about regular automobile check-ups	Standardizing garage time	Encourage the front men and maintenance men to improve their salesmanship	For the above purpose design and print check cards
3	When a service workshop reaches its target level, a managing director's prize should be given to the workshop in question	Do not refuse an order even if it is unreasonable	Encourage customers to telephone the repair shop when trouble or an accident occurs	Install a waiting room on the forecourt
4	Encourage salesmen to publicize the service station and distribute PR cards	Study the parking problem very thoroughly. (Provide convenient parking for customers)	Try to create an atmosphere in which customers enjoy coming to the workshop	Start night service and extend front reception time
5	Start a direct mail system whereby any customer with a mail card is given a present	Reduce the absentee rate	Employees who happen to be on the spot should be encouraged to welcome and send off customers cordially	Periodic checks for light trucks, taxis and heavy trucks should be done at night
6	Help maintenance men develop the ability to educate customers	Keep in touch with the sales department	Attach a sticker bearing the company's telephone number to user's keys	Reserve service system is opened and a PR campaign for the new system is started
7	Let sub-front man substitute for front men (spare parts sales counter personnel)	Start a group leader class on work distribution and delivery process control	Location of workshop is to be clearly indicated	Inform the public about the night service by radio advertising

Remarks: ● mark shown in the chart indicates the degree of effectiveness from upper to lower, and the same shown in the chart Indicates the degree of applicability from left to right.

[CHART 43]

21. SALESMEN'S CREDIT SURVEY REPORT FORM

Purpose

Sales and collection are as inseparable as the wheels of a cart and the efficiency and regularity of collections are largely dependent upon credit survey reports for determination of customers' credit worthiness. It must be borne in mind, however, that the preparation of credit survey reports should not be left exclusively to credit agencies.

It can be said that a salesman who regularly keeps in touch with customers is the most appropriate person for carrying out credit survey reports. Therefore, it is desirable for a salesman to collect and file the necessary information, using credit forms, such as shown on the following page, as part of his daily sales activity.

How to make

It is preferable for the sales department to prepare the blank forms for credit reports and if necessary, to design them in the form of hole sort cards.

The salesman should be instructed to make entries on the cards to record significant items regarding customers' credit status. The cards should be collected by the sales department for filing. The status of customers should also be indicated in a *RADAR chart* by which the entire picture can be assessed at a glance. The charts should be revised every six months as a customer's credit standing can change with shifts in ambient economic conditions.

Various relations

A salesman should not be sent out only for the purpose of completing credit surveys. These should normally be correlated in the course of his sales activities. The *credit survey report forms* or cards, after being completed, are to be filed for the common use of all members of the sales department. This means that particularly personal information should not be included. The forms are later to be transcribed onto a *RADAR chart*.

How to view and use

It should not be considered that a *credit survey report* has been completed with the recording of objective data. A salesman should have the ability to clearly perceive various danger signals regarding the financial affairs of business enterprise, by using common sense and experience. It is important for salesmen to make the company's credit policy effective by promptly determining the actual situation not just what is revealed by figures alone. It is desirable that each customer be graded according to his credit survey evaluation, and on the basis of such grading, credit policy should be arranged in advance.

(21) Salesman's Credit Survey Report Form

Customer's name			Code		Address	
Proprietor's name					How to contact by telephone	
Names of branches and field offices					Address	
Address of proprietor					Store employees	

Proprietor	Nature	gentle, excitable, open, devious, arrogant			Nature	short-tempered, patient, reserved, talkative		
	Hobby				Politically inclined	yes, no		
	School career	University graduate, junior high school graduate primary school graduate			Honorary posts			
	Intellectual standard				Home town			
	Previous career				Way of talking	Eloquent, slow, ordinary		
	Way of thinking	Middle-of-road, conservative, progressive			Habits	drinker, abstainer, smoker, non-smoker		
	Merits				Special ability			
	Demerts				Techniques	skilled, not skilled, 5 or 6 years' experience, knows a little		

	Age	Relations with the proprietor	Occupation	Age	Relations with the proprietor	Occupation	Mrs. X's nature	gentle, nagging, reserved, talkative
Family							Mrs. X's character	gentle, open, devious, arrogant, excitable, mean
							Mrs. X's hobby	
							Family	husband as center, wife as center, child as center
							Children	good training, bad training
							Home appliances	electric fan, electric washing machine, refrigerator, electric mixer, radio, record player
							Maid servant	have, have not
							Order	In good order, in bad order

	Customer's name	Date of first deal	Monthly purchases	Person in charge	Size		Frontage, depth	
Principal customers					Property		own property, rented store	
					Location		on main street, near main street, far from main street, in rural area	
					In the store		decoration: very good, ordinary, bad lighting lighting: very bright, ordinary, dark	
					Number of passersby		per hour, below 500, below 1,000, below 5,000	
					Insurance		Insured for ¥	
					Neighboring store of the same kind		address name	

		Items to deal in	Years and month when dealing began	Date of first deal	Remarks	Business experience		
Business side	**Items handled**					Date of first deal		
						Sales capacity	monthly units (in store), units (outside)	
						Actual personnel in the business	Proprietor, his wife, manager, sales clerk	
						Business areas		
						Shop sales clerk's name	Years of service	average monthly sales	Addresses

Accounting side	Banks						
	Bookkeeping system	Complete, incomplete (man in charge of accounting) nobody in charge of accounting		Property			
	Business organization	limited company, unlimited company, limited partnership, unlimited partnership, private management			Name	Address	Guarantee capacity
	Capital			**Guarantee**			
	Debit						
	Credit rating at banks	very good, good, ordinary, poor, very bad					
	Reputation among people in same type of business	very good, good, ordinary, poor, very bad					
	Reputation in the neighboring area	very good, good, ordinary, poor, very bad					

[CHART 44]

143

22.   SALESMAN'S VISITING SCHEDULE FORM

Purpose

A *visiting schedule* is of the highest importance for increasing the sales efficiency of a salesman, for rationalizing his activity rhythm to his daily routine. By preparing a schedule for each salesman, fruitless visits and time lags can be avoided and sales activities can be controlled and supervised from the office. Random sales activity without a *visiting schedule* is ineffectual and can result in much hard work being done in vain. It also contributes to lowering the morale of the entire sales department.

How to make the schedule

(1)   The names of customers to be visited are entered in the left hand column of the form by referring to individual customer cards. All customers to be visited during the month should be entered.

(2)   Place a small circle in the appropriate date column to denote a visit made on the same date last year.

(3)   Place a medium-size circle in the appropriate date column to denote a proposed visit during the month.

(4)   The form is now submitted to the sales manager, who gives approval by placing large circles against the names of customers in the appropriate date columns. The form is now returned to the salesman.

(5)   A horizontal line is to be marked in the visiting column after a visit is made.

(6)   A vertical mark is to be made if an order is obtained.

(7)   An oblique line (/) is to be made if the salesman receives payment.

(8)   A (\) mark is to be made if claims arise.

Accordingly, the mark ⊕ shows that the most favorable results have been achieved and also marks the completion of a transaction.

How to use

This is not only a schedule, but also the control chart for actual sales activity. In this way, a sales manager can precisely determine the actual nature of each salesman's activity from the schedule and can give precise instruction and supervision to each salesman individually. In addition, for the future visiting schedule, he can develop an overall picture in his mind.

(22) Salesmen's Visiting Plan Form (Example)

Area: Tokyo   Salesman in charge: Ichiro Tanaka   Period: May 1984

Customer \ Date	May 1	2	3	4	5	6	8	9	10	11	12	29	30	31
Hitachi, Ltd.		o	⊕			⊕			◎	o				◎
Noda Shoyu		⊕	o	⊕	o		⊕	o					◎	
Nippon Electric	o		o				o	o					o	o
Sekisui Chemical	◯		◎		◎		◯		◯	◎				o
Marubeni	o	o	⊕					o	o				◯	
Kyodo Printing			◎			⊕				◎				o
Nissan Automobile Engineering		⊕		⊕		◯								◯
Asahi Glass	◎		◯	o			o	◯	o	o	○		◯	o
Bridgestone Tire	⊕	⊕			◎	◎	⊕	o	o	o				o
Japan Travel Bureau		⊕		o			o	◯		◯			◎	
Nisshin Flour Mill		⊕	◯	◎	◎	◎	o	◎	o	◯			◎	◎
Tokyo Cellophane	⊕		◯	◎		⊕							◯	o
Citizen Watch						⊕	⊕							◎

o = Visiting programme on the same day of the previous year
— = Visited
○ = Visit at salesman's discretion
◯ = Permission from sales manager

| = Received order
/ = Collected bills
\ = Claim

[CHART 45]

23.   CUSTOMER PROFILE FORM

Purpose

In marketing, everything revolves around the customer. Success or failure in sales activity ultimately depends on the customer's yes or no. For any business entity, the customer is king. No one can succeed in sales without sufficient knowledge and information on the all-important customer.

Therefore, it is necessary to classify customers according to whether they are actual or prospective and then to collect and systematize information regarding customers for reference at each visit. The customer profile forms are designed for this purpose.

How to prepare

Cards with enough space for data concerning actual and prospective customers should be used.

If possible, they should be prepared in the form of hole sort cards. For printing and designing of the cards, it is recommended to consult several companies specializing in such work.

The merits of hole sort cards lie not only in their convenience for indexing, but also in the easy classification into area, scale, credit standing, condition, payment date, etc. It is advisable to learn the method of preparing the card, the principle of indexing, classification, sorting, etc.

Various relations

The cards of actual and prospective customers must be separated.

How to use

If it seems to take too much trouble to prepare the cards and maintain them on a daily basis, one is overlooking their great essential value. For example, to a group with good credit standing we may offer special terms; among a group of considerable size we may start a special sales campaign; on each collection day we may select certain customers and fix the order of the bill collection round; we may select customers by area and adopt a direct mail system for them; we may select customers by industry and find some unique sales points to introduce into the standard sales talk; or we may select prospects by class and plot specific strategies for sales campaigns. Sales efforts aimed at the right targets usually lead to success.

[CHART 46]

(23) Customer Profile Form

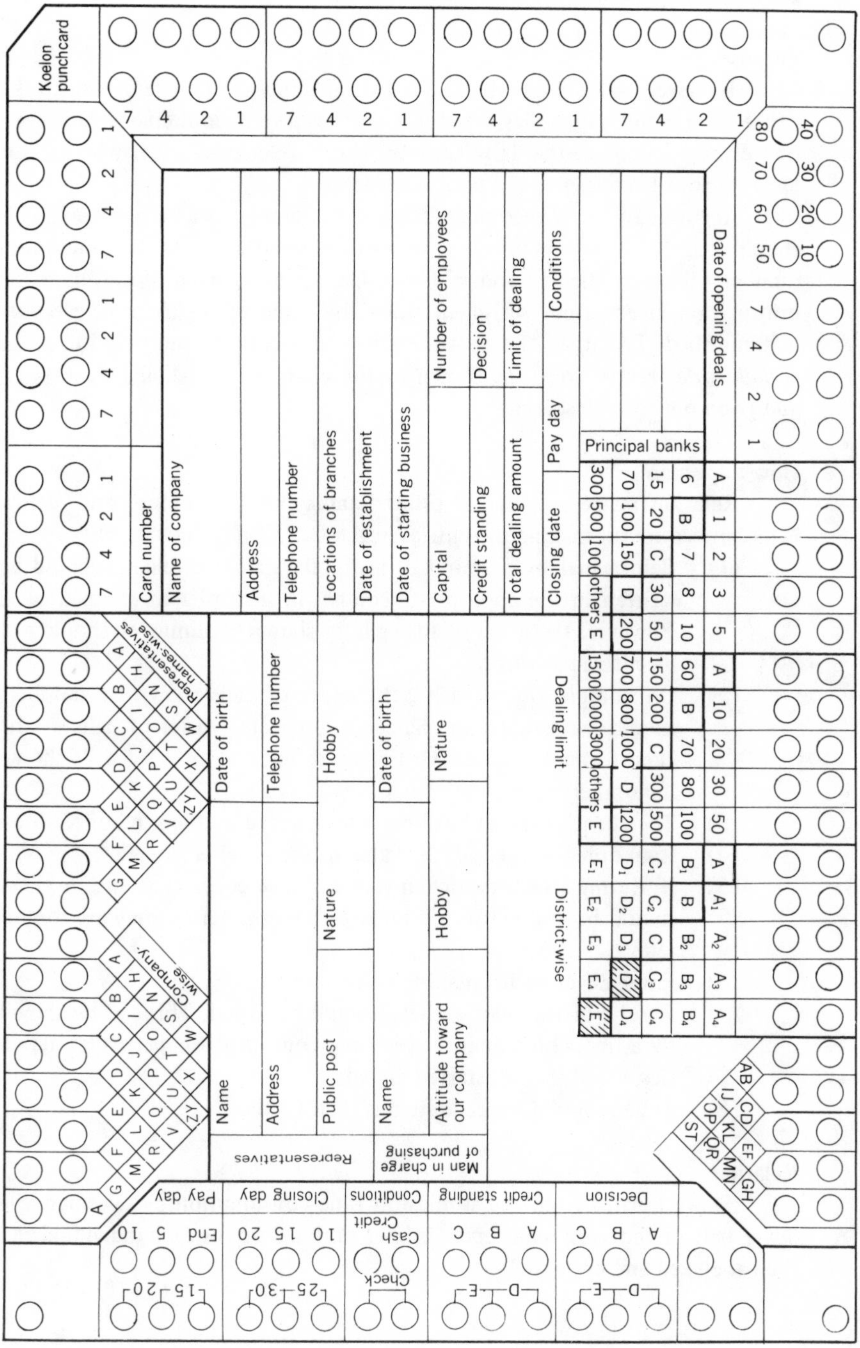

24. DAILY SALES REPORT FORM

Purpose

To have a salesman make a detailed sales report upon returning to the office after a full day's sales activity is a rather severe requirement. However, one cannot eliminate the daily activity report. A sales manager who cannot keep track of his salesmen is a poor manager.

Accordingly, it is recommended a *daily sales report* be prepared. This should consist of minimum length written reports, using the minimum number of letters, figures and symbols. On the other hand, however, if the information given is not sufficient, then the value of the *daily sales report* is diminished. To satisfy the above requirements, it is recommended to make a *daily sales report* form, as shown in the chart, which should be printed and given out to each salesman.

How to prepare

Relevant matters should be printed and symbolized beforehand. Below is the procedure for making the entries in the *Daily Sales Report*.

(1)   Before making a round of visits, the names of clients should be written in the appropriate column in the order of planned calls. However, the order of the calls, as shown by numbers, should not be entered at this time.

(2)   On completion of visits, the order of calls shown by numbers should be written in. Since the expected order of calls at the clients and the actual visits may differ, the order of calls shown in numbers shows the actual order of visits.

(3)   The client's type of business is then noted by the symbol X.

(4)   If an order is received, the value of the order is entered.

(5)   If, during a call, particular matters have come to attention, these should be entered in the remarks column before they are forgotten.

(6)   Enter expenses for making visits.

(7)   Results of the sales activity should be noted. This can be shown by a line which denotes the time consumed for particular activities, when the call started ended.

(8)   Time required for each item is then totalled.

Relation

As we learned from the studies on time consumption by salesmen, the lower half of the *daily sales report* is later summed up for each individual and then analyzed and evaluated.

How to view and use

As is evident from the given entries in the chart, the daily sales reports are easy to make and abundant information is provided by them.

Since the calling dates and the clients to be visited are known, such facts can be posted in the salesman's visiting schedule form mentioned previously. Also by aggregating the results of orders obtained and the amount of expenses incurred by each individual, a comparison can be made of expected and actual sales results.

(24) Daily Sales Report Form

Daily Sales Report

President:	Managing Director:	Dept. Manager:

Date:	Weather:	Name: Ichiro Suzuki

Target amount for the month: ¥5,400,000
Amount reached so far: ¥3,740,000

Order of Visit	Place of visit	Opening Up	Receiving Order	Checking	Estimates	Sending bills	Collecting bills	Remarks	Amount	Visiting expenses
3	Shimazaki Shoten				×			Rival companies seem to be D company and K company.		Taxi fare: ¥470
2	Kurushima Timber K.K.						×	Visit again next Monday.		Taxi fare: ¥470
1	Yamada Printing K.K.	×						Special specifications. Some possibility		Bus fare: ¥160
4	Yokoyama Measuring Instruments K.K.	×						Some possibility		
5	Takano Electric K.K.	×						Man in charge was not in and so couldn't meet him.		Taxi fare: ¥950
6	Tokitsu Bag Store		×					Succeeded on first visit	¥370,000	Bus fare: ¥160
7	Appolo Paint K.K.	×						Take actual product tomorrow morning		
								Total:		¥2,210

Special remarks:

On the desk of Manager Watanabe of Shimazaki Shoten I found estimates from D and K companies, two of our rivals, but couldn't see the amount.

[CHART 47]

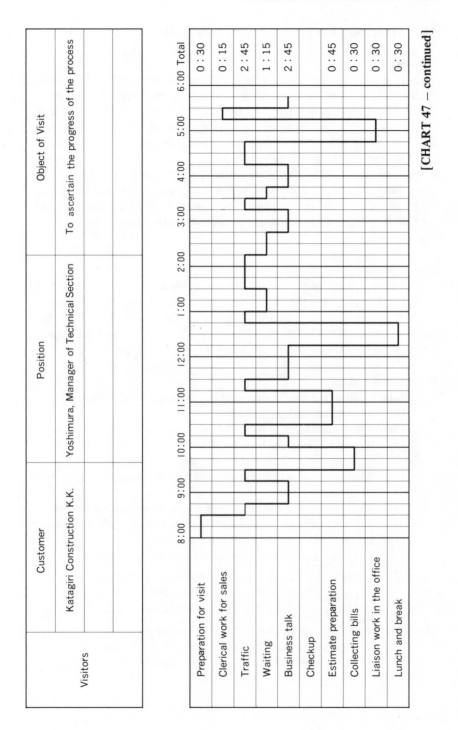

	6:00 Total
Preparation for visit	0 : 30
Clerical work for sales	0 : 15
Traffic	2 : 45
Waiting	1 : 15
Business talk	2 : 45
Checkup	
Estimate preparation	0 : 45
Collecting bills	0 : 30
Liaison work in the office	0 : 30
Lunch and break	0 : 30

Customer	Position	Object of Visit
Katagiri Construction K.K.	Yoshimura, Manager of Technical Section	To ascertain the progress of the process
Visitors		

[CHART 47 — continued]

151

25. ACCOUNTS RECEIVABLE CONTROL CHART

Purpose

If sales and collection can be considered the two wheels of a vehicle, it should be realized that a salesman also plays a vital role in the flow of funds. Accordingly, it is required to have always a clear picture of the status of sales and collection. However, by merely observing the figures in a given table or a chart, it is rather difficult to judge the state of the credit account, i.e., whether it is favourable or not. In order to comprehend the actual state of business affairs, to be able to see correctly the dynamic state of goods and funds (which are never immobile), to know at a glance the total amount of credit and due dates and in general, to control business scientifically and rationally, it is absolutely necessary to supervise credit activity by means of a graph.

How to prepare

To prepare this graph, it is necessary to prepare the Accounts Receivable Control Chart shown on page 153, which can easily accommodate the figures.

After this chart is drawn up, a graph can be drawn (page 154). The starting point on the sales line should be the graduated place from the original point in the vertical axis of credit balance and buyers' holding.

How to view and use

With regard to the lines shown on the chart, consider the following:

(1) What do the various lines show?
(2) Where should one look for the due date of an average bill?
(3) What conclusion can be drawn from the state of disparity between the lines of collection and settlement?
(4) What is the sales situation and what are the quantities of returned goods and discount?
(5) What is the relationship between sales line and settlement line?
(6) Which months are good, which are bad and what are the reasons?
(7) In July, what should the salesman do next?

The graph may be viewed vertically and horizontally:

Vertically:	Distance between A and B	Partial credit balance
	Distance between B and C	Bills receivable on hand
	Distance between A and C	Credit sales
Horizontally:	Distance between A and B	Period of partial credit turnover
	Distance between B and C	Bills receivable turnover period
	Distance between A and C	Period of turnover of credit sales

(25A) Accounts Receivable Control Chart

No. Line	1	2 Sales line	3	4	5 Cash line	6	7	8 Collection line	9	10	11 Settlement line
Remark	Sales	Cumulative sales	Balance of accounts receivable	Cash collected	Cumulative cash collected	Bills collected	Cumulative of bills received	Cumulative of cash & bills settled	Amount of bills settled	Cumulative amount of bills settled	(5) + (10)
Balance		180,000	70,000				60,000				
January	50,000	180,000	100,000	9,500	9,500	10,500	10,500	80,000	19,500	19,500	29,000
February	20,000	200,000	91,000	14,000	23,500	15,000	25,500	109,000	17,000	36,500	60,000
March	30,000	230,000	91,000	16,500	40,000	13,500	39,000	139,000	2,500	39,000	79,000
April	50,000	280,000	121,000	12,000	52,000	8,000	47,000	159,000	7,000	46,000	98,000
May	20,000	300,000	86,000	13,000	65,000	42,000	89,000	214,000	9,000	55,000	120,000
June	15,000	315,000	67,000	16,500	81,500	17,500	106,500	248,000	2,000	57,000	138,500
July	15,000	330,000	62,000	13,500	95,000	6,500	113,000	268,000	7,000	64,000	159,000
August	20,000	350,000	53,000	8,500	103,500	20,500	133,500	297,000	4,500	68,500	172,000
September	40,000	390,000	83,000	2,500	106,000	7,500	141,000	307,000	27,500	96,000	202,000
October	20,000	410,000	83,000	11,000	117,000	9,000	150,000	327,000	31,000	127,000	244,000
November	20,000	430,000	85,000	16,000	133,000	2,000	152,000	345,000	16,000	143,000	276,000
December	60,000	490,000	105,000	17,500	150,500	22,500	174,500	385,000	12,500	155,000	306,000

Remark for column 2: Including balance of accounts receivable and balance of bills at end of last fiscal term

Remark for column 8: Including balance of bills at end of last fiscal term

[CHART 48A]

(25B) Accounts Receivable Control Graph

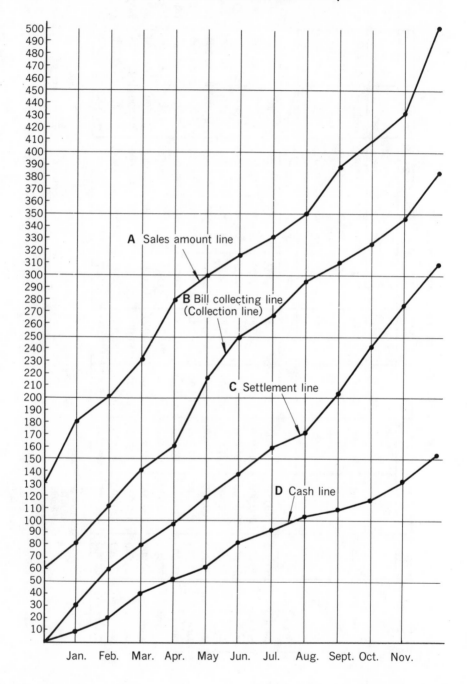

A Sales amount line

B Bill collecting line (Collection line)

C Settlement line

D Cash line

Jan. Feb. Mar. Apr. May Jun. Jul. Aug. Sept. Oct. Nov.

[CHART 48B]

26. SALESMANSHIP ASSESSMENT

Purpose

Sales promotion work carried out personally by salesmen, whether it, is the sale of production equipment or consumer goods, retail sales at a shop, or sales techniques, is a critical phase of marketing. This holds true despite the popularity of automatic vending machines. When competition, price-wise and quality-wise, has come to a dead end, the final work has to be done by a salesman or a service representative whose personality and salesmanship determine the outcome.

For this reason, it is highly recommended to continually assess, in the presence of the salesman or service representative, his skill and capacity and to give him instruction and guidance. A *RADAR* chart for assessing the techniques of handling customers at an automobile repair shop is shown on page 157.

How to construct

Periodically, an assessment chart of the technique of handling customers should be made to cover all the members of the shop. Each item is assessed on the basis of 100 maximum. If that marking is multiplied by the weighting factor, you get the point. By totaling these points you get the overall points. But before the points are multiplied by the weighting factor, they are transferred to the *RADAR* chart. By looking at this chart one can readily find merits and shortcomings and ascertain the mutual relations between the items to be evaluated, which will be useful for guidance.

Relations

Making the evaluations and marketing the points are not the only things to be done. It is also necessary to strengthen merits, correct weaknesses and take appropriate measures for the purpose of guidance and training. It is recommended to use also the training timetable of planned training or the *training progress chart* in order to enhance on-the-job or off-the-job training. (See Chapter VI.)

How to view and use

It is important that all assessors, if there are more than one, use the same grading system for giving marks. For instance, assessment should be done as follows:

Very good . . . . 100 − 90
Good . . . . 90 − 80
Fair . . . . 80 − 60
Bad . . . . 60 − 40
Very bad . . . . 40 and less

(26A) A Check List for Salesmanship

Name: Taro Yamano

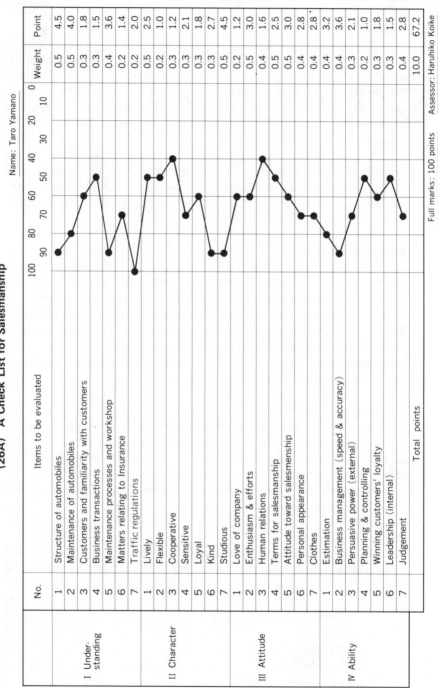

	No.	Items to be evaluated	100 90 80 70 60 50 40 30 20 10 0	Weight	Point
I Under-standing	1	Structure of automobiles		0.5	4.5
	2	Maintenance of automobiles		0.5	4.0
	3	Customers and familiarity with customers		0.3	1.8
	4	Business transactions		0.3	1.5
	5	Maintenance processes and workshop		0.4	3.6
	6	Matters relating to Insurance		0.2	1.4
	7	Traffic regulations		0.2	2.0
II Character	1	Lively		0.5	2.5
	2	Flexible		0.2	1.0
	3	Cooperative		0.3	1.2
	4	Sensitive		0.3	2.1
	5	Loyal		0.3	1.8
	6	Kind		0.3	2.7
	7	Studious		0.5	4.5
III Attitude	1	Love of company		0.2	1.2
	2	Enthusiasm & efforts		0.5	3.0
	3	Human relations		0.4	1.6
	4	Terms for salesmanship		0.5	2.5
	5	Attitude toward salesmenship		0.5	3.0
	6	Personal appearance		0.4	2.8
	7	Clothes		0.4	2.8
IV Ability	1	Estimation		0.4	3.2
	2	Business management (speed & accuracy)		0.4	3.6
	3	Persuasive power (external)		0.3	2.1
	4	Planning & controlling		0.2	1.0
	5	Winning customers' loyalty		0.3	1.8
	6	Leadership (internal)		0.3	1.5
	7	Judgement		0.4	2.8
		Total points		10.0	67.2

Full marks: 100 points   Assessor: Haruhiko Koike

[CHART 49A]

(26B)   RADAR Chart for Salesmanship Assessment

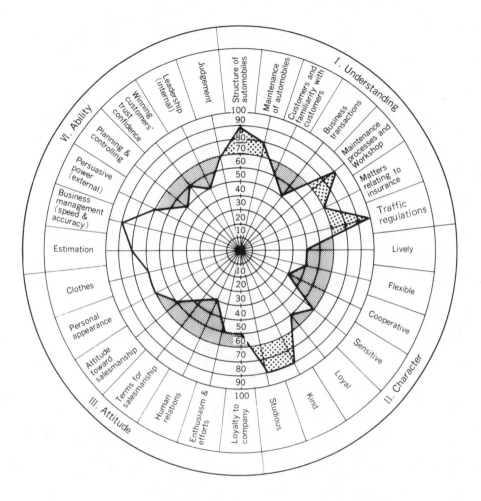

Name: Taro Yamano   Age: 23 years old

[CHART 49B]

Chapter 4
CHARTS ON INDUSTRIAL ENGINEERING

What is industrial engineering?

In 1961, an 'IE Symposium' was held under the sponsorship of the IE Association of the United States. A uniform view on the definition of industrial engineering was announced. It read something like the following:

Industrial Engineering deals with problems related to the planning, improvement and installation of an integrated system of manpower, materials, and machinery. That is to say, it takes recourse to the technical knowledge of mathematics, physics, and social sciences as well as engineering-oriented analysis and the principle and method of design for the purpose of clearly stating, forecasting, and evaluating the results obtainable from such a system.

Industrial Engineering (I.E.) has made remarkable progress in the last 70 years with the scientific management of F.W. Taylor as its starting point. Now, the scope and extent of industrial engineering have grown enormously and fully justify the above definition but its essential nature, on the other hand, still remains vague and indefinite.

Careful consideration of the purpose of I.E. would lead us to a belief that it is 'a technique for promoting productivity through management improvement and creativity'.

Its purpose may be expressed in two words – cost reduction. In this chapter, you will be introduced to 23 charts which will serve as instruments to achieve the goal.

These charts have been prepared chiefly by a work study method – the fundamental I.E. technique – for all the techniques of VA, QC, EE, PERT, OR and so forth will be nothing more than a 'house built on sand' if the various techniques, constituting the most fundamental basis for factory administration, are not firmly established.

It is, in effect, a set of techniques to be applied for the improvement of plant efficiency and to elevate plant administration. If this fundamental problem is given a satisfactory solution, it will be possible to prevent delay in delivery, to reduce costs and to attain an epoch-making improvement on the reliability of product quality.

Unless a fundamental system like this is firmly established, a sporadic application of partially precise techniques cannot be expected to produce any considerable effect. Therefore, it would be necessary first to subject the existing manufacturing processes and methods to a thorough analysis and appraisal. Thereafter, each manufacturing process should be subjected to an energetic review to re-arrange the processes or to combine them in such a way as will ensure the most effective performance of the projected function assigned to each process.

Work study may be roughly divided into qualitative analysis and quantitative analysis. F.W. Taylor's motion study and time study may be considered to correspond to these divisions. The qualitative analysis (motion study) is devoted to finding, establishing, and standardizing the only and best way to produce a given product or to perform work. The quantitative study (time study), on the other hand, is devoted to setting a standard time for the performance of work by a working method thus established.

In other words, the qualitative analysis concerns itself with finding answers to the question of 'how to do?', while the quantitative analysis concerns itself with finding answers to the question of 'how much to do?' which relates to the time required for the performance of a given volume of work.

The I.E. techniques are divided into these two phases as indicated by the broken line in the *organic chart of I.E. tools.*

At the present time, the qualitative phase of work study is called 'method study', and its quantitative phase is called 'work measurement'. The various techniques given above the broken line are those employed for method study, while those shown below the broken line are the different techniques applied to work measurement.

Method study is intended for a systematic recording, analysis and evaluation of both the present working method and an improved working method for the future and for finding and applying an easier and more effective method. In other words, it may be understood in terms of the following three steps.

(1)   Removing unnecessary work,
(2)   Re-arranging the remaining processes in the best sequence, and
(3)   Performing analysis of work for the purpose of standardizing a proper working method

How to conduct method study

In conducting method study, we have to follow the following six steps:

First Step: Select the processes or jobs to be studied (to be improved).
Second Step: Carefully observe and record all the facts related to the

processes or jobs.

Third Step: Examine all the facts related to the processes minutely in a certain fixed sequence and additionally, by the most pertinent method.

Fourth Step: Take proper account of all the conditions that may possibly occur and develop the most practical, economical, and effective way to deal with these conditions.

Fifth Step: Install the improved and standardized method developed in step four.

Sixth Step: Conduct regular and periodical inspections for the purpose of maintaining the standardized method.

I.E. staff should be thoroughly acquainted with these six steps. Now explanations for each of these steps are given.

First step: SELECT

We cannot just proceed with a method study, saying, "We have learned the various techniques of method study. Now, let's practice them at once." The task is not all that simple and clear-cut.

First, attention should be devoted to the systematic performance of the method study techniques, following an orderly sequence based on certain priorities. Random attempts at improvement will not lead to the desired end results. The first step in the work-study procedure is to select the jobs to be improved.

The following three criteria should be used for selecting the jobs to be improved.

    (1)   Economic criterion: Greater economic effect
    (2)   Technical criterion: Technical feasibility
    (3)   Human criterion: Unlikeliness to cause human resistance

Second step: RECORD

In this step, all the facts concerning the selected jobs should be recorded without exception. In doing so, it is important to record the facts on the basis of direct observation. Be careful not to proceed on the basis of assumptions. It will be unproductive to record what you think is occurring, just because you are reluctant to take the trouble to make actual personal observations on the spot. There are various methods for the recording of facts, depending on the nature of the objects of analysis.

    (1)   Outline process chart
    (2)   Flow process chart
    (3)   Flow diagram
    (4)   Multi-activity chart
    (5)   Man-machine chart
    (6)   Two-handed process chart
    (7)   Therblig chart

Third step: EXAMINE

A study presupposes questions. The questions may be represented by the following five Ws and one H.

Why — (reason), What — (substance), When — (time), Where — (place), Who — (person), How — (method)

These questions serve as 'sieves' to filter the facts collected and to rate them in proper perspective. Various hidden factors will be brought to light by these questions.

Fourth step: DEVELOP

This is the stage in which you work out a plan for improvement. It is at this stage that the work-study person displays his expert skills.

The details of the jobs which failed to satisfy the above mentioned questions should be understood and improved. The direction of improvement should be in line with ECRS; the term, ECRS, represents:

E: Eliminate C: Combine R: Rearrange S: Simplify

Fifth step: INSTALL

Once an improvement plan is devised, it requires implementation and practice. A 'work-study' individual or consultant should be aware that as such, he has no authority to issue directives. This is the task of the person in command. It is his responsibility, however, to persuade, motivate and instruct others to take action. His task is to encourage all to make a bold start.

> "It requires the ability of 10 men to generate an idea. It requires the energy of 30 men to develop the idea into a project. And it requires the power of 100 men to put it into practice."
>
> —Kiyoshi Ichimura

Sixth step: MAINTAIN

Once a plan is put into practice, continue all efforts toward its full realization. Failure to follow the plan leaves a sense of frustration and discourages volition for improving factory operations. Besides, deviation from the plan can weaken the overall effort.

Organic Chart of I.E. Tools

All the analysis charts to be explained in this chapter are those which will be used in the second stage of the six steps — namely, 'record'.

'Record does not mean going around with a pencil and paper in hand aimlessly to make a prosaic description of actual conditions. Such an attempt will prove utterly futile, for the I.E. techniques necessarily entail a unique methodology and premises of their own. These factors will be introduced to you in the form of analysis charts, each of which has its own respective objective and range of application. In the following paragraphs, these charts are explained systematically.

Now, let's have a look at the *Organic chart of I.E. tools:*

The main products classification chart (1) will be prepared to indicate the specifications of the products manufactured at the factory, their respective outputs, and their process requirement (i.e., the machine/hours required).

When several main products (two or three product items) have been selected, the next step is to make up an *assembly chart* for the products. An *assembly chart* is designed to show at a glance how the components produced at the factory are built into the products one after another in a certain fixed sequence.

Then, circular symbols are used to represent what specific kinds of processing are applied to each one of the components given in the assembly chart and what kinds of work are performed in relation to the processing thus described, and we obtain *the outline process chart* (2).

This is the most simplified of all the procedures adopted for process analysis with all subsidiary data omitted. This single chart alone will be sufficient to give an overall picture of all processes and operations relating to the product described. This *outline process chart* represents only "work" out of a total list of work-process symbols. A chart which is prepared employing all these work-process symbols is the *product process chart* (4), comprising "O" = work, "$\Rightarrow$" = transport, "D" = delay, "$\square$" = inspection, and "$\triangle$" = storage.

This chart may be regarded as a complete and detailed work-process analysis, as it represents not only the work-processes carried out at the factory, but also all transportation, delays, inspections and storage which take place in connection with the manufacture of the product.

The *product process form* (3) is used for specifying basic materials and information which are required in the preparation of a *product process chart.* When it is found necessary as a result of this product process analysis to conduct a more detailed study, it is desirable first to divide this into a main component analysis and a subsidiary component analysis as well as to prepare various types of charts for each one of these two areas.

When it is desired to find out more detailed facts about the work processes of particular parts or components, the *flow process chart* (5) will be useful. Flow process charts may be prepared for both the flow articles' and the 'motions of workers', but the two must not be combined in the same chart.

This chart will be useful for formulating a more effective improvement plan when it is used in conjunction with the *flow diagram* (6).

The *flow process analysis chart* (7) is convenient as it is capable of presenting an all-inclusive summary view of the processes which some or all of the main products or parts pass through. Furthermore, in addition to

Organic Chart of I.E. Tools

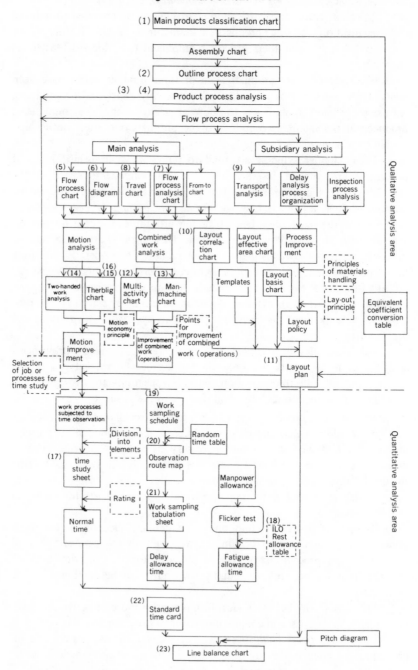

its application from the Industrial Engineering point of view, the chart will be very useful in the preparation of a manpower plan or a machine-loading table, as it is capable of showing the work-load for each process.

The *travel chart* (8) is a chart designed chiefly for an analysis of 'the travel of workers' rather than the flow of articles. The chart is, therefore, helpful in providing a clear understanding of the travel route, travel distance, and travel frequency of the worker subjected to analysis. With the help of this chart, it will be possible to have a better idea of any wastefulness or inconsistency in the worker's motions. In short, the chart will be useful in improving the efficiency of the motion of workers.

When it is intended to bring about a more thorough rationalization of the transport processes, placing an emphasis on it as part of the subsidiary analysis, it will be feasible to undertake the *transport analysis* (9). Above all, latent transport (the transport work conducted by workers other than those specially assigned to transport work) steals productive hours; it causes considerable loss in the working hours and increases transportation cost. For this reason, it is certainly desirable to concentrate efforts for improvement on this phase.

At this stage, the problems of plant layout are considered in the preparation of the *layout correlation chart* (10). Needless to say, a factory layout plan should be a blueprint for factory management. At the same time, it should sufficiently incorporate a scientific approach and wisdom for business administration.

Factory layout also depends on an ideal process-design. To phrase it another way, factory layout may be considered to be a physical arrangement of a process design. Consequently, on a qualitative basis, factory layout depends on an ideal work-process design; an ideal work-process design, in turn, depends on main process analysis and subsidiary factory including, above all, product work-process analysis.

In the process of a transfer of ideal process design to a special physical arrangement, it is necessary to make reference to the principles of material handling and of layout.

The fundamental principle of material handling

(a)   Unnecessary handling costs money and does not increase the value of the products.

(b)   Try to eliminate as much handling as possible. If it is required, try to use mechanical methods instead of manpower whenever possible.

(c)   A handling process should be adequately incorporated with the processes of work, inspection, storage, and other handling processes that precede or follow it.

(d)   In order to minimize the cost incurred for handling, ordinary working processes should include as many automation processes as possible.

165

(e) All the handling systems should be integrated.

(f) An active effort should be made to update the facilities and procedures for material handling whenever new equipment which promises higher efficiency is introduced to the market.

The principles of factory layout

(a) *Principle of total integration:*

The best factory layout is achieved when manpower, articles, machinery, processes, and the other related factors are integrated in a way that ensures the most harmonious of each and all factors.

(b) *Principle of the shortest travel distance:*

All other conditions being equal, the best layout is the one which ensures the transport of articles over the shortest distance between one process and another.

(c) *Principle of flow:*

All other conditions being equal, the best layout is the one which features an arrangement of the working areas in the same sequence as that followed in the shaping, processing, and assembly of the materials.

(d) *Principle of three-dimensional space:*

The maximum economy is secured when all the available space is utilized effectively not only on the horizontal plane but also vertically.

(e) *Principle of satisfaction and safety:*

The other conditions being equal, the best layout is the one which satisfies the projected work standard and ensures the safety of all workers.

(f) *Principle of flexibility:*

Other conditions being equal, the best layout is the one which permits adjustment or rearrangement at the lowest cost and with the least inconvenience.

In designing a plant layout, judgement should be based on quantitative data in addition to the qualitative approach mentioned above. That is, we should find out in advance how much material will flow through the factory. To fill this need, an equivalent coefficients conversion table would be used.

The preparation of a conversion table is indispensable to determine the factory capacity relative to its layout. Equivalent coefficients are assigned to the number of manhours required for one unit of another product based on a certain standard product's manhour requirement expressed as 100. The number of units of the standard product that corresponds to a certain unit volume of the other product when converted in terms of the equivalent coefficients should then be determined. Sufficient allowance for future as well as present work loads are an important consideration.

When qualitative and quantitative data have been collected in this way in preparation for designing a factory layout, a policy for the prospective layout can be formulated. A factory layout plan would be incomplete without a guiding policy. The policy should be based on an aggregation of objectives such as productivity improvement or the achievement of efficiency. In addition to the combination of the factory manager's information and knowledge, however, the policy also should reflect a manager's ability to integrate and efficiently utilize them within the context of the factory's overall operations.

Only on the basis of such a policy will it be possible to create an ideal plant layout plan (11). Plant layout may be considered to be the terminal point in the application of the various techniques for process analysis, both in its initial design and in the case of any subsequent revisions.

In the area of method study, the discussion thus far has dealt with those methods, which primarily concern themselves with the flow of articles, and may be grouped under an all-inclusive term, 'process analysis'. In this area, such nonproductive work processes (represented by the symbols, ⇒, D, ∇, or □), are thoroughly reviewed so that a large-scale improvement may be achieved by eliminating the unnecessary processes, combining others, and re-arranging or simplifying still others.

On the other hand, the process represented by ○ — the remaining part — concerns itself primarily with manpower or the processing work with machines; it is in this area that more elaborate improvement is required from the standpoint of motion analysis.

The following charts are intended for such motion improvement:

The *Multi-activity chart* (12) represents in terms of a time scale the working procedure involving the cooperative work of two or more workers. The problems arising from the cooperative work of multiple workers are the interference of their work with one another and the resulting idle waiting. This chart, which gives a comprehensive picture of the actual conditions of cooperative work itself, will provide a considerably useful hint for the improvement of team-work.

In most factories, the manufacture of products is not necessarily performed by manual operation alone. In many cases, production is performed by workers operating machines. Under such circumstances, the *man-machine chart* (13) will play an important role.

When workers perform their jobs operating machines, there are usually two heterogeneous tasks: on-the-machine and off-the-machine work. The former is work performed while the machine is in motion, and the latter is work performed while the machine is not in motion. The advantages of the man-machine chart lies in the fact that it shows that a dexterous combination of the two types of work can be arranged to improve the operation rate of the machinery. In many cases, such arrangements can lead to large increases in productivity.

(14) The two-handed process chart will make a significant contribution to the improvement of hand work by eliminating the wasteful movements, as it is capable of representing the precise movements of the right hand and the left hand in working situations involving two-handed work. Consequently, it can also aid the design of tools and instruments and the planning of holding devices.

Another approach to promote motion economy still further would be to use *(15)* the *Therblig symbols* to prepare a *(16) Therblig chart.*

This chart, devised by Frank Gilbreth, features a classification of all the movements of the hands into 17 types, all rendered in a system of symbolic representation.

This system offers a procedure, as it were, for eliminating immoderateness and wastefulness at the ultimate level of movements and for rearranging them into the most feasible and economical procedure. Compared with the techniques of work-process analysis, it is, indeed, microscopic in scale. Microscopic analysis is intended for an analysis of repetitive work with a short cyclic time. However, it would be totally erroneous to assume that a microscopic analysis will bring about less improvement when compared with a macroscopic analysis.

For instance, in case of a work process which has a recurrent cycle of two minutes, a reduction of 15 seconds as a result of a Therblig analysis will, in effect, increase the output by 14.3 per cent as shown in the following equation:

$$\text{Output:} \quad \frac{120}{120 - 15} = 1.143$$

Within the area of the work measurement, the objectives are:
(a)   To assist method study with time data
(b)   To establish standard times

The various techniques of method study already presented such as the *multi-activity chart,* the *man-machine chart* and the *two-handed process chart,* etc., require time data.

Now a technique for setting up a standard time — the backbone of work measurement — is needed and is used for the following purposes:
(a)   Basis for production planning
(b)   Determining factor of unit price estimate
(c)   Introduction of an incentive wage system
(d)   Setting up standard cost.

Furthermore, the following schematic representation will serve as reference to your understanding of the composition of standard time.

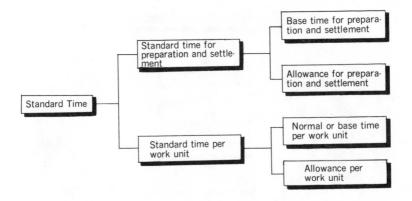

Standard time is defined as follows:

'The time that a full-fledged worker who has completed a certain period of skill-training requires in performing the work at a standard pace according to a certain fixed working method under prescribed standard working conditions.'

In other words, the definition of standard time includes the following four points as its essential requisite:

(1)   Standard working method
(2)   Standard working conditions
(3)   A worker having standard skills
(4)   Standard working pace (speed)

The various work measurement techniques employed in setting up a standard time are:

(1)   Predetermined time standard
(2)   Standard time data method
(3)   Memo-motion study
(4)   Direct time study method (time study)
(5)   Work sampling method
(6)   Others

The direct time study method, which is the most orthodox of all these techniques and procedures is discussed here. For a more detailed treatment of the subject matter, the reader is encouraged to consult special reference works.

The direct time study method is a means of analytical study conducted chiefly with a stop-watch for determining the time required for efficient performance of a given work following the sequence in which the work elements are performed.

The main steps of what is appropriately called time study may be explained as follows:

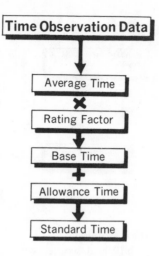

(a) The first step to be taken, prior to the observation of time, is to divide the cyclic work subjected to measurement into elements.

(b) Time observation will be repeated several times. This will be used as a basis for estimating a certain parameter to be used in determining the total frequency of measurement. This will also clarify the duration of the intended time study period.

(c) Time observation will be repeated as often as required over a pre-determined period of time study.

(d) The workers subjected to this measurement are rated in relation to the normal pace of an average worker.

(e) Allowance time will be given to allow for various kinds of interference with work and delay. The allowance time is determined either on the basis of a policy or by an independent measurement.

(f) Standard time is thus composed of the average time determined by observation, the rating factor, and allowance time. Chart (17) illustrates an example of the *time study sheet* with descriptions entered. This sheet will clearly show the procedure starting from time observation to the determining of a standard time.

According to the theory of allowance by M.E. Mundel, the allowance to be added to the normal time includes the following:

(a) Personal allowance
(b) Fatigue allowance
(c) Delay allowance

In this connection, the *ILO system rest allowance percentages table* (18) is distinguished from all the other measurement techniques of rest allowance by easier application and understanding of fatigue allowance. In the meantime, work sampling which has been already discussed can be used as a survey technique of delay allowance.

Work sampling is the procedure and/or techniques to determine the ratios of times appropriate to each one of the different types of activities performed by each individual employee, by conducting random observation studies on the entire range of a given work. In other words, this technique is based on the following 'law of probability' found in statistics.

'The samples selected at random from any given large group (population) display characteristic features similar to the original population; if the selected samples are sufficiently large in number, the characters of the samples coincide with those of the original group (population).'

The basic aim of work sampling is to make an estimate of the proportions of time spent respectively for the different forms of activity involving various production factors such as machines, facilities and workers. Consequently, this technique has been used, regardless of the type of industry, for a wide range of applications including the following:

(1) To indicate the work areas for which it should be recommended to conduct a method study

(2) To show the structure of the work distribution in multi-activity work

(3) To estimate the utilization ratios of similar machinery and equipment groups

(4) To show the status of the utilization of materials handling facilities

(5) To determine the ratios of productive factors and nonproductive factors in office work

(6) To set up a standard time for repetitive work, using the work sampling technique in place of the direct time study method performed with a stopwatch

(7) To provide a basis for a time standard applicable to the indirect personnel

(8) To determine time allowance to be included in a standard time.

Out of these eight basic objectives, it is intended here to explain work sampling as a means to determine delay allowance.

In short, the purpose corresponds to (8) given at the end of the list above. The next step is a discussion of the procedure of work sampling.

First step: Define the problem

It is important to clarify the purpose of the study and also to specify the items to be subjected to measurement. For instance, specify what items contribute to delay allowance. In this case, the study will yield futile results unless the concept of delay is strictly defined so that the concerned staff may have a uniform interpretation of this basic concept.

Second step: Seek the approval of the supervisor of the workshop to be subjected to the study

The second step is to obtain the approval of the supervisor in charge of the workshop selected for the study and to have the purpose of the study fully explained to the workers so that they may cooperate.

Third step: Determine the accuracy to be expected of the results

Now, fix the desirable accuracy or an allowable absolute error for the study which is necessary to have a measure of reliability.

Fourth step: Estimate the ratios of the activities to be subjected to the measurement

The ratios of the work activities may be estimated on the basis of past experience, but it would be better to conduct a preliminary study for a day or two whenever it is possible. The preliminary study will also be carried out by the work sampling technique. This data may be added later to the main study.

Fifth step: Map out a measurement plan

Specify the size of the samples (N), the number of workers involved, the period of observation study, daily frequency of the observation tours, the route of the observation tour, the departure time for the observation tour, etc. Then, prepare an observation sheet.

Sixth step: Conduct random observation study according to the plan

Seventh step: Analyze the results

Sort out and compute the data collected daily. Find out the control limit, and develop a control chart. Eliminate any extraordinary value found in the data, and represent the cumulative results in a chart. When constant and coherent results have been obtained, check their accuracy and discontinue the observation.

Eighth step: Put the results in order and report — If necessary, work out a recommendation for improvement

Now, return to the *organic chart* of I.E. tools and consider the following:

The first step: 'the definition of delay', the third step: 'the desirable accuracy and absolute error and reliability', and the fifth step: 'the size of the samples' mentioned above are presented in connection with the *work sampling schedule* (19).

Similarly, the fifth step: 'the daily frequency of observation and the daily frequency of observation tours, and the departure time for the observation tours' are presented in relation to the *random time table*.

As for 'the route for the observation tours' found in the fifth step, the *work sampling observation route map* (20) is given, and the *work sampling tabulation sheet* (21) is presented for convenience in making a summary report of the results obtained in the eighth step.

When the marginal delay allowance ratio is determined in this way, it will be added, together with the fatigue allowance time, to the base time to calculate the standard time.

This information will be transferred to the *standard time card* (22) to be frequently and effectively utilized for daily factory administration.

When it comes to employing these time data for organizing work processes, the *line balance chart* (23) will be helpful to effect a macroscopic improvement in the factory and a drastic reduction in cost.

At the end of the present section, you will find a factory improvement system which the author prepared for an electronic instrument manufacturer. The system chart will be helpful to the reader in gaining an idea of some other I.E. techniques which the scope of the present work ruled out of this discussion.

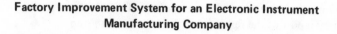

Factory Improvement System for an Electronic Instrument Manufacturing Company

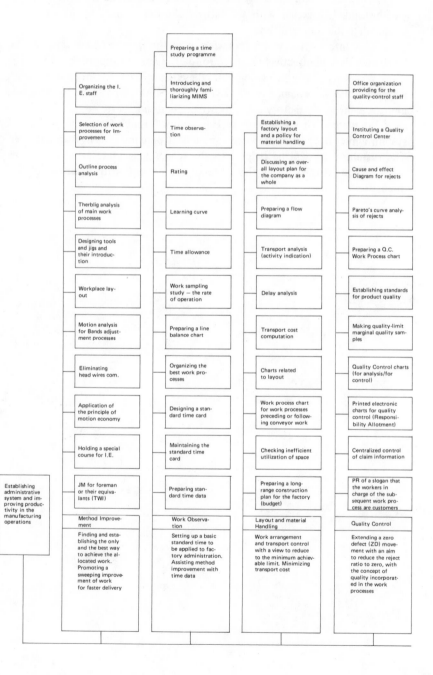

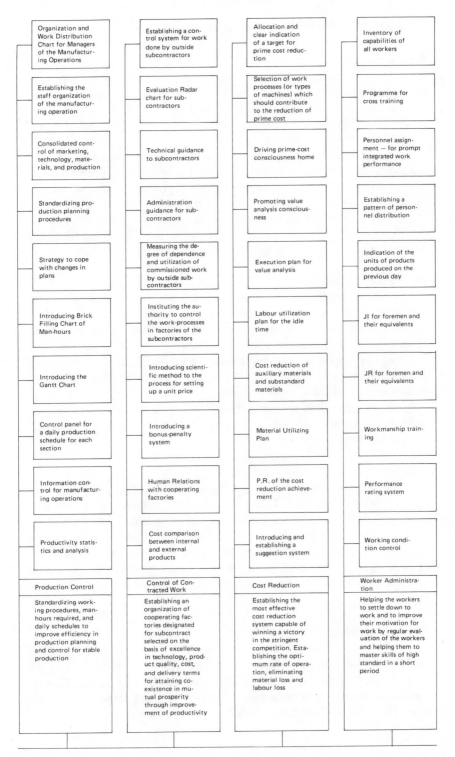

Column 1 — Production Control

- Organization and Work Distribution Chart for Managers of the Manufacturing Operations
- Establishing the staff organization of the manufacturing operation
- Consolidated control of marketing, technology, materials, and production
- Standardizing production planning procedures
- Strategy to cope with changes in plans
- Introducing Brick Filling Chart of Man-hours
- Introducing the Gantt Chart
- Control panel for a daily production schedule for each section
- Information control for manufacturing operations
- Productivity statistics and analysis

Production Control

Standardizing working procedures, manhours required, and daily schedules to improve efficiency in production planning and control for stable production

Column 2 — Control of Contracted Work

- Establishing a control system for work done by outside subcontractors
- Evaluation Radar chart for subcontractors
- Technical guidance to subcontractors
- Administration guidance for subcontractors
- Measuring the degree of dependence and utilization of commissioned work by outside subcontractors
- Instituting the authority to control the work-processes in factories of the subcontractors
- Introducing scientific method to the process for setting up a unit price
- Introducing a bonus-penalty system
- Human Relations with cooperating factories
- Cost comparison between internal and external products

Control of Contracted Work

Establishing an organization of cooperating factories designated for subcontract selected on the basis of excellence in technology, product quality, cost, and delivery terms for attaining coexistence in mutual prosperity through improvement of productivity

Column 3 — Cost Reduction

- Allocation and clear indication of a target for prime cost reduction
- Selection of work processes (or types of machines) which should contribute to the reduction of prime cost
- Driving prime-cost consciousness home
- Promoting value analysis consciousness
- Execution plan for value analysis
- Labour utilization plan for the idle time
- Cost reduction of auxiliary materials and substandard materials
- Material Utilizing Plan
- P.R. of the cost reduction achievement
- Introducing and establishing a suggestion system

Cost Reduction

Establishing the most effective cost reduction system capable of winning a victory in the stringent competition. Establishing the optimum rate of operation, eliminating material loss and labour loss

Column 4 — Worker Administration

- Inventory of capabilities of all workers
- Programme for cross training
- Personnel assignment — for prompt integrated work performance
- Establishing a pattern of personnel distribution
- Indication of the units of products produced on the previous day
- JI for foremen and their equivalents
- JR for foremen and their equivalents
- Workmanship training
- Performance rating system
- Working condition control

Worker Administration

Helping the workers to settle down to work and to improve their motivation for work by regular evaluation of the workers and helping them to master skills of high standard in a short period

1. MAIN PRODUCTS CLASSIFICATION CHART

Purpose

Apart from the production shops, it is important for the job shops to find out exactly the main flow of the manufactured products if the standard for factory administration should be improved, for the ability to create an efficient flow in the process of production is a valuable step toward productivity improvement.

Group technology, which has recently attracted much attention, represents an attempt to improve production efficiency in job shops. It aims to promote efficiency in the small-quantity production of many product items, to the same degree as achieved in the area of mass production of a few items, by classifying the production processes into a given number of groups on the basis of the similarity existing in the shapes, materials, and production processes. The present chart is prepared for this purpose.

How to prepare the chart

First of all, list all the products which are to be produced in your factory at present and in the future. Next, determine the average monthly sales for the products achieved in the last three months on the basis of the figures in the sales account book (by product category). Then, calculate the sales component ratio of each product, representing the total amount of sales as 100. Identify those products you consider to have a high sales component ratio in brackets.

In the case of the following chart, it will be found that the six product items shown in brackets occupy 72 per cent of the total sales components in a product line consisting of 26 product items.

Relations

This chart will be used as a basis for calculating the man-hours required for each product. Taking the man-hours required for the standard product as 100, we may obtain coefficients for all the other products in terms of the standard ratio. The coefficients obtained may be used as conversion coefficients. And when we obtain a conversion coefficient for each product, it may be very usefully applied to planning the number of required man-hours for given work-loads and to calculating manufacturing cost.

How to read and apply the chart

Either in improving production methods or in improving a plant layout, the first requisite is to understand the primary concentration of the product mix of items manufactured in the factory. In the case of the above-mentioned chart, it was quite easy to identify A grade products. However, when the volume of products to classify are too numerous at a glimpse, it is recommended to apply pareto analysis to classify the products into one of three groups, Group A (80%), Group B (15%), and Group C (5%). The products that are to be subjected to analysis are chosen on the principle of concentrating improvement efforts on the most profitable products.

(1) The Main Products Classification Chart

Major category		Medium category	Product name	Unit price (excluding the motor)	Quantity	Sales Amount Unit 1,000 yen	Sales component ratio
Non-stop trans-mission	with motor	4-speed	MSD-402	30,000	6	180	0.6
			MSD-405	31,300	220	6,886	(22.7)
			MSDT-408	40,200	33	1,327	4.4
		8-speed	MSD-806	50,100	3	150	0.5
	Unit (with-out motor)	3-speed	KM-5	29,110	15	437	1.4
			KM-82	35,900	10	359	1.2
		4-speed	MS-402	23,000	120	2,760	(9.1)
			MS-405	24,200	195	4,719	(15.6)
			MST-405	29,400	60	1,764	(5.8)
			MS-415	59,000	10	590	1.9
		8-speed	MS-802	38,500	98	3,773	(12.5)
			MSUT-802	39,080	41	1,602	(5.3)
			MS-805	43,200	26	1,123	3.7
Coleny speed reduction		1/5	MG-05-100T	2,400	30	72	0.2
		1/10	MG-10-65S	2,660	30	80	0.3
			MG-10-100S	2,680	30	80	0.3
			MG-10-100T	2,500	30	75	0.2
		1/20	MG-20-100T	3,500	10	35	0.1
		1/30	MG-30-65S	3,660	60	220	0.7
			MG-30-100S	3,680	160	589	1.9
			MG-30-100S	3,560	70	245	0.8
		1/50	MG-50-65S	3,660	60	220	0.7
			MG-50-100S	3,680	160	589	1.9
			MG-50-100T	3,500	170	595	2.0
Disposer			YDA-08DB	76,100	20	1,522	5.0
			YDA-08D	29,800	10	298	1.0
			Grand Total		1,677	30,290	

[CHART 50]

177

2. OUTLINE PROCESS CHART

Purpose

If you gain an overall view of the systematic assembly procedure of each part, the next step is to keep record of the existing conditions related to the manufacturing processes through which each product passes for assembly.

The present analysis is called 'outline process analysis.' It concerns itself only with the operation processes and the inspection processes out of a total of five processes including operation, transport, delay, inspection and storage. The advantage of this segmentation is that it is possible to analyze and evaluate the most essential part of the whole production process because it directs attention only on the operation processes without being troubled with the subsidiary processes.

It is advantageous to carry out elimination, combination, rearrangement and simplication of the operation processes at this stage.

How to prepare the chart

Using the assembly chart as a basis, arrange the operation processes of each part in a vertical line in the order of the actual production procedure. In doing so, it would be convenient to list the operating time required for each unit on the left side of the ○ process mark and to give the name of the operation processes or the name of the machine and the name of the operator, etc. on the right side of the ○ symbol.

This analytical chart should be prepared from direct observation of the actual processing work and should not, under any circumstances, be drawn up on the basis of memory. It will serve later for recording the actual conditions of the production work for the purpose of its analysis, evaluation and improvement.

Relations

As the *outline process chart* involves an analysis of operation processes based on the assembly chart, outline process analysis is not applied to a production procedure in which the products are completed through a single flow of processes. This type of procedure will be dealt with in a *flow process chart.*

The *outline process chart,* furthermore, can also grow into the *product process chart* with the addition of other kinds of processes. Product process analysis will be discussed later.

How to read and use the chart

Since this chart affords a bird's eye view of all the operating processes of the product, it is possible to have a clear general picture of the wastefulness and inefficiencies that may be found in the interrelations between one work process and another. This, in turn, will facilitate a reorganization of the operation processes directed toward their elimination, rearrangement, combination, and simplication.

An improvement plan for a plant layout, too, can be most practically developed by means of outline process analysis.

(2) Outline Process Chart Assembly of Transmission Shaft

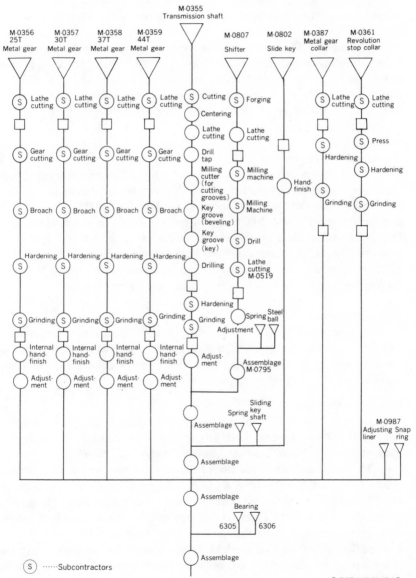

[CHART 51]

179

3. PRODUCT PROCESS ANALYSIS FORM

Purpose

An outline process analysis is conducted for the purpose of a subjective process analysis. This technique may then be further extended and developed into the product process analysis, which also includes analysis of the subsidiary processes. It is necessary to apply this analytical technique to expose and examine every feature of each process of transport, delay, inspection and storage, which are considered to be nonproductive processes and to subject these processes to a thorough review for energetic improvement.

As chances for achieving improvement advances as the volume of information made available grows, it is important to take the utmost care not to overlook any relevant bit of information in collecting data. To this end, a form such as the Product Process Analysis Form should be used. This analysis serves as an indispensable survey for the preparation of the *product process chart.*

How to prepare the form

The first step is to prepare a printed form and to record precisely on the basis of direct observation all of the features of the process to be improved. Above all, such factors as the delay time in the delay process and the transport time in the transport process should be recorded without fail. Furthermore, data on the actual conditions of the jigs and tools and how the transport containers are placed can provide much useful information in connection with the designing of jigs, tools and instruments, and also for a survey of live-load indices to be carried out at a later stage.

Various relations

As mentioned above, this analytical form is framed as a preparatory step for preparing the *product process chart,* which will be discussed in the following section. However, once this form is completed, the form may be used by itself to develop improvement plans.

How to use the form

Each process will be subject to in-depth review. In that case, five W's and one H will prove useful. Each process should be analyzed in terms of the questions, 'why?', 'what?', 'where?', 'when?', 'who?' and 'how?'.

The 'why' and 'what' questions relate to the reason why a given process should exist. If a given process does not satisfy the questions, it is targeted for elimination. Furthermore, the questions regarding 'where' (location), 'when' (time), and 'who' (person) will lead to the combining and rearrangement of processes, whereas the question 'how' (method) will give a clue to a simplification of working method. Improvement thus becomes a process characterized by elimination, combination, rearrangement, or simplification.

(3) Product Process Analysis Form

No.	Rough sketch									Process No.	4892-02-461	No. of unit produced	One Unit
										Product name	Small bus	Part No.	2435-D-47
	Back					Front				Material	Steel frame	No. of parts for one unit product	21 parts for a frame parts 25
		Frame Assembly Sketch								Title of survey	Frame assembly process	Date of survey	Nov. 9-Nov. 12 1965

No.	Unit	Distance	Time	Symbol	Process (Place)	Number of Workers	Equipment	Tools/inspection tools	Method of Placing containers	Processing part/ Processing conditions/special remarks for improvements, etc.
1				▽	Parts warehouse					
2	for five buses	÷ 80m		⇨		2 persons			Truck	
3			70′	D	Parts storage				Loading in bulk	
4	//			◯	Marking the position for hole drilling	1 person		Gauge bench		
5			15′	D	Parts storage					
6	//			◯	Hole drilling	1 person		Electric drilling		Holes of small diameter only
7			35′	D	Beside the drilling m/c					
8	//	70m		⇨		2 persons			Truck	
9			5′	D	Beside the drilling m/c					
10	//			◯	Drilling holes	2 persons		Drilling m/c		Large-diameter holes (approximately 12 m/m or more)
11	//	70m		⇨					Truck	
12			120′	D	Parts storage					
13	//			◯	Welding of parts			Electric welding m/c		
14			30′	D	Workshop					
15	//	80m		⇨		2 persons			Truck	
16			5′	D	Beside the Parker (Anti-corrosive treatment)					
17	//			◯	Anti-corrosive treatment					Specially assigned worker
18			10′	D	Beside the Parker					
19	//	80m		⇨					Truck	
20	//			◯	Red corrosion resistant painting (anti-corrosive)			Spray		Specially assigned staff

[CHART 52]

4.   PRODUCT PROCESS ANALYSIS CHART

Purpose

As the *product process form* is prepared for each one of the parts that are used to make a given product, an all-inclusive process analysis would require unification of all the data collected by the individual analysis forms in one chart to afford an integrated overview of the whole process. In order to satisfy this requirement, it is necessary to prepare, on the basis of the assembly chart, another chart which clearly illustrates in what sequence all the parts are assembled, how each part is worked upon, and what subsidiary processes the parts go through.

How to prepare the chart

Using the assembly chart as the basis, the particulars recorded on the *product process form* regarding the processing of each component part will be transferred to this chart.

The result of this manipulation is a three-sectioned structure primarily composed of process symbols in which the process, etc. are shown on the right side of each work-process symbol. Transport distance will be shown on the left side of the transport process symbol. On the left side of each process symbol for operation, inspection and delay, the time which elapses during the performance of the process is represented. Necessarily, the *product process chart* will be a large one.

Relations

This chart will present a comprehensive view of all the processes which take place in the factory in the course of producing the product subjected to the survey. However, it should be recognized that the analysis achieved by means of this chart presents a macroscopic picture of the entire process. As such, it does not by itself provide detailed analysis and improvement in individual processes. However, it will be possible to make an initial drastic cut in the processes for improvement, by following the flow from materials to products in this chart along with reference to the machinery arrangement chart for the factory.

How to read and use the chart

The processes which should be examined first upon the completion of the *product process analysis chart* are the subsidiary processes which include transport, delay, inspection, and storage. It is only after these subsidiary work processes are thoroughly analyzed and improved that we should proceed with an effort to improve the operation processes (the production processes).

When a given operation process is performed through cooperative work by two or more workers, multi-activity analysis will be employed.

When the process analyzed involves both man and machine, the man-machine analysis will be used. If the work process under analysis involves bench work by one worker, the two-handed work analysis or the Therblig analysis will be applied.

(4) Product Process Analysis Chart for the Total Assembly Procedure of Small Bus

(Symbol)   (Work Process)

	Frames	
6m	(Frame storage)	
2'	Transport to the assembly bench	
20'	① Fixing the frame on the bench with pins[1-2] Hammer	
	I Delay	

On the left side
14m Strorage at the side
120' 3 To the frame
2 Set against the frame[2-4]

On the right side
Storage at the side
2 To the frame[2-4]

3'	② Clamping the right side panel with the frame[2-3] vice
22'	I Height measurement (positioning)[1-2] Tape measure iron bar
I'	③ Right side panel Frame welding[1] Electric welding machine
12'	④ Bending correction[1-2] Hammer

The main unit represents the entire structure made up by combining the parts
Show-window jig
(jig storage)
Show-window
4 To the main unit[1-2]
(Workshop)
7m 5 To the main unit

2'	⑤ Left side panel Main unit calking[2] Vice
2'	2 Height measurement (Positioning)[1-2] Tape measure Iron bar
10'	⑥ Left side pannel Main unit welding Electric welding
20'	⑦ Bending correction[1] Hammer
4'	⑧ Show-window jig Main unit calking[2] Vice
4'	3 Framing (size measurement)[2] Measure
15'	6 Taken off from the bench and transported to the grinder
3m	⑨ Cutting with a grinder[1] Grinder, Scissors
4'	7 To the Main unit

Roof
(Roof storage)
18w B Above the the main unit[4-6]
(Work performed in parallel)
⑬ Main unit rivet calking
18 ⑭ provisional rivet setting 1—2
30' ⑮ Rivet positioning 1—2
14' ⑯ Makin holes[1] g
8' ⑰ Main unit and rivets calking 2
Reinforcing material
Preparation
17' ㉖ Preparation
Back part

5m	⑩ Show-window Main unit welding[2] Gas welding	Step frame
13'	⑪ Making hoist, rivet clamping[2] Drift gun	
20'	⑫ To be placed on the main unit[4-6]	⑲ Preparation
6'	⑱ Door stay removed[1]	6m 9
13'	⑳ Fixed to the main unit ( )[1]	Step side panel
20'	㉑ Fixed to the main unit (clamping)[2]	Step foundation plate
10'	㉒ Fixed to the main unit (clamping)[2]	Front window frame
210'	㉓ Fixed to the main unit (welding)[1]	Front part
35'	㉔ Fixed to the main unit (welding)[1]	The tools used are the same as that used in the above
15'	㉕ Fixed to the main unit (clamping)[2]	
210'	㉗ Welding of reinforcing material[1]	
40'	㉘ Correction[1-3] Hammer/grinder	

Steering wheel and related parts
6m 10
Tire housing (cover)
28m 11
Back part equipment
30m 12

35'	㉙ Back part main unit calking
45'	㉛ Back part Welding
65'	㉛ Back part Clampling
48'	㉜ Correction
35'	㉝ Fixes to main unit (Welding, Clamping)
15'	㉞ Clamping to the main unit
205'	3 Back part equipment left as it is untill assembling is finished
100'	㉟ Fixed to the main unit (welding, clamping)
18'	㊱ Tire housing cover fixed to the main unit (welding, clamping)
	▽ All the assemblage completed

[CHART 53]

183

5. FLOW PROCESS CHART

Purpose

In dealing with the *outline process chart,* we discussed the necessity and procedure only with regard to operation and inspection. However, if the operation and the inspection are efficient, it does not necessarily follow that the entire procedure is also efficient. There may be a long delay between one operation process and another, or the equipment for transport may be quite inadequate, the frequency of transport may be too high, etc.

As these conditions are not represented in an *outline process chart,* a *flow process chart* may be used for both (a) flow of materials and for (b) operation processes of one worker. The quantity of data represented in this *flow process chart* will be considerable, and, therefore, it would be uneconomical to include all components and parts to be assembled in this chart. It would be better to restrict this analysis to the flow of important parts and of those parts for which delay is frequently recorded.

For example, the *outline process chart* will be generally more effective as a means of analysis for such complicated assembly products as motors, power generators, engines, watches and so forth. In analyzing a *flow process chart* — especially when attention is focused on the transport distance, i.e. on the layout of the machinery — it is recommended to carry forward an improvement plan with the aid of the *flow diagram* and other more visual methods. Like using a map for travelling, these should be easier to follow.

How to prepare the chart

Prepare a form like the one on page 185 and record the actual performance of work in the order of the sequence of the processes involved through direct observation of the work processes. Be sure not to overlook even the smallest item. Jot down every finding in your memorandum at this time. When you have finished recording every feature of the actual processes, assign each process to one of the columns under the appropriate process symbol by drawing a dot. Then connect the dots with a line as shown in the chart. In doing so, enter the actual measured time for the transport process and write down the delay time for the delay process on the basis of inquiry.

Relations

It is recommended to prepare the *flow diagram* explained on the following pages at the same time. This diagram depicts the actual flow of work and enables you to obtain more concrete hints on improvement.

How to read and use the chart

Analytical charts are prepared to provide information which will

(5A) The Flow Process Chart (Prior to Improvement)

Chart / Sheet /		Summary			
Product/material	Activity		Present	Proposed	Saving
Dehydrator Component Parts (ND-250)/ SS-34	Work ○		5		
Activity/	Transport →		14		
Press Processing	Delay ◻		8		
Method: Present /	Inspection ☐		—		
	Storage ▽		2		
	Distance (m)		80		
Workshop First Press Section, First Press Group	Time				
Workers Work shift no.	Cost				
Prepared dy: Kurosaki	Labour expenses				
Approved by: Date: Nov. 9, 10 1972	Material cost				
	Total				

	Description	Quantities (sheets)	Distance (m)	Time (dm)	Symbol ○ → ◻ ☐ ▽	Remarks
1	Storage position (beside the 300 ⊛ press machine)				▽	
2	Placed beside the squares shears	400	14		→	Crane
3	Square shears temporary delay	400		( )	◻	
4	Cut with the square shears	1			○	Two workers
5	Transported to the front of the square shears	1	2		→	Manual
6	Square shears temporary delay	2		( )	◻	
7	Transported to the side of the 300 ⊛ press	400	12	5.45 Hr	→	Crane
8	Temporary delay	400		( )	◻	
9	Placed in front of the 300 ⊛ press	400	2		→	Crane
10	Punching on the 300 ⊛ press	1			○	Three workers
11	Transported to the front of the 300 ⊛ press	1	2		→	Manual
12	300 press temporary delay	400		( )	◻	
13	Transported to available room	400	7		→	So far based on oral inquiry Crane
14	Temporary delay	400			◻	
15	Transported to the left side of press No. 1	400	5		→	Crane
16	Z-bending processing of press No. 1	1			○	Four workers
17	Placed on the right side of press No. 1	1	2		→	Manual
18	Press No. 1 Temporary delay	400		(24Hr)	◻	
19	Transported to the left side of press No. 1	400	4		→	Crane
20	Joggled-lap processing on press No. 1	1			○	Four workers
21	Placed on the right side of press No. 1	1	2	310	→	Manual
22	Temporary delay	400		140	◻	
23	Transported to available room	400	3		→	Crane
24	Placed in front of press No. 3	400	7	612	→	Crane
25	L-bending processing	1			○	Four workers
26	Placed at the side	1	2		→	Manual
27	Temporary delay	100	8		◻	
28	Transported to available room	100	8	230	→	Crane
29	Storage	100			▽	

[CHART 54A]

185

reveal areas for potential improvement. Charts can visually highlight specific points to which we can direct attention. For instance, a chart can make apparent a high frequency of transport and long transport distance, which are likely to be the most unproductive of all the processes. While transport requires cost, the value of the transported goods does not increase by being transported. Then, how can we reduce the frequency of this transport process? To achieve this goal, it is necessary to subject the processes to a thorough review with the 5 W's 1 H questions and to subsequent rearrangement of the processes for improvement.

(5B) Flow Process Chart (After Improvement)

Chart / Sheet /				Summary			
Product/Material			Activity	Present	Proposed	Saving	
.Dehydrator Component Parts (ND-250)/SS-34.			Work ○	5	5		
Activity			Transport →	14	9	5	
Processing			Delay ▢	8	–	8	
Method:			Inspection □	–	–		
			Storage ▽	2	2		
			Distance (m)	80	40		
Workshop: First Press Section,First Press Group			Time				
Workers : Work shift number:			Cost				
Prepared by: Kurosaki			Labour cost / Material cost				
Approved by: Date: Nov. 12, 1972							
			Total				

	Description	Quantities (sheets)	Distance (m)	Time (dm)	○ → ▢ □ ▽	Remarks
1	Storage position (Warehouse)				▽	
2	Placed beside the square shears	400	5		→	Crane
3	Cut on the square shears	1			○	
4	Placed in front of the 300 〒 press	400	12		→	Crane
5	Punching on the 300 〒 press	1			○	
6	Transported to the 300 〒 press	1	2		→	Manual
7	Transported to the left side of the 10 feet brake press	400	11		→	Crane
8	Z-bending processing on the brake press	1			○	
9	Placed on the right side of the brake press (loaded on the push cars)	1	2		→	Manual
10	Transported to the left side of press No. 1 (As loaded on the push-cars)	400	2		→	Manual
11	Joggled-lap processing	1			○	
12	Placed on the right side (Placed on the push-cars)	1	2		→	Manual
13	Transported to the left side of Press No. 2 (as loaded on the push-cars)	400	2		→	Manual
14	L-bending processing	1			○	
15	Placed in front	1	2		→	Manual
16	Transported to the half-made product storage				→	Crane
17	Storage				▽	

[CHART 54B]

186

6. FLOW DIAGRAM

Purpose

When the *flow process chart* is completed, there arises a necessity to visually ascertain the actual conditions of the flow of the material through each process by developing the data into a ground plan. The *flow diagram* is prepared in order to fulfil this need.

This diagram will give hints or clues for job method improvement such as whether there are crossing or backtracking in the flow of articles, whether the articles are transported over an unnecessarily long distance, whether there is immoderateness or wastefulness in operation, inspection, or in storage places, or whether a rearrangement is required of the places where these processes take place. The *flow diagram* may thus be used with advantage as a supplementary means in conjunction with the *flow process chart* to visualize improvement at the time of job method improvement or work-process rearrangement.

How to prepare the diagram

First, ascertain the divisions and the range of the processes through which the products pass from the point where the analysis begins to the point where it is completed in the *flow process chart* and arrange all the elements in a ground plan using sufficient space. Draw all the machines, equipment, facilities, tables, benches and so forth which occupy this space in the ground plan. Then, tracing the work processes one after another in the order of the work flow from the starting point of the *flow process chart,* write the actual conditions of the flow in the ground plan. In this case, describing the work processes in terms of the five process symbols on the flow line would lead to a *flow diagram. Flow diagrams* are prepared in this way for the manufacturing process both prior to improvement and after the improvement.

Relations

Both the *flow process chart* and the *flow diagram* discussed here are designed for a macroscopic analysis centring around the flow of articles. It is only after a macroscopic improvement is accomplished that we can advance into the area of microscopic analysis and improvement as motion study. And at that point, the man-machine analysis, the two-handed process analysis, the Therblig analysis, etc., will be useful.

How to read and use the diagram

The first thing to be careful about in reviewing the *flow diagram* describing the conditions prior to improvement, is that the component parts or the products subjected to the analysis do not necessarily represent all of the parts and components the production departments are producing.

187

Therefore, it is not advisable to change the plant layout only on the basis of the information and data presented here. Initial efforts should be made to eliminate, combine, rearrange, and simplify production processes and transportation, before considering a change in plant layout. The flow diagram before improvement should serve as a work sheet for improvement, and entries or other necessary notations for analysis and examination will be useful.

(6) Flow Diagram: Dehydrater Component Part (No. 250)

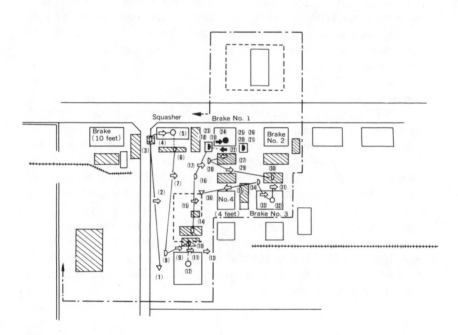

—— · —— · ——	Border line between work groups
————————	Transport work with a crane
— — — — — —	Manual transport work
▢	Press shaping machine
▨	Work bench
➡ ● ▶	Processed two times

[CHART 55]

7.   FLOW PROCESS ANALYSIS CHART

Purpose

The ordinary process analysis techniques clarify the processes and assembly required for each component of a given product. The *flow process analysis chart* discussed here, however, presents the correlative flow of the manufacturing processes for each component part by means of a single chart.

Since this chart reveals similarities existing in the manufacturing processes as well as the sequence of the processes, the potential for achieving *group technology* effects by grouping together similar work processes can be more readily assessed. Furthermore, the man-hours or machine hours required for one unit of components are marked in the circle. It is helpful to vertically sum the man-hours for each process and to work out a total man-hours for one unit of the product. By multiplying man-hours with the number of units produced, it is possible to calculate the work-load for each process for advantageous planning of manpower.

How to prepare the chart

First, fill in all the manufacturing and operation processes which each component part undergoes. It is desirable to arrange these in a processing sequence which may be considered to represent 'the greatest common measure' sequence for all the component parts as far as possible. Then, write a relevant component name in each row for the component parts on the left side of the form for each partial assembly unit. Following the regular order of assembly, the sequence in which a given component is progressively processed from the raw material stage is represented with circles and lines combining them. The man-hours required for a unit of a given component is written in the circle. Finally, the man-hours given in each operation process column will be totalled for total man-machine hours involved in the entire processing operation.

Relations

The *flow process analysis chart* will be completed by merely transferring the contents of *outline process charts* to this form. Needless to say, it is possible to prepare the chart by direct observation of the actual production situation. This chart will give many hints for working out a new arrangement of work processes or for designing a factory layout.

How to read and use the chart

The advantage of this chart is that it is capable of presenting the total man-hours required for a product unit for each production process. On the basis of this analysis, you are able to formulate adequate machine loading plans and man-hour plans. In addition, you can have reliable spare capacity control through comparison between prospective work loads and existing plant capacity. You can group parts and components on the basis of process similiarity, and accordingly, you can change the plant layout so that equipment and machines are placed sequentially with the normal flow of the production processes. Here again you can realize the effects of a mass production system in spite of the existing job shop production style. You can utilize this system further by developing common jigs and fixtures.

(7) The Flow Process Analysis Chart

Process							
28 Packaging							
27 Inspection							
26 Filling oil	⑩	⑮	⑧	⑩	⑧	⑩	105
25 Painting							
24 Assembly							
23 Decomposition					⑤.7		5.7
22 Washing							
21 Welding							
20 Plating							
19 Hand finish							
18 Adjustment	⑦.5	⑤.7	④.5	⑤.7	④.5	⑤.6	33.5
17 Grinding	⑳-②	⑳-②	⑳-②	㉚-⑮	⑳-②	⑳-②	130 25
16 Hardening							
15 Spot facing							
14 Broach	⑮	⑮	⑮		⑮	⑮	7.5
13 Gear cutting	⑧	⑥.8	⑥.5	④.6	⑦.3	⑧.4	43
12 Key groove				④.5			4.5
11 Press							
10 Tap							
9 Reamer							
8 Drilling							
7 Boring							
6 Lathe cutting	⑱	⑯	㉒	⑱	⑯	㉜	112.8
5 Centering				⑮			1.5
4 Milling m/c							
3 Cutting				⑦			7
2 Forging							
1 Casting							

	34 teeth Driving shaft gear	20 teeth Driving shaft gear	22 teeth Driving shaft gear	Driving shaft	17 teeth Pinion gear	26 teeth Driving gear	Total
Total work units	82	70	65.5	97.5	66.3	94.5	475.8
No. of work units of outside order	49.5	46.3	43	75	46.8	63.9	324.5
No. of in-factory work unit	32.5	23.7	22.5	22.4	19.5	30.6	151.2
Lot number	500	500	500	300	300	300	
Chart No.	M-0354	M-0353	M-0352	M-0390	M-0389	M-0391	Total

[CHART 56]

8.   TRAVEL CHART

Purpose

The activity analysis chart records more or less detailed information on the activities of a worker or a group of workers engaged in a series of processes. In pursuing a study of the activities involving nonrepetitive and nonstandardized work, a practical format to follow will be a *travel chart*. By transferring the loci found in the movement of the workers to a ground plan, it will be possible to obtain a distinct representation of the places where some backtracking or crossing of flow takes place.

How to prepare the chart

Now, let's draw an example from the traffic patterns in a hotel kitchen. The movements of a waitress preparing for breakfast follows the procedure below. As may be understood from the *travel chart* describing the situation prior to improvement, there is considerable inefficiency in the working procedure for the waitress.

1. Enter the kitchen by the entrance
2. Fetch a pushcart
3. Take tray and place on the pushcart
4. Place knives and forks on the tray
5. Take a glass for fruit juice and place it on the tray
6. Pour fruit juice in the glass
7. Take a bowl for cornflakes and place it on the tray
8. Pour cornflakes in the bowl
9. Take a warm plate and place it on the tray (egg dish)
10. Take a coffee jug and place it on the tray
11. Pour coffee from the pot on the stove into the coffee jug
12. Take toast from the toast shelf and place it on the tray
13. Take a milk jug and place it on the tray
14. Take a butter plate and a marmalade plate and place on the tray
15. Take milk from the refrigerator and pour it into the milk jug
16. Take butter from the refrigerator and place it on the butter plate
17. Take a cup and a saucer for coffee and place on the tray
18. Take a toast plate and place on the tray
19. Place marmalade on the marmalade plate
20. Take a sugar pot and place it on the tray
21. Put sugar in the sugar pot
22. Take seasoning and place it on the tray
23. Return the pushcart to its depository and take the tray by hand
24. Leave the kitchen by the exit.

The random working procedure results in a considerable delay in the serving of breakfast and the guests register constant complaints. The waitresses threaten the hotel manager with a group resignation because of the shortage of workers.

How to use the chart

Trace the movement of a waitress with pins and thread and eventually obtain a string diagram of a *travel chart*. One can imagine that the total length of the thread can be considerably long. In order to rectify this situation, we only have to rearrange the places for each item in the order of the procedure given above. It goes without saying that the kitchen is not used only for the preparation of breakfast. However, we may leave the immovable utensils and equipment, such as the stoves and sinks, and place every other item on a pushcart with casters. It will also be apparent that a change in the sequence of the preparation procedures, where possible, may be more practical than altering the physical layout. The *travel chart*, after an improvement, represents a reduction of the travelling distance to the minimum.

(8) A Travel Chart: Hotel Cuisine (Existing Condition)

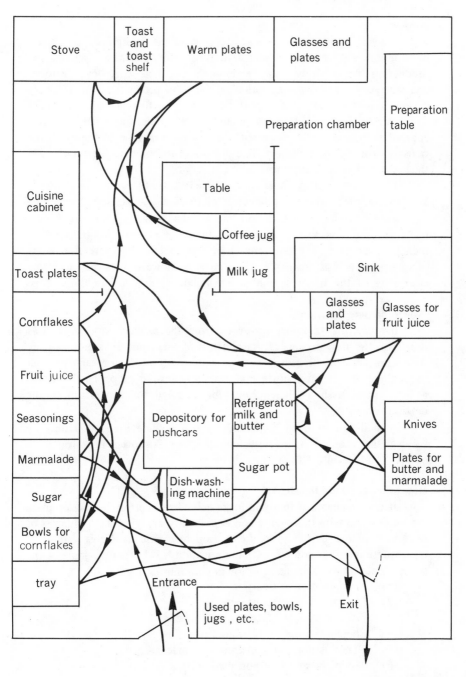

[CHART 57]

9. TRANSPORT ANALYSIS (PRINCIPAL PRODUCTS TRANSPORT FLOW CHART)

Purpose

Transport may be defined as a change in the position of the objects of production — chiefly subsidiary to production activities — among the production means of machines, equipment, facilities, workshops, factories and storage. It is essentially a principal factor of production. For this very reason, it is the target of transport rationalization to achieve improvement in the various factors of transport including the articles transported, workers engaged in transport, the means of transport, the method of transport, the transport routes, the transport time etc. so as to combine these factors in the best interface with each other.

In order to achieve this goal, it is advisable to conduct a transport analysis for each principal product item to find out particulars regarding the transport routes, the transport means, the quantity transported each trip, the total transport quantity, and the time required for transporting each product item. The following chart represents one of several varieties of transport analysis techniques. This chart is, however, designed to give a clear view of the transport routes for individual principal product items.

How to prepare the chart

Identify the transport processes from the *product process analysis charts* or the *flow process charts* and spread them out on a ground plan. As the production procedure follows a different route for each product item, the lines are given different characteristics. In preparing this chart, a form, such as shown here, should be prepared to keep record of the details for review.

In addition to these materials, try to calculate live-load indices by varying the product items, research ideas for improvement through an observation of a shift in the vertical distance.

How to read and use the chart

It is recommended that you make an energetic effort to develop plans for improvement by thoroughly and consistently applying the 'principles of material handling' explained in the introductory remarks in this chapter. It is also desirable that you consider the possibility of integrating some of the following steps toward standardization in your improvement plans.

    (1)   Specialization of transport
    (2)   Mechanization of transport
    (3)   Adopting appropriate transport means
    (4)   Standardization of the transport means
    (5)   Consolidation of the maintenance machinery
    (6)   Comprehensive transport planning

(7)   Setting up a vehicle operation plan
(8)   Intensification of transport work
(9)   Improvement on the work distribution
(10) Standardization of the road surface and the tracks

Transport process	From	To	Item transported	Person in charge	Container	Weight	Dist.	Freqcy

(9) The Principal Transport Flow Chart

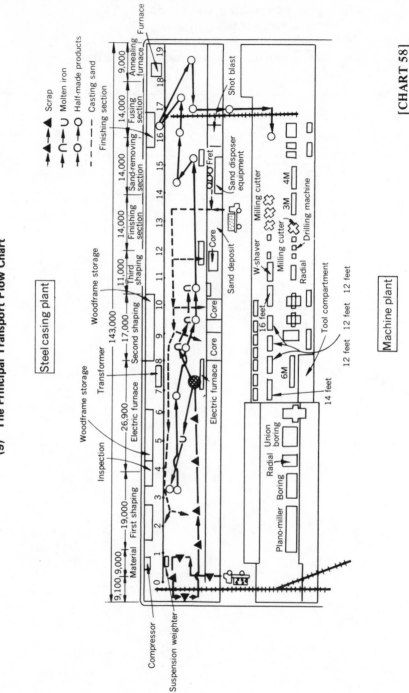

Steel casing plant

Machine plant

[CHART 58]

10. LAYOUT CORRELATION CHART

Purpose

Repeated extensions of plant buildings to accommodate the development of the corporate business result in something like the complex and monstrous streets of Casbah. It often happens that the work sections, which should naturally be operating closely together, are separated from each other and require transport over a long distance, while entirely unrelated work sections operate side by side. Under such circumstances, it is impossible to expect either high efficiency or high productivity.

Periodically it becomes necessary to re-evaluate the geographical interrelations of entire sections of the factory. Within the restricted physical space available, it is desirable to seek a rearrangement of each work section. The *layout correlation chart* is intended for such evaluation.

How to prepare the chart

Arrange all the work sections in the plant at the base of an equilateral triangle as shown in the following chart. The order of arrangement may be determined on an arbitrary basis. The triangular area that spreads to the right from the column is designed for evaluating the degrees of interdependence among the work sections. Each work section has mutually intersecting areas as we trace the line falling to the right and the line rising to the right, respectively. The intersecting areas are where you are expected to make an evaluation of each section in terms of its interrelation with every other section. In making that evaluation, it would be helpful by securing an all-inclusive view of the entire production processes at a glance by rating sections either with symbols or in colours. (Refer to the chart.)

Relations

Using this chart as a basis, group together the work processes and/or departments displaying high correlation to each other and enter them on the chart. Some of the processes will fall naturally into groups; others will not. Moreover, it will be found that some work sections or groups are related to all the groups and sections. The practical layout design is accomplished by filling in all these factors in the available space on the basis of a certain layout policy.

How to read and use the chart

When the *layout chart* is completed, select the work processes and/or department that require the most frequent contact and represent them in red. Then examine those processes having less contact and represent those in, say, orange. It does not matter to any significant degree if you ignore the work processes and/or departments represented in, for instance, green or blue, for they do not require any close contact. An ideal layout plan

197

should be prepared even when it is reasonably inferrable from the actual situation that such a plan could hardly be implemented. Improvement is attained during the course of the effort to reach a compromise with the actual situation and with the closest possible approximation to the ideal plan.

(10) The Layout Correlation Chart

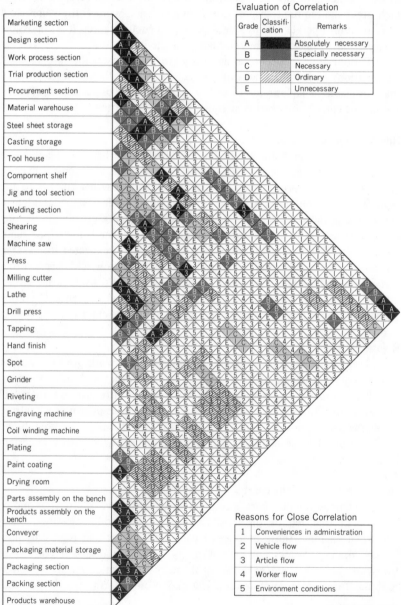

Evaluation of Correlation

Grade	Classification	Remarks
A		Absolutely necessary
B		Especially necessary
C		Necessary
D		Ordinary
E		Unnecessary

Reasons for Close Correlation

1	Conveniences in administration
2	Vehicle flow
3	Article flow
4	Worker flow
5	Environment conditions

Marketing section
Design section
Work process section
Trial production section
Procurement section
Material warehouse
Steel sheet storage
Casting storage
Tool house
Comporment shelf
Jig and tool section
Welding section
Shearing
Machine saw
Press
Milling cutter
Lathe
Drill press
Tapping
Hand finish
Spot
Grinder
Riveting
Engraving machine
Coil winding machine
Plating
Paint coating
Drying room
Parts assembly on the bench
Products assembly on the bench
Conveyor
Packaging material storage
Packaging section
Packing section
Products warehouse

[CHART 59]

198

11. PLANT LAYOUT PLAN

Purpose

There is no other expression that more accurately describes the importance of a plant layout, its essence and its role than, "A plant layout is a blueprint of plant management," for knowledge, wisdom and experience concerning production techniques and production control should be condensed in a *plant layout plan.* Good plant layout calls for an integrated control of the entire production procedure and for this reason, it should provide the shortest transport distance, a uniform and consistent flow of work and the reduction of crossings and backtracking to a minimum. It should also afford a multi-dimensional utilization of space, ensure safety, give satisfaction to the workers and permit highly flexible conditions for rearrangement to adapt to the changing conditions in the environment.

How to prepare the plan

A layout plan that embodies the layout principle outlined on page 166 may be naturally considered to be of maximum efficiency. It is indispensable to prepare a *layout correlation chart* and to establish a layout policy both for trying to improve an existing layout and for designing a new plant layout. In making an effort to improve an existing layout, the first thing that should be done is to represent the actual present situation as it is in a diagram. Then, the actual situation is reviewed in terms of the diagram to draw up a plan for improvement.

Moreover, an actual layout plan starts with a ground plan for the factory building. All the walls and unmovable facilities should be included in the ground plan beforehand. Then, using the same reduced scale as the one used for the ground plan, make templates for movable machines and facilities. This can be done with cardboard cutouts. The templates are then placed on the available space of the floor plan on the basis of the *layout correlation chart* and the layout policy. When a layout plan is finally accepted, the templates are pasted to the floor plan.

Furthermore, it is desirable to represent the flow of each component part and the materials with an arrow.

Various relations

The ideal layout diagram is nothing but a concrete representation of the results obtained through a thorough consideration of the *outline process chart,* the *flow process chart,* the *layout correlation chart,* the layout policy and so forth.

How to read and use the plan

The ideal layout chart as completed will be the target for the layout improvement to be achieved in the plant from now on. It will depend on the policy of the factory management whether the transfer of machines and facilities is carried out stage by stage or is accomplished in a single step. Whichever the case may be, all the workers in the factory should be thoroughly informed of this layout chart beforehand. Besides, it is advisable to secure the positive understanding of all workers about the advantages and effects of the proposed layout.

(11) An Ideal Plant Layout Plan of Facilities at a Circuit Breaker Manufacturing Factory

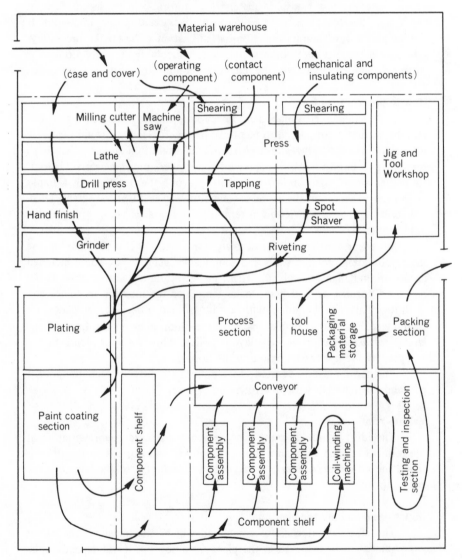

[CHART 60]

12. MULTI-ACTIVITY CHART

Purpose

A chart which depicts teamwork is called a *multi-activity chart*. In more strict terms, it may be defined as: 'A *multi-activity chart* is a kind of procedure chart designed to record mutually correlated activities performed by several workers and/or several machines.'

It is made by representing the passage of time in terms of a scale on paper and by graphically showing the work activities of each employee in the column provided for the individual worker. This chart clearly shows how individual workers assist one another, which workers are overloaded, which workers are underutilized and what the actual rate of operation is for each worker. This type of information will be helpful in achieving more rationalized work allocation, reduction of work cycles and more properly balanced work quantity.

How to prepare the chart

First, fill in the name of the worker or the job title on the upper part of the form as shown in the chart. Mark a time scale on the vertical lines on the right and the left sides of the form. Then, record the particulars of the work performed by each worker and the time spent. When the time cycle is short, it will be necessary to have one observer exclusively assigned to one worker for time measurement. However, when the time cycle is extremely long, as in the case of the example, it will be possible to have one observer perform time measurement for two or more workers simultaneously. The results of such observations will appear something like the following chart. The cited chart is a *multi-activity chart* for the assembly processes of tank lorries showing the results of an improvement. It took 17.5 hours to complete this one cycle in the assembly procedure as shown in the *multi-activity chart* prior to the improvement.

How to read and use the chart

As a hint to the nature of improvement achieved through a multi-activity analysis, I would like to draw upon the example of the discussion between President Roosevelt and Dr Alexander Sachs in 1939 concerning the way to divide the work required for the production of the atomic bomb (Manhattan Project).

President Roosevelt was anxious to know whether nuclear weapons would be made available in time to decide the course of the war. Before the discussion started, Dr Sachs had told the President that the project would require a period of 25 years for its completion at a cost of $2 billion if ordinary methods were employed. Dr Sachs explained that he had conducted a survey of actual examples showing how, in the course of human endeavours, time could be cut short. Dr Sachs found a relevant actual example in music.

Composers know how to use time in three layers. Dr Sachs told President Roosevelt to recall the waltz which he had the habit of humming. In this piece of music, three melodies flow side by side in a harmonious relation. Dr Sachs recommended that this was exactly the step to be taken for the atomic weapon project. Dr Sachs said: "When we take up a part of the project, let's consider we have already made a success of it. And we take up the subsequent part immediately." In fact, the project was carried out in just this way. Perhaps, it was the first time that the step was ever applied to an enterprise of this magnitude and indeed, the attempt was a big success. (Cited from: Ernest Dale, The Planning and Developing of Corporate Organization Structure.)

(12) Multi-Activity Chart: Tank Lorry Assembly Group

	First Group		Second Group			Third Group		
(hour)	Ishiwatari	Maebara	Yamamoto	Nakajima	Oono	Yamaguchi	Nozaki	Atarashi
	(1) Shell plate, tack-welding, regular welding	(1)	(1) Mirror centring	(1)	Size measurement	(1) Reinforcement marking-off, melting and cutting	(1)	(1)
					Undergoing inspection			
1	(2) Bottom valve marking-off	(2)	(2)	(2)	Adjustment			
	(3) Revolution	(3)	Reinforcement attached to the mirror			(2) Insulating plates marking-off, melting and cutting		
2	(4) Mirror No. 1 tack-welding	(4)	(3) Partition plates carried into the shell plates	(3)		Carry out		
	(5) Finish plates 1, 2, 3, 4, tack-welding	(5)	6 m/m rod wound around partition plates 1, 2, 3, & 4		(1)	(1) Manhole installation fixing and regular welding	(3)	(2)
3	(6) Mirror No. 2 tack-welding	(6)	(4)	(4)	(1)			
	(7) Ladder, marking-off, boss installation	(7)	(5)	(5)	(2)	(2) Oil basin transport, processing, tack-welding and regular welding	(4)	(3)
4	(8) Drain pipe positioning, marking-off and fixing regular welding	(8)	Partition plates regular welding of the inside parts (the lower parts on the opposite side)					
5	(9) Step stay fixing, tack-welding, regular welding	(9)				(3) Handrail marking-off the position, fixing, and welding	(5)	(4)
6	(10)	(10)	(6)	(6)	(3)	(4) Bottom valve hole-punching, tack-welding, and welding	(6)	(5)
	Hose box parts, marking-off, processing, fixing regular welding		(7) Partition plates welding of the inside parts (the upper parts on the opposite side)	(7)	(4)			
7						(5)	(7)	(6)
						(7) Support legs fitting the reinforcing plates		
			(8) Insulating plates Positioning and welding	(8)	Support	(7) legs	(9) welding fixing	
8	(11) Tail lamp, tack-welding, regular welding	(11)		(9)		(8) Support legs tack-welding	(10)	(9)
9					(7) Main legs regular welding	(9)	(11)	(10)

Suport legs positions marking-off

[CHART 61]

13.   THE MAN-MACHINE CHART

Purpose

The *man-machine chart* is an operation analysis-type chart intended for recording the time sequence of workers' operations in relation to the machine operations observed in work processes where workers and machines are combined in the performance of work (i.e. where workers operate machines).

The chart consists of vertical columns for the workers and the machine, respectively, with a time scale provided either in the centre or on both sides of the chart. Along the lapse of time, the operations of the workers or the machine(s) are filled in the blank columns. In this chart, the time expended for the operations of the workers and the machine(s) are represented in terms of corresponding areas, appealing directly to the intuition of the observer for potential improvement. Consequently, it will be possible to improve the rate of operation of the machines by altering certain details of the work cycle. This analytical chart will be highly useful when one operator is running several machines at the same time.

How to prepare the chart

This chart is prepared by the same procedure as applied to the *multi-activity chart* discussed earlier. The only difference is that time measurement is applied chiefly to machines. You will find an example of work improvement on the following pages showing successful improvement of the operation rate to 82 per cent through a reduction of the cycle time to one half. This is achieved by having unskilled workers taking charge of process No. 1 and process No. 6 in a work procedure involving work with a spot welding machine, whereas the operation rate of the machine was less than 42 per cent prior to this improvement. (The work procedure is shown for your reference.)

Process No. 1	Fixing a component part on the jig	2.00 minutes
Process No. 2	Positioning on the machine	0.25 minutes
Process No. 3	Welding (one hand is used to operate the machine, while the other hand is used to operate the jig).	1.50 minutes
Process No. 4	Taking the component off the machine	0.25 minutes
Process No. 5	Loosening the jig	0.375 minutes
Process No. 6	Taking the component off the jig and placing it (in a designated place)	0.375 minutes
	Total Cycle Time:	4.75 minutes

Relations

As this chart may be applied to all cases that involve combined work of man and machine, it will be a powerful means of work improvement in machine factories and so forth. When it is desired to make a more detailed analysis of the actions of the workers, the *Therblig chart* will be useful.

How to read and use the chart

Whichever of these two charts may be used, the purpose is to improve the operation rate of work processes. If the operation rate of workers remains at a low level, it will not be possible to allocate more work or to assign workers to an additional machine. However, the chart will at least provide a focal point for the solution of existing problems. Furthermore, when the operation rate of the machine is low, some part of the process may be allocated to less skilled workers. By this and other methods, it will be possible to balance the operations of man and machine, and this in turn will work toward efficiency in machine utilization in the long run.

(13)   Man-Machine Chart: Spot Welding

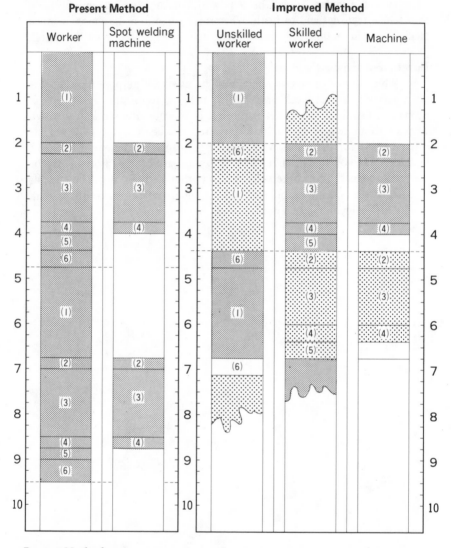

Present Method | **Improved Method**

Present Method

Processes (2), (3) and (4) take up 2 minutes of the spot welding machine's time in a work cycle of 4.75 minutes, or less than a 42% operation rate.

Improved Method

Processes (2), (3) and (4) still take up 2 minutes, but the work cycle is now reduced to 2.375 minutes, with processes (1) and (6) for the next operation done by unskilled workers at the same time. Machine operation rate is therefore 82%.

[CHART 62]

14. THE TWO-HANDED PROCESS CHART

Purpose

The *two-handed process chart* is a variation of the *product process chart* designed to record the work performed with two hands. The chart is designed to clearly represent the motions (or repose) of both hands of a worker in terms of the correlation between the right hand and the left hand or in relation to a time sequence. Actually, the chart may be considered to be a special type of analytical chart. The time scale provided in the chart will be convenient for recognizing the specific actions of each hand at any given moment with the aid of the symbols.

The prepared analytical chart will give many hints on the economy of motions.

How to prepare the chart

In the two-handed process chart, the work process symbols should be restricted to two or three for the entire process being analyzed. The symbols assigned to either the left hand or the right hand action will represent a broad activity category. The example chart presented here employs one symbol for both operations and inspection, another for transport and another for delay (or idle time). Inspection is combined with operations as it involves related actions of the hands, i.e., work. The restrictions to two or three classifications permit observation of inefficiencies of either hand occurring during simultaneous activities. The object, of course, is to improve productivity in the process under observation. This will be achieved by compressing the number of necessary hand actions either through improvement, or, in the case of delay time, through elimination.

Now, let's discuss the procedure for the preparation of the chart.
(1) Start describing the motions of one hand.
(2) The time when the worker picks up a component at the beginning of the work process is a good time to start recording the motions. The other column is reserved for describing the work performed by the other hand.
(3) The operations performed at the same time are written down on one and the same line.
(4) The operations which take place in a sequence should be written on separate lines. Make close observation of their relations in terms of sequence. Remember to describe all the operations of the workers.

How to read and use the chart

Pay particular attention to the 'holding' of the left hand. The act of holding is unproductive and does not in itself make any contribution to increasing the value of the product. For this reason, it is advisable to design a holding device operated with a pedal. The left hand, liberated from the holding operation, may now be utilized for other productive work. In the example shown in the chart, productivity was improved by an additional 70 per cent as a result of improvement.

(14A) Two-Handed Process Chart (Present Method)

Chart 1 Sheet /	Workshop Layout
Drawings and component parts: Window Pillar of a bus **Work:** Correction Pressing on a Press **Workshop:** Second Press Section Friction Press No. 3 **Workers:** **Prepared by:** Takeshi Orihara **Date:** November 12, 1982	Component parts Unit: m/m 150 Inspection boad (panel) 100 Lever currently used 20 50 Operated by hand Window pillar Length: 760 40 Thickness: 1.2 Supporting point

No.	Action of the left hand	Symbols		Actions of the right hand
		Left hand	Right hand	
1	A component is placed in a metal mould	◯	◯	A component is placed in a metal mould
2	Holding the component	◯	⇨	The hand is streched to the lever
3	Holding the component	◯	◯	Lever is opearated
4	The component is taken out of the metal mould	◯	⇨	The hand is put back to the component
5	The component is held for finding distortion	◯	◯	The hand holds the component to detect distortion
6	Holding the component	◯	⇨	The hand takes up the inspection board
7	Holding the component	◯	◯	The inspection board is used to detect distortion
8	Holding the component	◯	⇨	The inspection board is put down
9	The component is placed on the floor	⇨	D	Idle waiting of the hand
10	The return of the hand to its original position	⇨	⇨	The hand is streched to the next component part
11	Idle waiting of the hand	D	⇨	The component is brought to to the press

	Remarks				
Method	Present		Revised		
	Left hand	Right hand	Left hand	Right hand	
Operations	8	3	3	3	
Inspection		1	1	1	
Transport	2	6	2	2	
Delay	1	1			
Total	11	11	6	6	

[CHART 63A]

(14B) Two-Handed Process Chart (Improved Method)

Chart 2 Sheet /	Workshop
Drawings and component parts: Window Pillar of a Bus	Component parts Unit: m/m Pedal-type operation
Work: Collection Pressing on a Press	
Workshop: Second Press Section Friction Press No. 3	
Workers:	
Prepared by: Takahashi Orihara Date: November 12, 1982	

No.	Actions of the left hand	Symbols		Actions of the right hand
		Left hand	Right hand	
1	Placing a component part in a metal mould	○	○	Placing a component in a metal mould
2	Holding the component part (pedal operation)	○	○	Holding the component
3	Inspecting distortion while taking out the component part	○	○	Inspecting the component to detect distortion while taking it out from the mould
4	Setting the component against the inspection board	○	○	Setting the component against the inspection board
5	Placing the component on the floor	⇒	⇒	Extending the hand to the next component (the right hand does not have to wait for the left hand)
6	The hand is returned to its original position	⇒	⇒	Bringing the component to the front of the press

Method	Remarks			
	Present		Revised	
	Left hand	Right hand	Left hand	Right hand
Operations	8	3	3	3
Inspection		1	1	1
Transport	2	6	2	2
Delay	1	1		
Total	11	11	6	6

[CHART 63B]

15. THE THERBLIG SYMBOLS

Purpose

There is a big difference between the motions of skilled workers and those of beginners. The difference is presumed to be the result of their respective achievement, but a closer observation of the details of their motion would reveal that the motions of the latter show a mixture of many wasteful elements as compared with the motion of the former.

Mr. and Mrs. Gilbreth (F. B. & L. M. Gilbreth) classified those fundamental actions which are considered to be common to all kinds of work into 17 categories as an auxiliary means to improve motions and gave the name 'Therblig' (Gilbreth spelt in reverse order) to the classification. This Therblig classification concerns physical activities used for the performance of work and as such is based on the principal objectives of motions. Most of the elements of the Therblig classification represent momentary actions taking less than a second. Therefore, it will be difficult to analyze motions, not to speak of measuring the required time, by an ordinary method of measurement. Consequently, a method of measurement with the aid of film is sometimes adopted. But because of the expense and techniques involved, naked-eye analysis is not infrequent.

The symbols used for the Therblig classification are as shown in the following chart.

How to learn the symbols

In order to prepare a *Therblig chart*, the first thing you have to do is to acquire a perfect mastery of the 17 symbols given in the chart.

The *Therblig symbols* are relatively easy to master as their forms are designed to reflect the formal characteristics of what they stand for. Here, it is required that you memorize all 17 symbols. It is helpful to both read and write the symbols repeatedly. Additional reinforcement can be gained by practicing the motions these symbols represent. Do the right hand and the left hand, separately, on the basis of a careful observation of the motions of other people.

Relations

All tasks, all operations and all jobs consist of the Therblig elements. In other words, the Therblig elements are the minimal analyzable units and the 17 types of Therblig elements are combined in various ways to make up various types of operations. The different operations thus composed will fall into such categories as action elements, work units, unitary operations, and work processes on the basis of their respective sizes. These relations are shown in the chart given on the following page.

(Work Area Analysis)

Title: Work
Area analysis

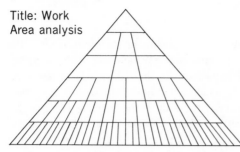

← Work process

← Unitary operations

← Work units

← Work elements

← Motion

← Therblig elements

(15) The Therblig Symbols

No.	Description	Letter of symbols	Therblig symbols		Example Take a pencil from the desk and write letters
			Symbols	Description	
1	Search	SH	👁	A form of an eye looking for something	Look around for a pencil
2	Select	ST	→	A form pointing to the thing selected	Select an adequate pencil out of several
3	Reach	R	◡	A form of an empty dish	Put out the hand (to the place where the pencil is placed).
4	Grasp	G	∩	A form of a grasping action (Magnet)	Grasp the pencil
5	Move	M	◡○	A form of a dish with something placed in it	Take the pencil and bring it to the place where it is used
6	Position	P	9	A form of a hand holding something	Position the pencil in a position ready for writing
7	Assemble	A	⌗	A form of combination	Put a cap on the tail of the pencil
8	Use	U	∪	A form of a glass in up-right position	Write letters (use the pencil)
9	Disassemble	DA	╫	A form showing one line detached from the form representing combination	Take off the cap from the tail of the pencil
10	Release Load	RL	◠○	A form of a dish held up-side down	Put down the pencil
11	Inspect	I	◇	A form of a lens	Examine how well the letters are written
12	Pre-position	PP	₰	A form of a bowling pin in its upright position	Change the direction of the pencil for easier writing
13	Hold	H	⌂	A form of a magnet attracting something	Keep holding the pencil
14	Unavoidable delay	UD	⌐○	A form of a man falling down	It became impossible to continue writing letters because of power failure: idle waiting
15	Rest	RE	⚲	A form of a man sitting on a chair	Take a rest as the person is tired
16	Avoidable delay	AD	─○	A form of a man lying down	Do not write letters, looking away
17	Plan	PN	⚲	A form of a man thinking with a hand on the head	Think what words to write

[CHART 64A]

211

16.   THE THERBLIG CHART

How to prepare the chart

Prepare a Therblig analysis form as shown in the chart. Then, after having observed motions to be analysed over several cycles, start analyzing the motions of the more active hand (usually the right hand). It that case, no attention is paid to the other hand. After having analyzed the motions of the one hand completely, proceed to analyze the motions of the other hand. Above all, direct your attention to the points in which the two hands act in concert with each other. Thereafter, analyze the remaining motions of the hand one after another. When the analysis is completed, again go through the entire course of the operations to make sure that there is no mistake in the Therblig symbols in the chart or any time lag in the timing of the operations.

How to read the chart

As we consider the motions represented by the Therblig symbols, it is observed that these motions fall into three distinct groups: The first group includes the Therblig elements that are useful to the performance of work; the second group consists of those elements that have a tendency to obstruct the completion of work; the third group comprises those elements which do not perform any work. The following chart represents this classification.

Motions	Main points for analysis	Therblig		
		Group I	Group 2	Group 3
1 Put out the hand	Distance, direction	⌣		
2 Grasp	How the object is placed, shape, and size	⌢		
3 Carry	Distance, weight, destination	⌣ひ	⊙→	⌂
4 Assemble	Shape and size	9 ♯	⧖	⌣ᴑ
5 Use	Cutting conditions, processing methods	∪	( )	⌐ᴑ
6 Disassemble	Resistance, direction	++	⧍	ᴑ⌐
3 Carry	Distance, weight and destination	⌣ᴑ		
7 Release	How the object is placed, shape and how it is held	⌒\		
1 Put back the hand	Distance and direction	⌣		

The work elements which belong to the first group may be considered to comprise those which are useful, i.e. necessary to the completion of work. However, as the ideal situation is one where no work is required at all, it will be necessary to pay attention to these elements, too. Those elements which belong to the second group are psychological elements or those whose presence tends to interfere with the completion of work. In many cases, the presence of these elements tends to delay the time required for the performance of the basic elements which belong to the first group.

The elements which belong to the third group may be considered to be those which do not perform any work. Consequently, it would be most effective to eliminate the elements which belong to this third group at the time when an improvement of work is attempted. In many instances, holding and unavoidable delays — which are two major elements of the third group — may be eliminated by preparing a mechanical holding device, rearranging the work places, or changing the arrangement in the sequence of motions.

The first step in the improvement of the working procedure is to eliminate as many of the elements as possible which belong to the second and the third groups. The final step is to combine and rearrange the elements belonging to the first group in a way which will ensure the completion of the work in the shortest period of time.

(16)　The Therblig Chart

| Motion Study Analysis Form (A) | No. / |

Outline work arrangement charts		
Ashtray　□ Match box ◎		
A cigarette pack in the pocket on the left breast ——→ Smoker		

Name of the work process of work	Smoking work (?)
Work number	Chart number	Sheet number	Number of units
Unit　20 cigarettes	Name	Hi-lite
Date of survey March 7, 1972	Survey	Arrangement	Analysis
	Higashi-mura	Nishimura	Minami-mura

Points to be noted for improvement	Left hand			Right hand			Points to be noted for improvement
	Work elements	Description	Therblig	Therblig	Description	Work elements	
	Rest (1)	As it is			To the left breast	Taking out a cigarette pack from a pocket on the left side of the breast (1)	
		//			The cigarette pack		
		//			Out of the pocket		
	Holding the cigarette pack (2)	Draw closer at hand			Closer at hand		
		Cigarette pack			Passing on to the left hand		
		Cigarette pack			One cigarette	Taking out a cigarette from the pack and holding it in the mouth (2)	
		Cigarette pack			One cigarette		
		Cigarette pack			Out of the cigarette pack		
		Cigarette pack			To the mouth		
		Cigarette pack			Hold in the mouth		
		Cigarette pack			To the cigarette pack	Putting the cigarette pack in the pocket (3)	
		Cigarette pack			The cigarette pack		
	Open the pocket on the left-side breast (3)	To the left breast			To the left breast		
		The lip of the pocket			To the left breast		
		The lip of the pocket			To the pocket		
		The lip of the pocket			The cigarette pack		
	Holding the match while lighting a cigarette and closing the match box (4)	Closer at hand			To the match box	Taking the match box, taking out a match stick and making fire (4)	
		Closer at hand			The match box		
		The match box			Closer at hand		
		The match box			Push the bottom of the pack		
		The match box			Out of the match box		
		The match box			To the match box		
		The match box			One match stick		
		The match box			One match stick		
		The match box			One match stick		
		The match box			In order to light the match		
	Holding the match and passing it to the right hand (5)	The match box			Light		
		Until passed on to the right hand			Till the combustible substance is burnt out	Lighting the cigarette and putting out the fire on the match stick (5)	
		Until passed on to the right hand			To the tip of the cigarette		
		Until passed on to the right hand			Till the cigarette is lighted		
		//			The match stick		
		//			In order to put out the fire		
		//			The match stick		
		//			To the match box	Passing the match box on to the right hand and placing on the table (6)	
		//			The match box		
	Resting the left hand (6)	To the left side			The match box		
		As it is			The match box		
		//			To the cigarette held in the mouth	Taking the cigarette by hand (7)	
		//			The cigarette		
		//			The cigarette		
		//			The cigarette		

[CHART 64B]

17. THE TIME STUDY SHEET

Purpose

The techniques of setting up a standard time include the PTS method, the WF method, and other various methods. The most fundamental of these methods is the *time study sheet*. This method is conducted by direct time observation with a stop watch, with the measurement being repeated and recorded several times. A shorter work cycle calls for more frequent measurements. The results are added up and then divided for an average. To this, rating (rating of pace) and an allowance time will be added to set up a standard time.

As for allowance time, an explanation was already given in the introductory remarks to the I.E. area. The form intended for recording the basic time data is the *time study sheet* illustrated here.

How to prepare the form

The time observation method includes the snap-back timing method with a flyback stopwatch, and the cumulative method with a non-flyback stopwatch. Here, the latter method will be shown first. In the left hand column of the illustration, the cycle is divided into several work elements. Under ordinary circumstances, an object of measurement should comprise at least 4 − 5 DM.

First, stand at a place to the right in front of the worker and hold a stop watch so that the hands of the worker and the stop watch fall in the same field of vision. Then, start time observation. Read off the time at the end of each work element and record the time in the measurement form. At a stage when the time measurement is completed over 10 cycles (10 cycles of time observation), the time required for each work element is calculated. This is achieved by subtracting the time 'reading' for a given work element from the time 'reading' for the immediately preceding work element.

When the individual time requirement of each work element at each cycle is worked out, add up the figures horizontally to arrive at the total time for each work element. Divide the value of the total time by the number of the observations (10) to obtain the average time. However, since this value is nothing but the average time of each work element and its cycles as a whole for the workers have been subjected to the time measurement, this value should be adjusted, multiplied by a rating coefficient in order to determine the base time requirement which serves as a basis for a standard time.

Rating is, essentially, a rating of the pace (speed) of work performance. For this purpose, the data obtained by the measurement should be converted into a normal pace. For this rating, 100 will be taken as the mean value and if a given work element is performed faster than the mean, it will be rated above 100, while a work element whose performance is slower than the

215

mean will be rated below 100. One hundredth of the rating thus obtained will be the rating coefficient. (The chart represents a long-cycle work to which Dr. Mandel's an objective rating method was applied with the observation conducted three times.)

(17) Time Study Sheet

The Time Study Sheet												
Name of Work		Copper Nozzle Molding (No. 1)						Serial No.				

Drawing Number		44028-53											
Product Designation		Copper nozzle (manual setting)											
Machine, Device													
Workshop, Worker		First Foundry: Yanagida Ikeda, Kimura, Tokimoto											
Analyzed by: Date:		Komatsu January 23, 1969											

	Work element		1	2	3	Total time	Average time	First rating	Second rating	Base time	Fatigue allowance	Modified time
1	Placing the pattern (lower pattern)	Reading	141	163	119	423	141	0.9	0.1	140		
		Time	141	163	119							
2	Placing a metal frame	Reading	270	303	237	387	129	0.9	0.1	128		
		Time	129	140	118							
3	Sanding	Reading	1,027	1,074	980	2,271	757	1.0	0.08	818		
		Time	757	771	743							
4	Jolting	Reading	1,593	1,618	1,564	1,698	566	1.0	0.08	613		
		Time	566	545	587							
5	Reversed by a reverser (converter)	Reading	2,212	2,219	2,202	1,857	619	0.9	0.15	640		
		Time	619	600	638							
6	Passing CO_2	Reading	2,542	2,527	2,554	990	330	1.0	0.08	356		
		Time	330	308	352							
7	Placing a pattern (upper pattern)	Reading	2,681	2,662	2,697	417	139	0.9	0.1	138		
		Time	139	135	143							
8	Placing a metal frame	Reading	2,844	2,832	2,853	489	163	0.9	0.1	162		
		Time	163	170	156							
9	Sanding	Reading	2,981	2,951	3,008	411	137	1.0	0.1	151		
		Time	137	119	155							
10	Stamp	Reading	3,159	3,124	3,191	534	178	0.9	0.2	193		
		Time	178	173	183							
11	Passing CO_2 to the reverser (converter)	Reading	3,439	3,392	3,483	870	280	0.9	0.1	277		
		Time	280	268	292							
12	Stamping	Reading	4,169	4,112	4,223	2,190	730	0.6	0.15	503		
		Time	730	720	740							
13	Transfering to the mold finishing workshop	Reading	4,179	4,126	4,129	30	10	0.9	0.08	10		
		Time	10	14	6							
14	Finishing the upper and lower patterns	Reading	4,981	4,882	5,092	2,406	802	0.8	0.15	740	0.29	
		Time	802	751	853							
	Total		4,981	4,882	5,092	14,943	4,981			4,869	0.29	6,281

1. Base Time=Average Time×First Rating Coefficient×(1+Second Rating Coefficient)=4,869
2. Modified Time=Base Time×(1+Fatigue Allowance Rate)=6,281
3. Standard time=Modified Time+(Base Time×Allowance Delay Allowance Rate)
   Delay Allowance Rate: 12% Standard Time: 7,034 DM=1 hour 10 minutes 34 seconds DM

[CHART 65]

18. THE ILO SYSTEM REST ALLOWANCE PERCENTAGE TABLE

Purpose

If time has been calculated, the next step required is to measure the allowance time. Many different theories have been advanced as to the classification of allowance factors but the method commonly adopted is possibly the one based on the theory that allowance factors may be roughly classified into personal allowance, fatigue allowance and delay allowance. The delay allowance will be dealt with by a work sampling technique to be discussed later. At this point, the personal allowance and the fatigue allowance will be determined.

For this purpose, the *ILO system rest allowance percentage table,* as shown in the following illustration, will be of use. The gist of this procedure is to measure the fatigue brought about by the job performance of workers subjected to measurement during their work for each evaluation item listed.

Explanation

This constant allowance factor consists of physiological allowance as well as the allowance required for the recovery of the energy spent even during the time the work is not performed. These two kinds of allowance may be considered to comprise the above-mentioned personal allowance, though this will vary according to the nature of the workers involved. For instance, female workers could need a greater physiological allowance. On the other hand, variable allowance factors relate to the above-mentioned fatigue allowance and to the factors which vary depending on the types of work. The figures shown on the right side of the factor items indicate, separately for men and women, the rest allowance percentages for the normal time.

Relations

The following table is presented for the convenience of the reader in understanding various relations concerning the method.

Relation to the work	Name of allowance	Human/ Material	Contents of the allowance	Method of survey
No relation to the work	Personal allowance	Humanistic	Physiological allowance	ILO-system
Related to the work	Fatigue allowance		Fatigue allowance	
	Delay allowance	Materialistic	Workshop allowance Work allowance	Work sampling

While the ILO system has been introduced because it is comparatively easier to use as a method of rest allowance computation, it should be noted that there are also other methods such as the Dodge Company method, the BICC method, the Western Electric Company method, the Energy Metabolism method, the 3M (Minnesota Mining Manufacturing Co.) method and so forth.

As the calculation of a standard time requires a highly specialized knowledge in the field of Industrial Engineering, the reader is advised to consult other technical publications for dependable work measurement techniques.

Translator's note: The Japanese version of the above-mentioned table (shown on page 219), taken from "Introduction to Work Study" (ILO), was included by the author in his original book. The system was not an ILO one, however, but one recommended by the Personnel Administration, Ltd., London.

(18) ILO System Rest Allowance Percentage Table

1. **Constant Allowance:**

	Man	Woman
Personal allowance	5	7
Basic fatigue allowance	4	4

2. **Variable Allowance:**

A. **Standing allowance**   2   4

B. **Abnormal position allowance**

	Man	Woman
slightly awkward	0	1
awkward (bending)	2	3
Very awkward (lying, stretching up)	7	7

C. **Use of force or muscular energy (lifting, pulling or pushing)**

Weight lifted (in lb.)

	Man	Woman
5	0	1
10	1	2
15	2	3
20	3	4
25	4	6
30	5	8
35	7	10
40	9	13
45	11	16
50	13	20
		(max.)
60	17	
70	22	

D. **Bad light**

	Man	Woman
Slight below recommended value	0	0
Well below	2	2
Quite inadequate	8	8

E. **Atmospheric Conditions (heat and humidity)**

Cooling Power (Kata) Allowance (in millcalories/cm^2/sec.)

16	0
14	0
12	0
10	3
8	10
6	21
5	31
4	45
3	64
2	100

F. **Notes Level**

	Man	Woman
Fairly fine work	0	0
Fine or exacting	2	2
Very fine or very exacting	5	5

G. **Close Attention**

	Man	Woman
Continuous	0	0
Intermittant, loud	2	2
Intermittant, very loud, high-pitched, loud	5	5

H. **Mental Strain**

	Man	Woman
Fairly complex process	1	1
Complex or wide span of attention	4	4
Very complex	8	8

I. **Monotony**

	Man	Woman
Low	0	0
Medium	1	1
High	4	4

J. **Tediousness**

	Man	Woman
Rather tedious	0	0
Tedious	2	1
Very tedious	5	2

[CHART 66]

19. WORK SAMPLING SCHEDULE

Purpose

In planning work sampling, it is essential to prepare a fixed form, listing all the integral items of the plan beforehand in order to avoid confusion in conducting the work sampling.

The items to be included in such a form will be:

(1)   The classification and definition of the items to be measured: Designing a work sampling observation sheet.

(2)   The accuracy and dependability to be expected of the results
* The value when the reliability limit is set at 95%
* The accuracy desired . . . . S
* The ratio sought (The occurrence ratio in percentage) . . P
* The random observation frequency in that case . . . . . . N
(The size of the samples calculated according to the work sampling formula)

(3)   Schedule for carrying out the observation
* The number of the machines to be observed
* The daily frequency of the observation tour
* The number of persons available for conducting the observation
* The number of days to be spent for the measurement in conformity with the conditions represented by N calculated by the formula.

(4)   Fixing the route as well as the starting point for the observation trip.

Relations

The route of the observation trip is mentioned above as requiring a prior description and is explained in the *work sampling observation route map*. The starting time point for the observation trip is determined by using a table of random numbers. Taking random numbers of three digits, we convert the first figure into hours (for instance, 8 o'clock if we get 1; 9 o'clock if we get 2) and the second and the third figures into minutes (all the two figures are to be multiplied by 0.6), and we obtain a random timetable.

How to use

This work sampling sheet is prepared primarily for the purpose of scheduling, but secondarily, it may also be used for the orientation of staff engaged in work sampling. Above all, it is of importance to agree on a uniform definition of the items selected for the measurement, with clear delineation so as to allow no ambiguity in their interpretation before commencing the work sampling.

(19) Work Sampling Observation Sheet

1. The definitions of the items to be observed

Work Sampling Observation Sheet

Object: Workers

No.

Name of workshop:

Measured by:

Measurement Time:

Measurement Hour:

Disapproved delay (Nonworking)		Absence					
		Pausing					
		Idle talk					
		Walking					
	Personal allowance	Drinking water and wiping perspiration					
		Washing hands					
Approved delay	workshop delay	Waiting					
		Cleaning					
		Writing chits					
		Communication (Contact)					
		Drawing/examination					
		Previous arrangement					
	Operational delay	Inspection					
		Oiling					
		Removing chip					
		Minor repairs					
		Tool grinding					
		Tool adjustment					
		Product handling					
	Preparation for work	Material supply					
		Machine adjustment					
		Preparation (Arrangement)					
Net operation		Supervising					
		Net processing					
Observation frequency							

Workers or machines subjected to observation

Machine number: 1, 2, 3, 4, 5 ... 21

Total

Percentage

Remarks

[CHART 67]

2. The accuracy and reliability expectations

$$N = \frac{4P\,(100 - P)}{L^2}$$ is usually applied to the calculation of the observation frequency in work sampling. However, in order to further broaden the range of its application, the following formula is recommended.

$\sigma t = SP$ The standard deviation σ in working sampling is considered to be:

$$\sigma = \sqrt{\frac{P\,(1 - P)}{N}} \quad \cdots\cdots\cdots\cdots\cdots\cdots\cdots\cdots\cdots\cdots \quad (1)$$

Then

$$SP = {}^{t}\sqrt{\frac{P\,(1 - P)}{N}} \quad \cdots\cdots\cdots\cdots\cdots\cdots\cdots \quad (2)$$

In this case,
S: the desired accuracy (relative deviation)
P: the ratio to be sought
N: the random observation frequency (the size of the samples)
t: the value of t proportionate to reliability

For the present purpose, the probability of normal distribution will be used as it is to obtain t as reliability, and to calculate on the basis of the formulae mentioned above.

If we assume $S = \pm 3\%$, $P = 40\%$, and $t = 2$, the frequency of observation may be found by the following:

$$\text{Frequency of observation } N = \frac{4 \times 40\,(100 - 40)}{3^2} = 1{,}067 \cdots\cdots\cdots \text{ The required frequency of observation}$$

3. The measurement schedule

1. The number of the machines or workers to be observed: 25
2. The frequency of measurement trips per day: 28 times
3. The number of the staff members to be mobilized for the work sampling: 4
4. The number of days spent for the observations: 1 day
5. $N = (1) \times (2) \times (3) \times (4)$

$N = 25$ workers $\times 28$ times $\times 4$ persons $\times 1$ day $= 2{,}800$ times. Since 2,800 times of observation well exceeds the required number of measurement, 1,067 times, it may be considered that observation schedule is adequate.

[CHART 67 – continued]

20. THE WORK SAMPLING OBSERVATION ROUTE MAP

Purpose

When the measurement frequency which satisfies the desirable accuracy and confidence limits under a given occurrence ratio percentage is determined, the next step is to prepare the random timetable and the observation map. Unless the observation is carried out under a certain fixed agreement, errors could occur in the results of the measurement carried out by several persons.

For this reason it is necessary in work sampling to prepare a factory floor plan as shown in the illustration and to include in the floor plan a fixed route for the observation trip so that all the members engaged in the measurement will follow the exact same route. The *work sampling observation route map* is designed to meet this requirement.

How to prepare to map

First, it is important to decide clearly which of the two factors, 'the workers' or 'the machines', will be subjected to measurement. When the workers are to be measured, the usual fixed positions of these people should be clearly indicated on the floor plan and their names should be given to all the members of the measurement staff. And, in the case of machinery, the machines should be numbered along the observation route and their numbers should be clearly marked on the floor plan. By this means, all the measurement staff will be able to recognize the objects of observation with certainty and without confusion and mark scores in the appropriate columns in the *work sampling tabulation sheet.*

Relations

The *work sampling observation route map* is one of the instruments used for work sampling, together with the *observation sheet* and the *random timetable.* However theoretical the observation plan may be in conformity with the formula, it would be impossible to expect achieving the desirable results unless the plan is carried out consistently and efficiently at the stage of its actual employment.

How to use the map

A work sampling project, in which several or more than a dozen measurement staff members conduct sampling observations for many hours, tends to be a large-scale project. In order to have the observation staff members take uniform actions and obtain accurate data, it is advisable to give the staff a thorough orientation prior to the start of the observation.

Besides, when machine trouble or any other accident takes place during the observation, it will be helpful if the leader indicates the event on the floor plan, together with the time when the accident occurs.

This step should be taken to prevent each observer from asking the same questions in an attempt to establish the cause of the trouble.

(20) Work Sampling Observation Route Map
(Machine Workshop)

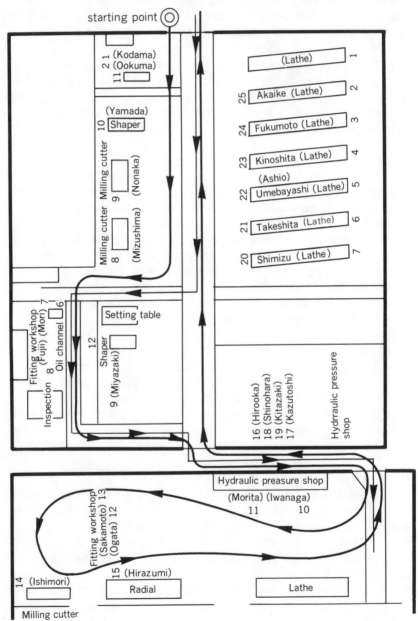

[CHART 68]

21. THE WORK SAMPLING TABULATION SHEET

Purpose

This is a tabulation of the *work sampling observation sheet*. It enumerates the operation rate of a machine or a worker, and may be used for computing data for the individual machine or worker at the stage of assembling the data. Although this is merely a representation of the score counts in terms of Arabic numerals, it will enable us to grasp the operating and nonoperating conditions of each machine or each worker over the period of observation for each work element.

How to prepare the tabulation

This tabulation gives us a number of interesting hints for daily factory administration. In designing a *work sampling tabulation sheet,* the most important elements are a theoretical classification applicable to the factors of measurement, and an accurate definition of the measurement factors without ambiguity. These conditions being satisfied, an observation can be performed by a group of observers with a uniform interpretation.

Here, the work performance will be roughly divided into net operation and 'delay'. 'Delay' is further divided into 'allowable delay' and 'unallowable delay.'

The classification could be divided still further, but the observers should master 'the allowance theory' thoroughly and accurately before they proceed to conduct observation. This being accomplished, they should repeat actual momentary observation, relying on the *random timetable* and the *work sampling observation route map,* and assign the conditions observed at the time of the momentary observation as applied to each work in the appropriate column. Upon the completion of the observation, all the scores will be converted to figures which will be added together vertically to obtain a total, and the calculations will be completed by deriving the percentage for each group.

Relations

The technique of work sampling is used for various purposes. Here, it is used for calculating the delay allowance rate which is a significant factor in setting up a standard time.

How to read and use the tabulation

As mentioned above, the results of this tabulation will be used here for the calculation of the delay allowance rate, though the same data may be used as material for individual guidance of workers as they contain information on the performance of each worker. Using the cited chart as an example, the delay allowance rate is found to be 19.3 per cent by the interpolation method, and this will be added to the base time together with the fatigue allowance to arrive at a standard time.

(21) Work Sampling Tabulation Sheet

Name of the Workshop: Machine Section Observation Hour: 8 hours Observation Date: December 20, 1971 Observation Time: From 08:00 To 17:00 Measured by: A Group

Machine No.	Workers subjected to observation	Observation frequency	Net Operation — Net processing	Net Operation — Supervising	Preparation Work — Preparatory arrangement	Preparation Work — Machine adjustment	Preparation Work — Material supply	Operation allowance — Product handling	Operation allowance — Tool adjustment	Operation allowance — Tool grinding	Operation allowance — Minor repair	Operation allowance — Removing chip	Operation allowance — Oiling	Approvable delay — Inspection	Workshop allowance — Previous arrangement	Workshop allowance — Drawing examination	Workshop allowance — Communication	Workshop allowance — Writing in chits	Workshop allowance — Cleaning	Workshop allowance — Waiting	Personnel allowance — Washing hands	Personnel allowance — Drinking water and wiping perspiration	Unapproved delay — Walking about	Unapproved delay — Idle talk	Unapproved delay — Pausing	Unapproved delay — Absence
1	Adams (Plano-miller)	224	14	(16)	41	7	12	1	4	5	0	7	0	0	0	0	0	0	0	0	4	0	0	1	0	1
2	Brown (Plano-miller)	224	66	17	32	(34)	12	1	6	21	0	3	0	0	11	0	1	1	21	0	0	5	1	1	0	5
3	Clard (Planner)	225	121	11	20	22	5	4	5	2	2	0	1	5	2	3	3	0	1	5	3	0	1	1	4	0
4	Davis (Radial)	224	(83)	0	49	7	17	0	(18)	1	0	4	1	2	5	3	0	0	3	8	2	1	1	2	8	2
5	Eagle (Lathe)	223	31	(134)	17	7	3	2	7	1	0	4	0	3	0	0	0	0	3	7	3	0	0	1	0	3
6	French (Shaper)	224	36	29	(82)	11	7	2	8	2	0	3	1	38	6	0	0	2	2	2	3	0	0	1	3	3
7	Gomez (Boring)	225	17	(33)	19	15	3	1	8	1	1	1	0	18	0	0	0	2	0	0	1	0	7	2	0	1
8	Harley (Shaper)	225	90	2	31	10	1	2	11	4	0	1	0	(34)	16	0	0	0	0	1	1	0	0	2	3	1
9	Irving (Hand Finish)	224	166	0	11	1	2	2	4	4	3	1	0	3	24	0	3	0	1	1	2	0	6	7	4	0
10	Jones (Hand Finish)	227	134	0	11	1	10	1	1	4	1	1	1	4	10	1	0	0	1	0	4	1	3	2	6	0
11	Kaz (Hand Finish)	222	153	0	4	0	13	2	10	2	0	2	0	(26)	3	1	0	3	2	6	1	6	3	5	10	1
12	Long (Hand Finish)	221	176	0	11	1	(39)	5	10	0	0	0	0	1	1	1	0	2	1	2	1	0	2	0	3	0
13	Mendoza (Hand Finish)	223	126	0	5	2	10	5	8	0	0	0	0	0	3	0	0	3	5	2	0	1	4	0	2	1
14	Nelson (Hand Finish)	225	150	0	5	2	10	5	5	0	0	0	0	0	4	10	0	2	8	14	8	0	12	0	9	1
15	Ohara (Inspection)	224	148	4	4	0	8	7	3	0	0	0	0	0	5	0	0	3	2	5	8	0	4	0	2	2
16	Peters (Inspection)	225	124	15	5	0	12	5	15	1	0	0	0	10	4	0	0	2	5	5	0	0	2	1	9	8
17	Quin (Hand Finish)	225	72	0	11	1	9	5	5	1	0	0	0	0	5	0	0	2	0	(23)	7	1	5	8	2	8
18	Retton (Welding)	224	72	15	(17)	5	20	4	1	0	3	0	0	3	0	0	2	5	0	0	3	1	7	8	8	3
19	Scott (Milling Cutter)	225	52	15	(45)	25	8	1	(16)	5	1	0	1	23	3	2	4	1	4	0	7	3	0	2	2	2
20	Towns (Lathe)	222	82	38	(63)	20	2	1	9	2	0	0	2	11	4	4	0	1	1	0	3	0	0	0	0	2
21	Uleman (Lathe)	222	36	28	34	(30)	3	3	5	8	0	0	0	45	4	1	1	3	4	4	2	0	0	0	1	0
22	Voughn (Lathe)	226	23	28	(66)	14	7	3	9	9	0	0	0	11	4	1	1	3	2	9	2	0	0	0	0	1
23	White (Lathe)	126	23	43	16	8	7	0	2	1	0	2	0	10	2	0	2	6	1	1	1	0	6	0	0	0
24	Xavier (Lathe)	224	66	45	26	14	7	3	6	4	0	6	1	14	1	6	0	0	6	3	10	0	6	2	2	0
25	Young (Lathe)	224	29	(109)	(82)	4	1	0	2	2	0	1	0	11	1	5	0	0	0	2	3	0	1	1	1	0
(1)	Total	5,503	2,247	759	680	241	217	60	177	82	5	40	13	258	124	38	20	41	97	102	62	10	69	32	97	39
(2)	Medium classification total		3,008		1,128			646						258	112						72		237			
(3)	Percentage		64.5%		20.5%			11.8%						19.3%	7.5%						1.3%		4.4%			
(4)	Major classification percentage		78%																	5.7%						

[CHART 69]

226

22. THE STANDARD TIME CARD

Purpose

It is a tremendous task to develop standard times for each and every operation process performed in the factory. Apart from the case of a factory operating on a few-item mass production basis, it is an onerous task to contemplate for a factory engaged in job-shop type production. With a view to standardizing this work, the predetermined time standard method and the standard data method have been developed in the field of work measurement in addition to the direct time study method conducted with a stopwatch.

Here, the results of time measurement with a stopwatch will be included in the previously designed card and a method of storing the cards under a well-regulated classification system should be developed. The *standard time card* has been devised so that the data once written on the cards and completed may be quickly referred to at any moment.

How to prepare the card

It is convenient to make use of this card as illustrated. The standard time for the work processes observed and measured with the *time study sheet* at hand can be transferred to this card. However, it should be pointed out that each line allocated to work on this card does not necessarily correspond to a work element recorded on the *time study sheet*. Each of the operations, which may combine several work elements, will fill the line. For instance, as is shown in the following illustration, it is the *time observation sheet* that covers operation and work elements which constitute operation, while it is the *standard time card* that covers operation which, in turn, constitutes job or process.

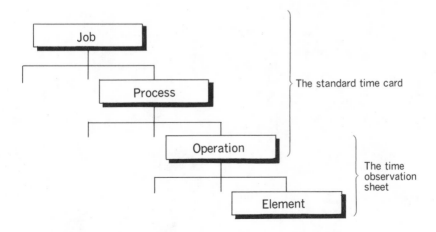

Relations

The *standard time card* may also be used for guidance (with a vinyl cover to keep it free from dirt and soil), for it shows all requisite items such as the processing procedure, the jig and tools to be used, the standard time for setting and preparation, the standard time per unit, etc.

How to use the card

As mentioned earlier, the standard time is useful for a number of purposes including (1) information for production planning, (2) basic data for estimating the unit price for sale, (3) a basis for calculating standard cost and (4) provide information for an incentive wage system. To facilitate the utilization of the standard time for a wide range of purposes, it is desirable to arrange the data by means of a card system to ensure quick reference to them. As one job is composed of a certain number of operations, it is possible to figure out the standard time for the job as a whole by a synthesis of the time achieved by taking out a required number of the *standard time cards* and combining them.

(22) Standard Time Card

Sketch			Drawing No. F-635e	Name: Groove cutting		

Remarks: S.E.

Material quality	Material size		Weight of the parts for one unit
	90.5φ ×40		4.35kg

Component number:	Component name:
TP-7635	Adjustment piece

Process name:	Product name:
Groove cutting with a milling cutter	Distance spacer for sliding unit

Number of pieces required for one unit: 4

Num-ber	Working method		Pro-cess name	Jig	Tool	Ma-chine used	Standard time		
	Processing	Working operation					Pre-para-tion	Main body	Total
1	Taking a component part from the table							min. 0.04	min. 0.04
2	Placing the compo-nent part in the vice							0.10	0.10
3								0.18	0.18
4		Starting the machine				Plain mill m/c No.16		0.02	0.02
5		Moving the table forward						0.13	0.13
6								0.03	0.03
7		Groove cutting						3.05	3.05
8		Stopping the machine						0.04	0.04
9	Putting back the table							0.23	0.23
10	Loosening the vice							0.21	0.21
11	Putting the compo-nent on the finished component table							0.08	0.08
12	Brushing off the vice with a brush					Brush		0.57	0.57
								4.68	4.68

Remarks: Tolerance of groove size ±0.01mm	Inspected by:	Total time:		4.68	4.68

Composition or assembly classification (category)	Work process or type classification:	Material arrangement division :	Completion & storage division:
III-136-22	F.H105	F.H.10544	3×5P

[CHART 70]

23. THE LINE BALANCE CHART

Purpose

The key factor in measuring and improving the efficiency or productivity of an assembly line, more important than the designing of the jig and tools, the improvement of working methods and the practising of motion economy, is whether or not a line balance is maintained throughout the entire course of the assembly line operation. The reason is that the output per unit hour will not increase at all, no matter how drastic an improvement may be made and how much reduction of time may be achieved in individual work processes, unless a time reduction is achieved through an improvement on the line balance. A failure to improve the line balance will merely result in a failure to derive advantage from waiting time. It follows, therefore, that it is absolutely necessary to prepare a *line balance chart* if it is desired to correct any imbalance in the line, to cut down the waiting time and to improve the rate of operation.

How to prepare the chart

First, prepare a section graph and mark a time scale along the horizontal axis and a scale of work processes in the flow of the assembly line on the horizontal lines. Fill in the name of the work process and the name of the machine or the worker, in the flow order of the work processes. Calculate the time cycle for each work process by time measurement. Although it is desirable to work out a standard time by applying an appropriate rating coefficient and by adding a marginal time, the base time alone will serve the purpose. Plot the time value thus obtained on the graph. If possible, note the particulars of the work elements, as shown in the illustration. Draw a straight horizontal line, parallel to the vertical axis starting from the work process which shows the highest time value. Then, the area represented by hatching corresponds to the nonoperational time through the entire work process, and the rate of operation may be calculated by the following formula:

[(The total of the cycle time for each work process) ÷ (the highest time value for all the work processes) × (the number of the work processes.)]

Relations

Although the preparation of a *line balance chart* will have an outstanding effect when attempting macroscopic and comprehensive improvement on an assembly line, it will be a prerequisite to this kind of study to conduct accurate time measurements. The reliability of a *line balance chart* will be low and its effect will consequently be slight, however diligently time measurements may be conducted, unless the rating of the working speed of the workers is correct.

How to read and use the chart

When the chart indicates that there is considerable nonoperating time, we should consider how we may reduce the area distinguished by hatching. To that end, focus efforts on an improved rearrangement or redistribution of each work process. In other words, try to make the time value of each work process as equal as possible to any other time value by shifting part of the work elements of a work process having a high time value to another work process having a lower time value. Such a step will progressively decrease the hatching area, consequently reducing the tact time (the time value found at a point where the vertical line crosses with the horizontal axis) by a large margin.

In the case of the chart shown as an example, the tact time after a rearrangement was reduced by 23 per cent while productivity increased by 30 per cent. At the same time, the number of workers was unchanged without sacrificing effectiveness in performance.

(23A) Line Balance Chart for An Assembly Line of Transistorized Radios (Before)

Scale: 0 10 20 30 40 50 60 70 80 90 100 110 120 130 140 150 160 170 180 190 200 210 220 230 240

#	Worker	Tasks (left to right)
1	Adams	Removing the mount — Inspection of mount surface — 80P replaced with 70P — Checking component fixing
2	Brown	Print surface inspection — Print surface solder correction
3	Clark	Building the rotary switch in the base — Soldering on the rotary switch — Soldering the lead wires, 5 pieces — Covering lead wire with a tube
4	Davis	Soldering 30P, 70P and 100P to rotary switch — Soldering three lead wires to the variable condenser — Soldering on the lead wire of the variable condenser — Threading nine lead wires through a hole in the base
5	Eagle	Wiring the lead wires on hand (red, white, yellow, green) — Wiring nine lead wires of the rotary switch — Arr. ld wrs.
6	French	Spare soldering on the base — Wiring the red, white, and pink lead wires — Putting the antenna lead wire in a tube — Wiring two lead wires of the variable condenser — Cutting 2P wiring to length
7	Gomez	Wiring the black lead wire — Wiring the yellow, white, pink and brown lead wires to the two terminals — Wiring red n ylw rotary wrs. 04 to tml. — Bond 3 places n arr ld wrs
8	Halley	Wiring pink, brn, lead wires — Arr. lead wires — Earthning lead wiring (long) — cut 04 wire — 3 earthning lead wiring (short) — Arr. lead wires
9	Irving	Conn. w/drum — Conn. speaker lead wires w/power source — Checking the working of five bands — Correction and data collection
10	Jones	Setting IF for AM — Adjusting IF for AM — Setting the band width of AM — Fixing the band width of AM and Marine bands — Taking off
11	Kaz	Putting in mold plane — Setting on the jig — Fixing IF for PB — Fixing IF for VHF — Tracking for VHF — Taking off
12	Lee	Setting — Fixing the band width of PB — Fixing the band width of VHF — Fixing the band width of FM — Taking off
13	Mendoza	Setting — Adjusting the tracking of FM — Tracking of PB — Taking off — Cutting the lead wires/test points Gum tape
14	Nelson	Fixing strut A, fastening with a screw vol 1 — Fix strut B. Fastening with a nut and arr ld wrs n hold w/nut put on a sub-pulley — Arr ld wrs n put on a tape — Inspecting the circuit
15	Ohara	Case inspection — Placing the indicator onto the drum — Fixing the indicator — Correction of the indicator position — Running test and correction — Fixing the lamps — Bonding the indicator — Graze up
16	Peters	Attaching a spring to the thread — Fixing a thread to the set — Bonding — Fixing the back plates
17	Quin	Polishing the case and the lens — Wiring two lead wires — Arr ld wrs n put on a tape — Fixing case B — Arr ld wrs n put in case — Insp lamps — Putting in the case again
18	Retton	Testing the wiring for two lamps — Putting on a tape (two pieces) — Wiring six lead wires for dial Indicator lamps — Insp Wiping the back lamps plate and bonding
19	Sields	Spare soldering 2 wires to sliding switch — Soldg. battery lead to neg terminals — Soldg 2 positive bat.lead terminals to vol.cont termls — Fix 3 struts by airscrew driver — Instg. a tube in 'rotary switch — Processing the strut into a tube (performed off the conveyer)
20	Tomson	Tightening the four screws on the base plate — Fixing the lamp base with screws — Arranging the resisters and condensers
21	Uleman	Fixing the volume control knob — Placing a label — Greasing — Fix switch & inspectg lamps
22	Vokt	Prev. adj to insert jack plugs — Adjusting the width of BC — Tracking of BC — Putting on paraffin — Checking — Tacking off the jack plug
23	White	Prev. adj. to insert jack plugs — Adjusting the width of marine band — Tracking marine band — Putting on paraffin — Cut test point
24	Xavier	Varnishing the high-frequency components, inserting jack plugs, and so forth — Adjusting the band width of FM — Tracking for FM — Removing the jack plugs
25	Young	Previous arrangement for inserting jack plugs, etc. — Adjusting the band width for VHF — Tracking VHF — Fixing the coil width sellbet — Remv jack plugs
26	Zaidi	Prev. adj to insert jack plugs — Setting the band width for the police band — Applying sellbet. for PB tracking — Disconn jk Plugs etc.
27	Asimov	Bonding the knobs placing the FCC label — Wiring the lead wires of the antenna — Arranging the lead wires — Bonding mold plane — Screwlock — Fix Knob
28	Bradley	Power on, rod antenna — Operation inspection — Ext. outfit insp
29	Cramer	Rotary switch inspection — Spare soldering — Soldering the 20P, 50P, and 80P two rotary switches — Spare soldering — Soldering three lead wires — Cut legs 30P,70P, 100P
30	Part-timer	Putting accessories in the gift box — Placing a set in a gift box and putting on the lid

[CHART 71A]

(23B) Line Balance Chart for the Assembly Line of Transistorized Radios (After)

Scale: 0 10 20 30 40 50 60 70 80 90 100 110 120 130 140 150 160 170 180 190

1 Adams — Removing the mount | Inspection of mount surface | 80P replaced with 70P | Checking comporment fixing

2 Brown — Print surface inspection | Print surface solder correction

3 Clark — Building the rotary switch in the base | Soldering on the rotary switch | Soldering the lead wires, 5 pieces | Covering lead wire with a tube

4 Davis — Soldering 30P, 70P and 100P to rotary switch | Soldering three lead wires to the variable condenser | Soldering on the lead wire of the variable condenser | Threading nine lead wires through a hole in the base

5 Eagle — Wiring nine lead wires of the rotary switch | Arranging the lead wires

6 French — Spare soldering on the base | Wiring the red white, and pink lead wires | Putting the antenna lead wire in a tube | Wiring two lead wires of the variable condenser | Cut and adj 2P wire

7 Gomez — Wiring the black lead wire | Wiring the yellow, white, pink and brown lead wires to the twn terminals | Wiring red n ylw rotary wrs. 04 to tml. | Bond 3 places n arr ld wrs | Arr. lead wires

8 Halley — Wiring pink, brn, lead wires | Arr. lead wires | Earthning lead wiring 04 (long) | cut wire | Wiring the three earthing lead wires (short) | Arr. ld wrs.

9 Irving — Connecting with the drum | Conn. speaker lead wires w/power source | Checking the working of the five bands | Correction and data collection

10 Jones — Setting | Adjusting IF for AM | Setting the band width of AM | Fixing the band width of AM and Marine bands | Taking off

11 Kaz — Putting in mold plane | Setting on the jig | Fixing IF for PB | Setting IF for VHF | Tracking for VHF | Wiring the lead wires' | Taking off

12 Lee — Setting | Fixing the band width of PB | Fixing the band width of VHF | Fixing the band breadth for FM | Taking off

13 Mendoza — Setting | Adjusting the tracking of FM | Tracking of PB | Taking off | Cutting the lead wires/test points Gum tape

14 Nelson — Fixing strut A, fastening with a screw vol 1 Fastening with a nut and screws with a sub-pulley | Fix strut B. arr ld wrs n put on n hold w/nut a tape | Inspecting the circuit

15 Ohara — Case inspec tion | Fixing the indicator | Correction of the indicator position | Running test and correction | Fixing the lamp | Bonding the indicator

16 Peters — Attaching a spring to the thread | Fixing a thread to the set | Bonding | Fixing the back plate | Graze up

17 Quin — Polishing the case and the lens | Arr ld wrs n put on a tape | Fixing case B | Arr ld wrs n put in case | Inspecting stains | Putting in the cases again

18 Retton — Testing the wiring for two lamps | Putting on a tape (two pieces) | Wiring six lead wires for dial Indicator lamps | Insp lamps | Wiping the back plate and bonding

19 Sields — Spare soldering 2 wires to sliding switch | Soldg. battery lead to neg. terminals | Soldg. 2 pusitive bat.lead terminals to vol. cont. termis. | Fix 3 struts by airscrew driver | Instg a tube in rotary switch | Processing the strut into a tube (performed off the conveyer)

20 Tomson — Tightening the four screws on the base plate | Fixing the lamp base with screws | Arranging the resisters and condensers

21 Uleman — Fixing the volume control knob | Placing a label | Greas ing | Fixing the switch knob and inspecting the lamps | Parts CR treatment lead wire inspection | Trimmer for PB

22 Vokt — Prev. adj to insert jack plugs | Adjusting the width of BC | Tracking of BC | Putting on paraffin | Check ing | Tacking off the jack plug

23 White — Prev. adj to insert jack plugs | Adjusting the band width of marine band | Tracking marine band | Putting on paraffin | Cut test point

24 Xavier — Varnishing the high-frequency components, inserting jack plugs. and so forth | Adjusting the band width of FM | Tracking for FM | Removing the jack plugs

25 Young — Previous arrangement for inserting jack plugs, etc | Adjusting the band width for VHF | Tracking VHF | Fixing the coil width sellbet | Remv jack plugs

26 Zaidi — Setting the band width for the police band | Applying sellbet. for PB tracking | Disconnection of jack plugs. etc.

27 Asimov — Bonding the knobs placing the FCC label | Wiring the lead wires of the antenna | Arranging the lead wires | Bonding mold plain | Screwlock | Fix Knob

28 Bradley — Power on, rod antenna | Operation inspection | Ext. outfit insp

29 Cramer — Rotary switch inspection | Spare soldering | Soldering the 20P, 50P, and 80P two rotary switches | Spare soldg. | Soldering the three lead wires | Cut legs 30P,70P, 100P

30 Part-timer — Putting accessories in the gift box | Placing a set in a gift box and putting on the lid

[CHART 71B]

233

Chapter 5
CHARTS ON PRODUCTION
CONTROL

WHAT IS PRODUCTION CONTROL

The scope of production control is, even now, not yet clearly defined. Some consider it to include production engineering, methods and standards, jigs and tools, quality control, etc., while others maintain these are not within the realm of production control.

In Japan, the latter has been popularly known as 'process control' for a long time. According to the ASME definiton of control terms, production control is the procedure for planning, programming, scheduling and promoting the flow of production from the materials stage (i.e., raw materials, parts, accessories and assembled parts) to the finished goods stage.

Production planning consists of:

(1) Producing goods effectively and economically and meeting targeted delivery dates by making a systematic schedule for men, materials and machines, using lead times, standard operations, delivery dates, output volume and other data.

(2) Order of operation and daily scheduling.

From this definition we can understand, in general, what is included. But, in reality, as the production control function is closely linked with each function of an enterprise, this definition alone does not express its complete meaning.

In American texts, the terms 'Production Planning and Control' or simply 'Production Control' are used, but in fact, every author looks at these terms quite differently, both in concept and content.

To gain a clearer understanding of what production control is, consider the straight forward fact that production control is the 'control' of 'production' activities; and if we look at control from its functional side, there is:

Plan ⎫

Organize ⎬ Planning

Direct Doing

Coordinate ⎫

Control ⎬ Checking

In short, to achieve the initial objectives of a plant that has already been constructed, we must plan, do and check the production activities of this plant.

The objective of a plant is to produce goods (or services) of the appropriate quality and quantity by the most economical method to meet predetermined dates of delivery.

When we attempt to effectively utilize the factors of production which are to be controlled, namely men, materials, money, machines, space, time and so on, production control will play the part of the nervous system of a human body.

These are, for instance:

(1) PLANNING AND ORGANIZATION OF PRODUCTION ACTIVITIES
  (a) Determine the types of goods to be produced and the order in which the work should be performed. (order of operation)
  (b) Appropriate the necessary time (day schedule), volume, position and priority for manufacturing component parts of a product.

(2) DIRECTIONS FOR PRODUCTION ACTIVITIES — To carry out a pre-arranged plan, provide instructions on the types of items which are to be produced and related details.

(3) PRODUCTION ADJUSTMENT
  (a) Clarify the scope, note the problems, and gather and provide the plant with data necessary for future production plans.
  (b) Check processing conditions in the plant, and by means of historic records and reports, assist and promote future control.

(4) CONTROL OF PRODUCTION ACTIVITIES
  (a) Continually study the situation and operating conditions of the work place, evaluate actual results and take quick action to close the gap between the desired and actual results.
  (b) Control production activities through to their successful achievement.

The diagrams A and B show varying amounts of effort required, represented by areas, in each level of the production control function. Of course, B would be more efficient in the long run. In short, concentrating effort in the planning stage of a project, can save time and energy in the actual control.

On the contrary, due to inadequate planning in the case of A, or lack of effort in preparing the plan, control work increases and may finally be resolved by doing the work all over again or finishing up the work partly undone. Therefore, the importance of production planning is stressed.

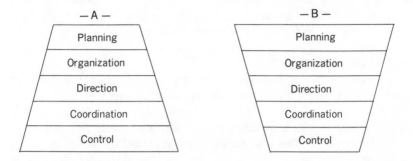

— A —	— B —
Planning	Planning
Organization	Organization
Direction	Direction
Coordination	Coordination
Control	Control

SUMMARY OF PRODUCTION PLANNING

Reviewing the definition of production control, it was stated earlier that it consisted of order of operation and daily scheduling.

Although these are, no doubt, the two big pillars of production planning, we must look at it more synthetically. For this purpose, we must refer to the five W's and one H for assistance.

A production plan may be sub-divided into the following:

Why	(Objective)	policy, direction
What	(Object)	parts, products
Where	(Place)	placement
When	(Time)	daily schedule
Who	(Person)	workers, machines
How	(Method)	process

Arranged in order of process and restated in proper production control terms, the plan includes:

(1) What   Material
(2) How   Production order
(3) Who   Man-hours (working hours and ability)
                Staffing plan
(4) Where   Layout
(5) When   Daily schedule, time order

Among the above, once personnel and layout have been set, they should not be frequently changed; therefore, they should not be included in the cycle of the routine production project.

Hence daily production control is mainly concerned with:

(1) Material
(2) Operation order (Process)
(3) Man-hours

(4)   Daily schedule

In simple terms, prepare a plan for obtaining the raw materials of the necessary quality and quantity required for production, decide the order for processing the raw materials, compute working and operation hours necessary for processing and set personnel and hours in the daily schedule.

FORMS OF PRODUCTION

Since the types, business conditions, scale of plant and forms of production processes differ, the method of formulating a production plan will differ, too. In other words, the manner of process control in each enterprise will vary in accordance with production volume, rate of production, the term or duration, high or low repeatability and stability of techniques. From these four points of view, the different categories of industries may be classified as follows:

(1) Job-order manufacturing (large variety & small quantity)	Mechanical Assembly Industries
(2) Intermittent manufacturing	
(3) Continuous (repetitive) manufacturing	
(4) Equipment (process) manufacturing	Equipment Industries

The 'A' group consists of industries with a small variety and large scale production, the 'B' group of industries with a medium variety and medium scale production, while the 'C' group covers industries with a large variety

Production Quantity

Repeatability

and small scale of production.

The difficulty or ease of production control will depend upon the type of manufacturing. Comparatively easy production control may be achieved when items are manufactured in large quantity but in small variety; and as we proceed from medium-variety, medium-quantity production to job-order manufacturing the difficulties in production control will increase. Considering the forms mentioned above, the higher an industry goes up, the more difficult production control becomes, while the lower it goes, the easier the production control.

Therefore, in this section, an attempt will be made to explain how to improve processes, in all types of production with production control as the focus.

IMPROVING PRODUCTION CONTROL OF JOB-ORDER MANUFACTURING

Many small and medium enterprises and subcontracting businesses inevitably follow the job-order system of production. More often than not, these kinds of businesses experience lower productivity and relatively high operating costs. But, with the introduction of new techniques of industrial engineering, namely, network planning and group technology, many deficiencies of job-order production can be overcome.

Network planning for PERT (Programme review and evaluation techniques)

This is the "age of huge projects", commencing with the days of the development of atomic bombs, the birth of 'Sputniks' and the progress of the 'Apollo' project. In Japan, the construction of the New Tokaido Super Express Line (bullet train) and the Wakato Great Bridge, etc., have been projected and materialized, one after another.

Effectively, a one-time job that is new, creative, and of large-scale proportions is classified as a project. A massive project is subject to severe constraints of cost, terms and techniques. In other words, the question is, how to utilize men, material, money, space and time within a certain budget, a certain period of time and a certain frame of technology. PERT may be compared to the 'Aladdin's lamp' of the modern age for assisting in the solution of such problems. It is a network project technique in which an 'event' is represented by 'O' and an 'activity' by '→'. For example, a PERT chart is drawn as follows:

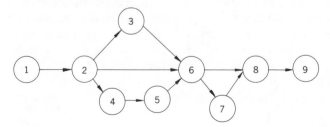

In this case, an 'event' should meet one of the following requirements:

(a)   It should indicate an outstanding or significant point of the project

(b)   It should be the beginning or end of a piece of work

(c)   It should consume neither time nor resources

An 'activity' means the actualization of a piece of work. It is the part of a PERT network where time is spent and which requires personnel, materials, physical space, equipment or other resources. The number of days or hours spent on an activity are represented by 'te', i.e., time estimate value calculated on the three-point estimate system (to be explained later). In the course of various processes of a project, a 'critical' path can be determined using the time estimated values.

PERT was originally conceived as a development and project technique for a large-scale project. However, it is now considered that this technique can fully demonstrate its effectiveness in job-order manufacturing.

For each job order, the required date of delivery, the possibility and method of parallel operation (or simultaneity) and 'slacks' in each event can be rationally estimated. It is very useful for operation order, working hours and daily schedule project.

Group Technology

Job-order manufacturing is, to some extent, the destiny of small- and medium-size enterprises. Compared to large-scale enterprises, their production processes tend to lower their rate of profit due to the complicated processes involved, the time lost by shifting from one process to another, the time spent in learning changed operations, the cost of gathering and providing necessary jigs and machine tools, and despatching and cutting of materials.

Consequently, the technique of group technology has evolved with the objective of overcoming this disadvantage of small-and medium-size enterprises, and enabling them to reap similar benefits to those of the mass runs of large-scale enterprises. This technique is widely adopted in Europe, and especially in the Soviet Union and West Germany, where industrial conditions are more or less similar to Japan – unlike the USA which basically employs mass production systems.

The principle of this technique is that semi-finished products, parts and accessories which are apparently quite different but have some common and similar features of materials, forms, manufacturing processes, machines and tooling requirements, are all grouped together into lots and adopted and channeled into a conveyor system. Group technology is, in essence, a group technique of assembled components and parts as well as a technique for arrangement, classification and unification.

PERT and group technology are used for solving various problems of small and medium manufacturing industries, especially in job-order manufacturing. These two modern techniques should be widely used in the future for production planning and control, together with the conventionally orthodox production planning technique. The following 11 charts are on production control techniques, presupposing the introduction and setup of these two methods.

Organic chart of production control tools

First of all, production control is a system and a standardized flow of processes. Due to different types of production as well as other reasons, this system will vary with the individual enterprise and plant. In a single enterprise or plant there should be only one standardized production control system, like the rhythm of life, with all the concerned persons. IBAM (Institute of Business Administration and Management) type flow charts can present a stabilized process control system in a production plant. This chart clearly indicates to the persons in charge what is to be done in a consistent flow. Those in supervisory positions should draw up such a flow chart to enable setting up a system which will be a major premise for effective process control.

The starting point of production planning is first to make, a major daily schedule and fix a *master schedule* (1) of production for a comparatively long period. (It may be roughly scheduled.)

A master schedule is a monthly production plan for a one year period; a medium schedule is a daily production plan for a one month period; a minor schedule is a daily and hourly production plan for a period of one week.

The master schedule, for a longer period basically shows the future programme and sometimes shows delivery dates too. You may indicate them with different colours. As the master schedule has columns for sales, cost and gross profit, it will also play the role of a production budget.

Next, for the job order for which a delivery date has been fixed or informally requested, we shall draw up a PERT *network planning chart* (flow diagram) (2). With this we can clarify how supply and purchased parts should go through the processes for domestic production and outside orders as well as how they are assembled. However, we have not yet entered the domain of the time and quantitative analysis from the planning and operating stage to completion.

It is the *event-activity chart* (3) which enables us to perform this analysis.

In each activity between the preceding event and the following event, the expected time is projected by three estimates, i.e., 'a', most optimistic time; 'm' most likely time; and 'b', most pessimistic time. The following formula is then used: $te = \dfrac{a + 4m + b}{6}$. The single time estimate (te) of every activity thus computed is again written on the flow diagram (2), adding the values of 'te' to obtain TE (earliest possible completion time) where a critical path may be found and the activities in that path may be rearranged in order to shorten the period of production.

Next, we draw up a *flow analysis and estimated man-hour table* (4), using the prepared process chart and standard time card. It is similar to the flow process analysis chart explained earlier in chapter 4, but here the objective of its use is somewhat different. As mentioned previously, this is used for group technology. In this system, the parts contained in a job order are grouped together according to similarity in processing.

Next, the process chart for each group is drawn up. Keep adding the necessary time for each process vertically to find the work hours necessary for each process or machine of that group.

Proceeding further to obtain the total shop order, obtain the work hours for each process and total these, to arrive at the total work hours. Then compile them into an *accumulated work load graph* (5). This will show the daily necessary work hours during a certain period, namely 'work load'.

A capacity line drawn on the same accumulated work load graph will serve as a method of work hour plan or spare capacity control.

A *parts routing chart* (6) within the PERT network can be developed by converting the arrow diagram into a date graph. In that routing chart, the routing number counted backwards from the delivery date is calculated for each part and drawn in the form of a chart. Based on this, the routing priority for each part will be decided.

Next, when all this information has been acquired, prepare a *pro-trol chart* (7), where 'pro-trol' is an abbreviation for production control.

By means of the medium schedule, a flow process analysis chart and machine-wise accumulated work load graph can be set in a concrete schedule; and control the work after it is put into practice, by using magnetic tags painted in different colours for different processes.

Then, a *machine loading chart* (8) will be drawn. This may be called a minor schedule which is divided further than a medium schedule. This will show, daily and hourly, what routing number part is loaded on a certain machine during a given week.

In this manner we advance to the order of production, man-hour planning and daily schedules. The daily schedule is constructed more precisely and minutely than a master schedule or a medium schedule. A concrete plan is then said to have been established.

Now, to start working in accordance with the plan, a *dispatching panel* (9). is utilized. At this stage, materials and parts have been pre-arranged. This is the time for materials and parts to come into and go out of warehouses.

On this occasion a *check file board and come-up system* (10) for checking is employed. Among supplies and purchased goods, the parts which are liable to late arrival are enumerated and the purchasing personnel should

Organic Chart of Production Control Tools

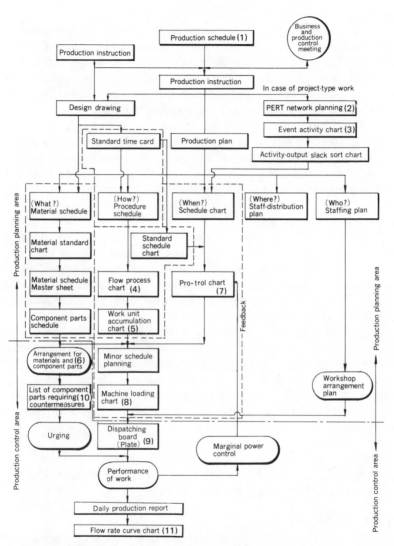

be informed of this likely delay as soon as possible.

In this manner the work begins. The state of progress and completion of operations will soon be fed back to the *pro-trol chart* and sometimes measures necessary for change in a plan are considered here.

The position of magnetic tags will be changed on the *pro-trol chart* and the results of operations will be plotted daily on the *flow frequency curves graph* (11). This will indicate that goods are leaving the warehouses, being handled during various processes and brought to the completed state. This plays a valuable role in the control of actual results.

243

1. MASTER SCHEDULE

Purpose

This is a production schedule for the whole year. However, the difference between this and an ordinary production schedule is that the former would show the desirable monthly output from the standpoint of the plant, while the ordinary production schedule will only indicate orders received, dates of delivery and those fixed in the schedule. In other words, what is usually termed 'orders in hand' is shown by month.

The schedule shown here will indicate number of orders in hand in terms of sales, production cost and gross profit. This will give the business department an indication of the desirability of acquiring more orders to fill any gap in the shortage of orders and also give the plant a signal for making preparations to process the orders already received.

How to draw up this chart

Keep entering all work necessary in the form of a list. If desired, enter prospective orders as well as definite orders and include them in the monthly total. In calculating the monthly total, sales volume should be defined as the value of goods manufactured and shipped and for which debtors have been established relative to their sales, while the production cost should be determined on the basis of sales.

Cost of sales should be defined as the cost, i.e., finished goods inventory at beginning of month + production cost of the goods manufactured during this month − month-end finished goods inventory. The month's production cost should be defined as semifinished goods inventory at beginning of month + this month's production cost − month-end semifinished goods inventory. Gross profit is calculated by subtracting cost of sales from sales volume.

Relations

A *master schedule* is subdivided into a medium schedule, which will be explained in chart No. (7) as a *'pro-trol' chart*.

How to use this chart

A chart such as this can be prepared on a blackboard when an order is made definite. In other words, this schedule must be kept continuous. It is desirable to total the complete delivery amount every month and know the sales amount in advance as well as the amount of production.

(1) Master Schedule

No.	Customer	Type of product	Sales amount		Month			Month			Month			Month			Month			Month		
					Sales	Cost	Gross profit	Sales	Cost	Gross profit	Sales	Cost	Gross profit	Sales	Cost	Gross profit	Sales	Cost	Gross profit	Sales	Cost	Gross profit
				Total																		
				Amount																		
				Total																		
				Amount																		
				Total																		
				Amount																		
				Total																		
				Amount																		
				Total																		
				Amount																		
				Total																		
				Amount																		
				Total																		
				Amount																		
				Total																		
				Amount																		
				Total																		
				Amount																		

[CHART 72]

2. PERT NETWORK PLANNING CHART

Purpose

First, the various definitions of PERT will be introduced:

(a)   To accomplish the objective of a project successfully and punctually, PERT will clarify what should be done and provide managers with tools for their use.

(b)   It is a technique which will assist a decision maker, but will never make a decision on his behalf.

(c)   When many activities of a project have been completed, it is a technique which will provide some statistical information regarding possible future uncertainties.

(d)   This is a method which draws the attention of managers to the utilization and control of time, resources and functions in order to increase the possibility of meeting the target date.

From the above objective and functions it is clear the chart will serve as a production project which takes the form of individual production or job shop system production, in which each activity is performed only once. The next issue is how to secure time and labour for drawing up an arrow diagram in network planning.

How to draw up this chart

To save time and labour, sheets of arrow diagrams can be preprinted (mimeograph printing is quite enough).

The example is from a subcontracting machine processing industry. Diagram sheets are printed in advance so that the names of parts in each flow (or the name of all parts) are entered and 'te' is computed for each activity. We then enter them in the sheet. TE (earliest possible completion time) and TL (latest allowable completion time) can now be computed in succession. TE is accumulated and TL is counted backward from the last delivery date. This should correspond with the routing number.

Relations

To decide TE and TL, it is convenient to use an *event-activity chart* which provides for a three-point estimate.

How to use this chart

As critical paths and slacks in each event will be found by computing TE and TL, it will contribute to the improvement of this arrow diagram. For example, as we shift the manufacture of a certain part (a critical item) from a subcontractor's to our own or vice versa, we can perform the most rational and effective treatment and control of resources, time and functions by cutting short critical paths and minimizing slacks.

246

(2) PERT Network for Tape-Type Automatic Controlling Machine Development (Drawn on 18th, March, 1982)

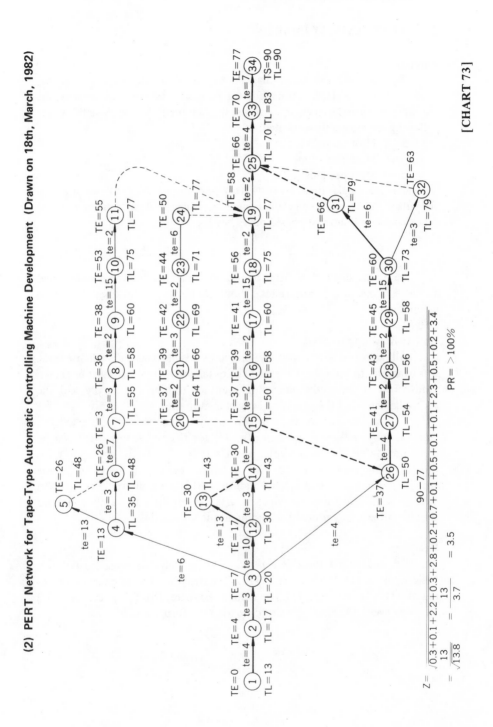

$$z = \frac{\sqrt{0.3 + 0.1 + 2.2 + 0.3 + 2.8 + 0.2 + 0.7 + 0.1 + 0.5 + 0.1 + 0.1 + 2.3 + 0.5 + 0.2 + 3.4}}{90 - 77}$$

$$= \frac{13}{\sqrt{13.8}} = \frac{13}{3.7} = 3.5$$

$$PR = >100\%$$

[CHART 73]

247

3. EVENT-ACTIVITY CHART

Purpose

To complete the arrow diagram explained in the previous page, we must find out 'te' (time estimated) for each activity. For this purpose, the three-point estimate technique is usually adopted. For each activity the following are separately estimated:

a   Most optimistic time
m   Most likely time
b   Most pessimistic

To get single time estimate (te) and dispersion (σ^2), we use two formulae. 'te' is an average time value, assuming that an activity is to be repeated many times and phased out. They are:

$$te = \frac{a + 4m + b}{6} \quad \text{or} \quad \sigma^2 = (\frac{b - a}{6})^2$$

'te' is the single time estimate of a certain activity repeated many times and σ^2 is a measure of uncertainty about an activity, in this case, of 'te' thus computed.

How to draw up this chart

All activities are shown by preceding events and succeeding events. For example, to indicate the activity of obtaining a supply, it must be shown sandwiched between the preceding event of routing the supply and the succeeding event of the supply arriving at a given spot.

The entire chart is made in this manner, and 'te' for each activity is computed by a three-point estimate. TE for the succeeding event can be computed as TE for the preceding event + te for the specific activity. TL for the preceding event is TL for the succeeding event − (minus) 'te' of the specific event and it is a symbol indicating the latest allowable completion date. It is the latest date on which a certain event should take place in order that the project may proceed according to the set schedule.

Relations

To understand the *PERT network* completely, we must master such basic terms as (1) PERT event, (2) PERT activity, (3) Preceding and succeeding events, (4) Network, (5) Three-point estimate, (6) TE of an event, (7) TL of an event, (8) Slack, (9) Critical path, (10) Dispersion, σ^2.

(3) Event-Activity Chart

Preceding event	Succeeding event	Activity	3-point estimate a	m	b	te	σ^2	Succeeding event, TE	Succeeding event, TL	Slack
1	2	Survey on computer function and tape system	3	4	6	4	0.3	4	17	13
2	3	Conference on overall function	2	3	4	3	0.1	7	20	13
3	4	Planning on mechanical function	4	6	10	6	1.0	13	35	22
3	12	Planning on electric circuit function	6	10	15	10	2.2	17	30	13
3	26	Planning on remodelling existing machines	3	4	6	4	0.3	37	50	13
4	5	Experiment on mechanical function	10	12	20	13	2.8	26	48	22
4	6	Survey on machine functional parts	1	3	5	3	0.2	26	48	22
6	7	Machine designing	5	6	10	7	0.7	33	55	22
7	8	Machine	2	3	4	3	0.1	36	58	22
8	9	Making of machine parts table	1	2	3	2	0.1	38	60	22
9	10	Machine parts survey	10	15	20	15	2.3	53	75	22
10	11	Machine part making	1	2	3	2	0.1	55	77	22
12	13	Experiment on electric circuit	10	12	20	13	2.8	30	43	13
12	14	Survey on electric functional parts	1	3	5	3	0.2	30	43	13
14	15	Electric circuit designing	5	6	10	7	0.7	37	50	13
15	16	Electric circuit part drawing	1	2	3	2	0.1	39	58	19
16	17	Making of electric circuit parts list	1	2	3	2	0.1	41	60	19
17	18	Purchase of electric circuit parts	10	15	20	15	2.3	56	75	19
18	19	Making of electric circuit parts	1	2	3	2	0.1	58	77	19
20	21	Conference on completion of machine and electric parts	1	2	3	2	0.1	39	66	27
21	22	Cage body designing	2	3	4	3	0.1	42	69	27
22	23	Making of cage body parts list	1	2	3	2	0.1	44	71	27
23	24	Purchase of cage body	4	6	10	6	1.0	50	77	22
19	25	Setting-in of cage body	1	2	3	2	0.1	66	79	13
26	27	Existing machine remodelling designing	2	4	6	4	0.5	41	54	13
27	28	Existing machine remodelling drawing	1	2	3	2	0.1	43	56	13
28	29	Making of existing machine remodelling parts list	1	2	3	2	0.1	45	58	13
29	30	Purchase of existing machine remodelling materials	10	15	20	15	2.3	60	73	13
30	31	Assembling of remodelled machines in existence	4	6	8	6	1.5	66	79	13
30	32	Wiring on the installation stand	2	3	5	3	0.3	63	79	16
25	33	Three element combination (remodelling inclusive)	2	3	10	4	0.2	70	83	13
33	34	Test operation for regulation (remodelling inclusive)	4	6	15	7	3.4	77	90	13

Unit: week date hour actual work hours No. D-8 Name Shigeru Inoue

[CHART 74]

4. FLOW ANALYSIS AND ESTIMATED MAN-HOUR TABLE

Purpose

The flow analysis chart has been explained in the chapter on industrial engineering. However, we shall employ it here to find similarity in the process system of each component part. The objective is to apply group technology to process control. Group technology is a method of 'group processing' in which goods, though different in type but similar in form, measurement and technical nature are combined and subjected to a single process as far as possible. Technical similarity means that, in production operations, there are similarities in installation, processing and measurement methods. Group technology can overcome those built-in problem areas of the job shop system and permit the attainment of productivity more in line with a mass production system. The graph shows how productivity will rise when lots are gathered in a group.

Man-hours/kg and Productivity

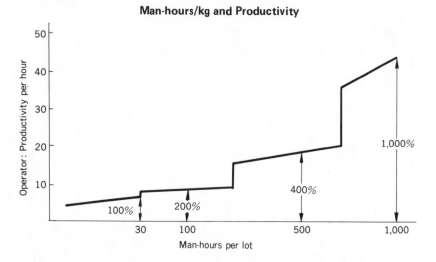

How to draw up the table

As explained before, we indicate in the chart the process to which each part is subjected. The symbols HT, L, HC, K & D represent the processes of heat-treatment, lathing, gear cutting, marking and drilling. Next, enter man-hours required for each machine. Multiply this by the number of machines and adding the figures vertically for each process, we obtain the total man-hours per process. If large quantity lots are gathered, productivity gains can be expected. Prior to such an operation, you are advised to cut and divide the flow process analysis chart into components or parts, and make appropriate groupings on the basis of process similarity. Here, the possibility of group processing will become evident and lead to the practical implementation of group technology.

(4) Flow Analysis & Estimated Man-Hour Table

Direction number	Customer					Production number					Type of machine					Production number				
Part number	Quantity	Material	HT	L	HC	K	D	MV	ML	SL	GC	F	GP	HF	SH	BL	P	HV B	Others	Total

[CHART 75]

251

5. ACCUMULATED WORK LOAD GRAPH

Purpose

The objective of a man-hour table is to plan work load and capacity. Work load is the time for the process to be completed, while capacity is the time to be allocated for the process. The work to be done (work load) and the ability to perform that work (capacity) are represented by time values which are to be compared.

For this purpose, first plot the work load on the graph. If a flow analysis chart already exists, we can find the man-hours necessary for each process. This will make its comparison with work load easier.

How to draw up this graph

The graph is the *accumulated work load graph* showing the piping operation of the oil pressure piping department in a machine tool plant. With a month divided into three parts of 10 days each for the piping work in a machine tool plant, man-hours are to be accumulated by each schedule. To make these accumulated man-hours practical, we must be accurate in the estimate of man-hours. Moreover, we must have basic data on standard times ready for use. Then, when the work load is estimated, we draw a capacity line parallel to the base. If one person works 10 hours a day (overtime work is expected) and we have 20 workers, we draw a capacity line at 200 hours a day.

Various relations

Consideration is given to the schedule, but an ordinary *accumulated work load graph* is an accumulated graph of simple man-hours before the schedule is planned. Based on it, a schedule is made.

How to use this chart

In comparing work load with capacity, spare capacity is indicated if the accumulated work load is below the capacity line. On the other hand, if it is above the capacity line, it shows that some countermeasures must be considered.

In the latter case, consider what countermeasures should have priority. The shortage of man-hours during particular periods can be overcome through overtime work, working on holidays, assistance from other divisions, utilization of subcontractors, or recruitment of outside workers. Capacity control is achieved by taking realistic measures to balance the flow of the workload.

(5) Accumulated Work Load Graph

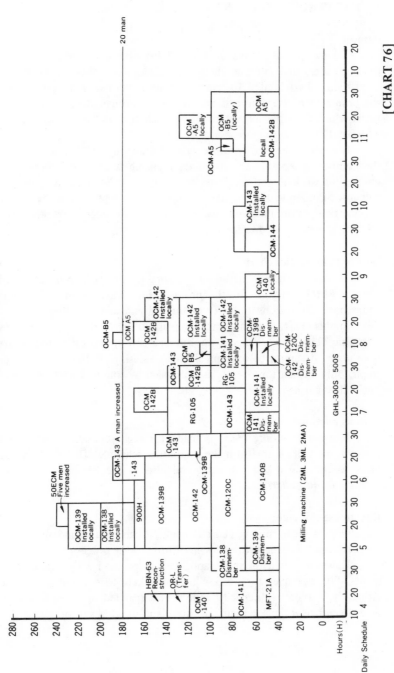

[CHART 76]

6. PARTS ROUTING CHART

Purpose

Taking the last event of a *PERT network* as 0, we count back the routing orders and compile them into a graph to obtain a *parts routing chart*. This chart is used for clarifying the relations among parts, such as, the orders of routing, process and starting. Through this, from the critical items which take the longest time, we shall arrange the order of each item with plenty of time to spare.

Note that the *parts routing chart* is drawn up on the assumption that the number of workers and machines available is unlimited. In reality, the number of workers and machines are limited and their mutual interference will grow. Consequently, in real cases, mutual interference must be minimized by changing it into a *machine loading chart* at the stage of weekly and daily scheduling and adjusted rationally.

How to draw up this chart

The most efficient method of drawing up this *parts routing chart* is to make a PERT network for the product. Following TL in each event, we count back the routing order from the tail end and plot them on a graph.

In this chart, some are under preparation and others in the process of operation. They are all mixed up, but as a three-point estimate has already been made, it cannot be too unrealistic as a desk plan. In the example in the graph, only the part processed in this plant is coloured so that it may be easily distinguished.

Various relations

If a *parts routing chart* is made for each production order or each product, we will be able to make a monthly schedule. This will serve as the basis for making a *pro-trol chart* and also as the key for drawing up a *machine loading chart*.

How to use this graph

Once a parts routing chart is made, it can be used indefinitely unless there is a drastic change in the design or form of the processes.

However, based on this graph, we can proceed with various improvements. For example, for parts which are likely to encounter bottlenecks, either the production capacity should be expanded or a decision must be made whether to make them at this plant or at a subcontractor's plant.

(6) Parts Routing Chart

Scale (top): 140 130 120 110 100 90 80 70 60 50 40 30 20 10 0

Part	Routing details
Change boss	97 — Routing base material (Kuroishi) — Nakagawa Iron Works — In our plant
Change arm	67 — Routing base material (Kuroishi) — Kawasaki Iron Works — Operation by milling machine
Change shaft collar	61 — Routing base material (Kuroishi) — Kubo Iron & Steel Works — Tenjin Industries
Casing & cover	46 — Routing base material (Nakamura) — Kubo Iron & Steel Works — In our plant
Pulley & flange	60 — Routing base Material (Kuroishi) — Processed at our plant — Teijin Industries
Shifter	80 — Routing base Material (Nishiuchi Steel) — Shikoku — In our plant
Axis	113 — Routing base Material (Nishiuchi Steel) — Ishimoto "Gear Cutting" Takamatsu Takahashi Die Casting
Gear	133 — Routing base material (Nishiuchi Steel) — Miwa Industrial Machine — Tokyo Heat Miwa Industrial Mori I.W. Machine — In our plant
Collar	100.5 — Routing base material (Nishimura Steel) — Choei Steel & Iron — Choei — Masu Press — Takamatsu Die C.
Supplementary axis	78 — Routing base material (Toshima & Co.) — Asahi Seisaku — Nakai Plating
Change shaft / Change fork pipe	76 — Routing base material (Toshima & Co.) — Nakai Plating — Nakagawa Iron Works
Change fork	73 — Routing base material (Toshima & Co.) — Takada Iron Works
Bearing	15 Ozaki & Co.
Oil seal & others	15 German & Co.
Snap ring	12 Iwamoto Enterprise
Slide key	54 Hashimoto Enterprise
Name plate	18 Meiji Mark
Key	22 Shikoku Spiizel
Oil	5 Taka
Package box	15 Niyodo Timber
Motor	55 Yasukawa Electric Works
Motor fastening boss	27 Kubo Steel

[CHART 77]

255

7. PRO-TROL CHART

Purpose

A *pro-trol chart* is employed as the control board for monthly programming and control. The special features of this board are:

(a) It proves effective in individual production characteristic of a job system.

(b) The visible recorders and the schedule of the manufacture instructions are combined.

(c) A weekly and daily schedule can be developed by utilizing coloured magnetic tags.

(d) A coloured flag hanging from the top indicates 'today'. If many coloured tags are found to the left of this line, the work is delayed. This is a very effective tool for delivery date control.

How to draw up this chart

On the left end of a blackboard made of steel, we make a rack for a visible recorder as shown in the graph. As the base of each (visible recorder) is made of acetate, if we insert a production specification in it, it serves at the lower end as an identification window for production number, type of machine and customer's name. From this recorder, a horizontal line extends to the right. Then, the vertical lines on the blackboard delineate a date column which is further divided into three parts: forenoon, afternoon and overtime. As lines are to be made according to production specifications, we shall set a tag on the line, which indicates the end of the process.

This particular chart was drawn up at a compressor repair shop and the principal processes for repairs of compressors are – overhaul, examine, repair, assembly and delivery. Accordingly, five different coloured tags will indicate the respective processes.

How to use it

On this *pro-trol chart*, dates are scaled vertically and varying coloured magnetic tags are positioned horizontally. We make a monthly or a weekly pro-trol planning. As the operation progresses, we remove the tags to show the degree of completion of operations. When there are some tags left on the left side of the date indicator flag (a red string with a weight at the end), the delay in the process is automatically evident. If you take a colour photo of this board every week, you can compile a file of the actual results of process control.

(7) Pro-Trol Chart, Monthly Schedule

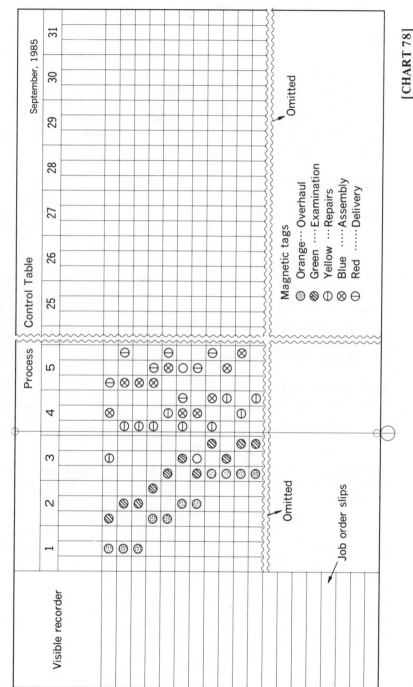

[CHART 78]

8. MACHINE LOADING CHART

Purpose

When production planning gets to this stage, it is no longer a mere plan, but consists of more concrete facts.

In this chart, we allot to each machine the parts to be processed for the next week, so it becomes a weekly (by hour) or daily schedule. If process controllers, foremen and workers are provided with copies of this chart, foremen will not have to direct their men repeatedly. Thus, the foremen's burden of control will be considerably lightened.

How to draw up this chart

Blank forms of this chart are printed in advance. Each machine column is divided into a planning column and an actual results column. Each column is again divided into a regular column and an overtime column and a day is further divided into eight hours each.

When you project a weekly or a daily schedule, use this form. First, determine this week's work by the *pro-trol chart* and then check if there is any possible interference among production specifications by going through the *parts routing chart.*

Then, referring to the *flow analysis and estimated man-hour table,* load the work on to each machine. On this occasion, each routing number and part is painted in different colours.

How to use this chart

As the work proceeds, cover the actual results column with colours, one by one. It is better to use the same colour for each routing number and part respectively so that you can compare them with the machine loading of the planning column more easily. By tracking the actual results, you will obtain the project achievement rate per head. Therefore, it becomes very useful for foremen to get a grasp on the work and to control their personnel. For this purpose, the machine loading in the planning column should be based on the standard times set by the proper techniques.

(8) Machine Loading Chart

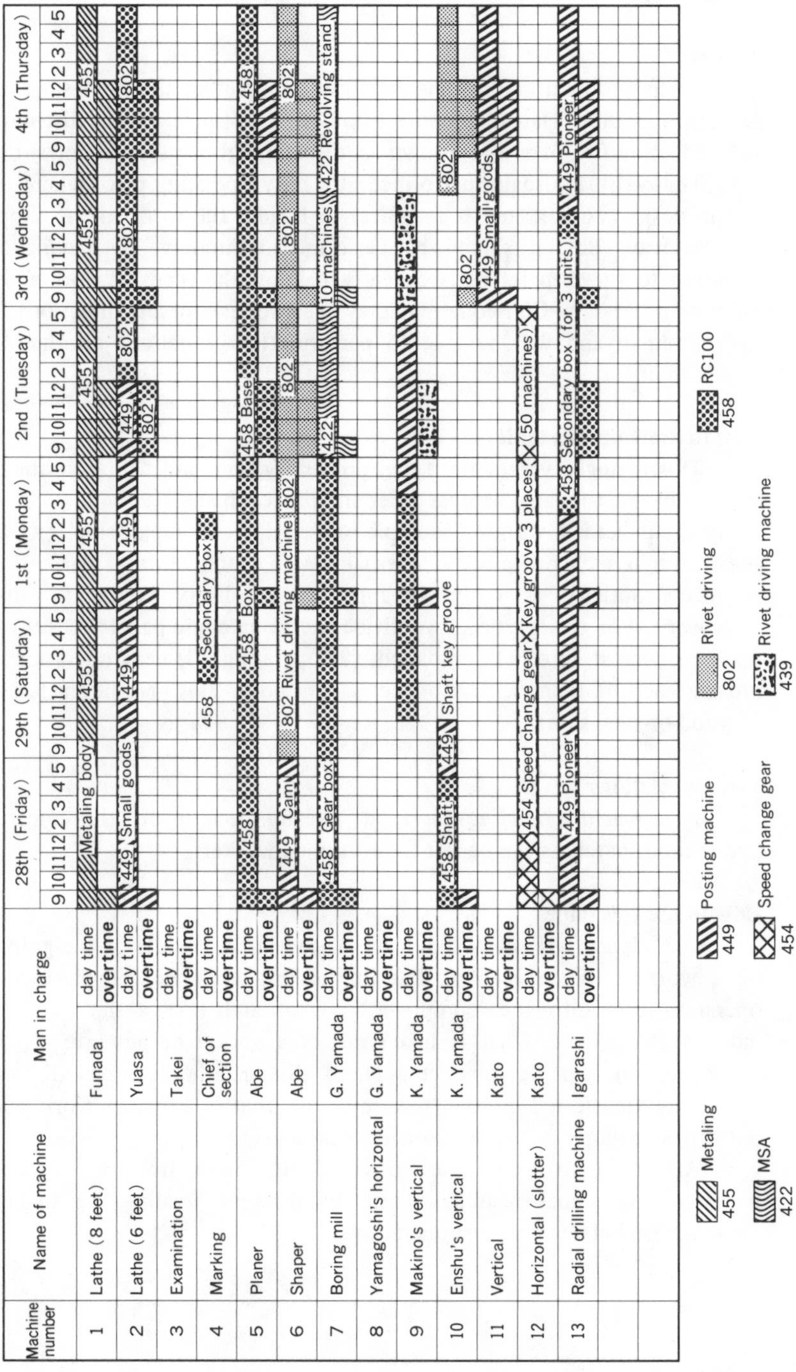

Machine number	Name of machine	Man in charge	
1	Lathe (8 feet)	Funada	day time / overtime
2	Lathe (6 feet)	Yuasa	day time / overtime
3	Examination	Takei	day time / overtime
4	Marking	Chief of section	day time / overtime
5	Planer	Abe	day time / overtime
6	Shaper	Abe	day time / overtime
7	Boring mill	G. Yamada	day time / overtime
8	Yamagoshi's horizontal	G. Yamada	day time / overtime
9	Makino's vertical	K. Yamada	day time / overtime
10	Enshu's vertical	K. Yamada	day time / overtime
11	Vertical	Kato	day time / overtime
12	Horizontal (slotter)	Kato	day time / overtime
13	Radial drilling machine	Igarashi	day time / overtime

Day columns: 28th (Friday), 29th (Saturday), 1st (Monday), 2nd (Tuesday), 3rd (Wednesday), 4th (Thursday), each divided into hours 9 10 11 12 1 2 3 4 5.

Legend:
Metaling 455 · MSA 422 · Posting machine 449 · Speed change gear 454 · Rivet driving 802 · Rivet driving machine 439 · RC100 458

[CHART 79]

9. DISPATCHING PANEL

Purpose

When production planning has been completed, the next stage is to get into operation. Here, the control process which includes the distribution and allocation of operations known as 'dispatching' plays an important role.

This work is usually performed at a busy operating place where there are no desks available and it is easiest to handle the work in the simplest possible way. But, it should be performed accurately. By paying close attention to the dispatching, workers will know the types of work and the order of processing. Consequently, they need not ask for any directions from their foremen and will be able to perform their functions on their own responsibility.

How to draw up this table

This is single-type (series type) process system, and will serve the type of work having the same process order and process name.

The panel is a working example in a compressor repair ship. The work goes through such processes as overhauling – examination – parts routing – process routing – assembly – examination – delivery – repairs – painting – delivery. For this purpose, we divide the dispatching panel vertically and further divide it into (1) completed, (2) operating, (3) next operation, and provide each of them with a pocket (a slip box). This may be made either of wood or steel sheet.

Various relations

If a *machine loading chart* has already been made, the control of operation dispatching can be left to less skilled workers.

How to use this table

The *dispatching panel* should be placed in the middle of the group of plant workers. When each worker finishes his work, he will place the 'in operation' slip into the 'completed' pocket and take a slip out of the 'next work' pocket. What is taken out of a pocket or put into a pocket are operation slips, graphs, etc. Those slips in the 'completed' pocket should be transferred to the 'next process', that is the next work pocket in the next column or the subsequent work pocket.

As the foreman continues to record those items from the dispatching panel in the actual results column of machine loading, he maintains coordination between process operations.

(9) Dispatching Panel

Dispatching Panel									
(1) Overhaul	(2) Examina-tion	(3) Part routing	(4) Procees routing	(5) Assembly	(6) Examina-tion	(7) Delivery repairs	(8) Painting	(9) Delivery	
5	5	5	5.	5	5	5	5	5	
4	4	4	4	4	4	4	4	4	
3	3	3	3	3	3	3	3	3	Pocket
Operating	Operating	Operating	Operating	Operating	Operating	Operating	Operating	Operating	
in operation	In operation	In operation	In operation	In operation	In operation	In operation	In operation	In operation	
Completed	Completed	Completed	Completed	Completed	Completed	Completed	Completed	Completed	

[CHART 80]

10. CHECK FILE BOARD AND COME-UP SYSTEM

Explanatory note

An assembly operation requiring a large number of parts cannot be completed, if even a single part is unavailable.

Parts may be broadly divided into four categories, namely, purchased goods, goods processed at subcontractors, goods supplied by subcontractors and goods processed at the plant. Of these we should keep an eye on those critical items which can cause bottlenecks. If, for example, there are parts which are not yet ready for use five days before the assembly date, we should indicate them on the board and take the necessary remedial measures. It is desirable that this blackboard be used together with the *come-up system* in purchasing. Thanks to the set-up of the control function, clerical work can be performed according to a schedule prepared several days in advance instead of being tackled when the need for such work arises. In consequence, following the schedule and daily programme, the action can be smoothly performed and handled automatically.

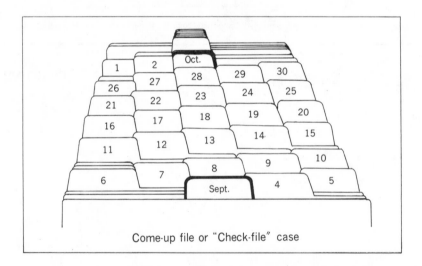

Come-up file or "Check-file" case

For example, consider the case of the *come-up system* in purchasing. When an order is made for certain parts, you must ensure delivery of those parts 10 days before the delivery date. On that occasion, insert a copy of the order slip in the come-up file, dated 10 days before the delivery date.

(10) Check File Board & Come-Up System

Check File Board

O O Industries & Co., Ltd. Assembly Work Shop

[CHART 81]

| Direction number | Kind of machine | Purchased article | | Processed articles & supplies from subcontractors | | | | | | | Name of part | Articles processed at own plant — Process-wise delivery date | | | | | | Date & day | |
		Name of article	Date	Name of article	Date	Name of article	Date	Name of article	Date			Process	Date	Process	Date	Process	Date	Priority order	Completion of Assembly
	(Unit)																		
	(Unit)																		
	(Unit)																		
	(Unit)																		
	(Unit)																		
	(Unit)																		
	(Unit)																		

263

11. FLOW FREQUENCY CURVES GRAPH

Purpose

When the production process has been standardized and the process set in motion, the *flow frequency curves* shown hereafter will serve as a progress chart, and at the same time, also serve to control semi-finished products in each process. In other words, the *flow frequency curves* can combine the flow and stick conditions of several processes into a single graph.

How to draw up this graph

This is a triangular graph based on the total line and if this cumulative line is plotted into several lines for the several processes, these will show the semifinished goods (stocks) in each process and serve to control them. First, from the starting point 0 we draw the cumulative line of the number of finished goods completed. This is the cumulative line of the number of finished goods in the fourth process. Next, for those carried over from the third process, namely, semifinished goods ready for the fourth process, we plot upwards from the starting point, and from there we keep on plotting the cumulative line of the number of finished goods in the third process. In this way we go on drawing cumulative lines for the second process, the first process and materials ex-store.

Do not forget that these cumulative lines play the role of bridging various processes. In short, the cumulative line ① of the graph is not only the completed total line of the first process, but also the starting cumulative line of the second process.

Various relations

In the chapter on management in general, the curves of current purchase, stock, manufacture and sales were explained (p. 70). The concept here is the same.

How to use this chart

The vertical distance relating to the total number in this graph will show the quantity of semifinished goods (stocks) and the horizontal distance will show the turnover period of semifinished goods in each process.

For example, in the graph, the production capacity of the second and third processes will fall on the fourth, fifth and sixth days; for the period of the seventh day to the 14th day, the production capacity of the first process will begin to sag and in the fourth process, production capacity will be lowered throughout. At the beginning of the month there were 14 tons of unfinished goods while on the 16th this quantity had increased to 24.5 tons. In this manner, by balancing the production capacity of each process with the other processes, this table will become a very useful tool for effectively controlling the flow throughout the entire process.

(11) Flow Frequency Curves Graph

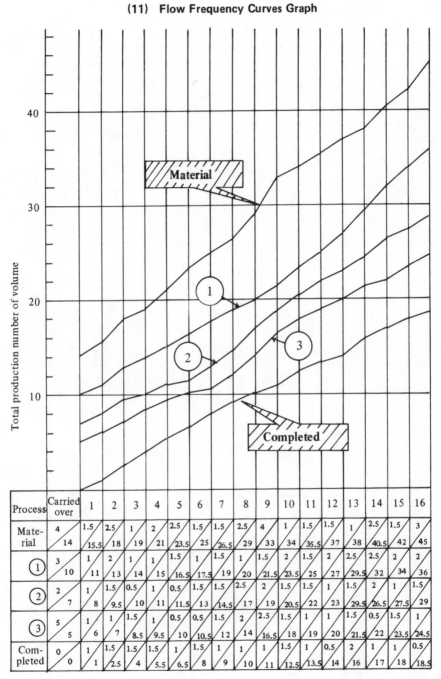

Process	Carried over	1	2	3	4	5	6	7	8	9	10	11	12	13	14	15	16
Material	4 / 14	1.5 / 15.5	2.5 / 18	1 / 19	2 / 21	2.5 / 23.5	1.5 / 25	1.5 / 26.5	2.5 / 29	4 / 33	1 / 34	1.5 / 35.5	1.5 / 37	1 / 38	2.5 / 40.5	1.5 / 42	3 / 45
①	3 / 10	1 / 11	2 / 13	1 / 14	1 / 15	1.5 / 16.5	1 / 17.5	1.5 / 19	1 / 20	1.5 / 21.5	2 / 23.5	1.5 / 25	2 / 27	2.5 / 29.5	2.5 / 32	2 / 34	2 / 36
②	2 / 7	1 / 8	1.5 / 9.5	0.5 / 10	1 / 11	0.5 / 11.5	1.5 / 13	1.5 / 14.5	2.5 / 17	2 / 19	1.5 / 20.5	1.5 / 22	1 / 23	1.5 / 29.5	2 / 26.5	1 / 27.5	1.5 / 29
③	5 / 5	1 / 6	1 / 7	1.5 / 8.5	1 / 9.5	0.5 / 10	0.5 / 10.5	1.5 / 12	2 / 14	2.5 / 16.5	1.5 / 18	1 / 19	1 / 20	1.5 / 21.5	0.5 / 22	1.5 / 23.5	1 / 24.5
Completed	0 / 0	1 / 1	1.5 / 2.5	1.5 / 4	1.5 / 5.5	1 / 6.5	1.5 / 8	1 / 9	1 / 10	1 / 11	1.5 / 12.5	1 / 13.5	0.5 / 14	2 / 16	1 / 17	1 / 18	0.5 / 18.5

[CHART 82]

265

Chapter 6

CHARTS ON ORGANIZATION AND PERSONNEL MANAGEMENT

Here we will consider the framework of management and various techniques for planning, practice and control pertaining to personnel. Labour management is usually studied in the following 12 fields:

(1) Labour policy.
(2) Labour management organization.
(3) Labour relations.
(4) Employment and posting.
(5) Transfer.
(6) Wages and salaries.
(7) Performance rating.
(8) Education and training.
(9) Benefits and welfare.
(10) Safety and sanitation.
(11) Publicity and information.
(12) Labour survey.

Obviously, we could draw up 100 charts on this field alone. Here, because of space limitation, we'll construct a time series and explain the contents.

As an example it will be more understandable to compare labour management to horticulture.

Step 1: In order to cultivate plants, we must have a field or garden. This means we must cultivate a field which has suitable soil and geology for the nature of the plant.

In personnel management this is analogous to the planning of the organization. Organization planning is a suitable means of management and its formation constitutes the central part of this problem.

(1) Analysis of soil ————➤ analysis of duties.
(2) Improvement and mixing
         of soil ————➤ allotment of duties.

(3)   Construction of paths and
ridges of paddy-fields.———————➤ formation of organization.

Step 2:   Next comes the choice and selection of the seeds to be planted. This is 'employment' in a business organization. If we make a wrong choice here, it is extremely difficult to correct later. The plant will die because of poor resistance to insects and being unsuitable for the soil. Choosing good personnel, fit for the object and constitution of the business, is the most important step and it precedes all others.

Step 3:   Next comes the process of sowing. It is of use to scatter seeds at random. Plant them one by one with care. This is the posting in the business organization. It is also important for the structure of a workshop to take in new workers. It depends on this sowing (posting) whether these new workers will turn out to be good workers with the drive to perform.

Step 4:   Let us suppose the seeds were sown in good soil. The soil should contain balanced nourishment and just enough water for the plant to absorb that nourishment. Wages should not be excessive, but should be adequate.

Step 5:   The plants which have begun to grow should be well taken care of. We must sometimes examine the condition of stems and roots and if we find insects there, we must get rid of them as soon as possible. In the world of business this is equivalent to 'performance rating'. Later, we should check the workers according to various rating factors and if we find anything wrong with their way of thinking, attitude, ability, or working method, we should correct this at the earliest date possible.

Step 6:   Looking around the field frequently, we must pack the soil hard and trim stems and leaves according to their particular growing condition. In the world of business this corresponds to 'education and training'. This 'education and training' involves seminars outside the plant, study overseas, lectures in the plant and on-the-job training (OJT).

Step 7:   It is necessary to have plenty of sunshine for the growth of plants. Carbonic acid gas is turned into nutrition here. This corresponds to the problems of leadership and communication of the managers and supervisors in the workshop.

Under good leadership, worker's techniques will improve, their desire to work will be heightened and they will finally become men of the character. The core of leadership is the knowledge of work by an administrator (the brightness of the sun) and human love for his men (the heat of the sun. Brightness and heat will change even carbonic acid gas (harmful thoughts and acts in the workshop) into nutrition (productivity) through adequate guidance (assimilation).

Step 8:   A rich crop of fruit will sooner or later be harvested. In business, this fruit corresponds to labour productivity. The object of labour management is to get employees to achieve higher productivity and at the same time to let them have spiritual and material happiness.

If we neglect to make management efforts from **Step 1** to **Step 7** the plants will not grow and labour productivity will not rise. In consequence, we cannot afford to buy even fertilizer. Then, labour trouble will erupt over the fruit and fertilizer (productivity and wages).

Step 1 to 8 can be graphed as follows:

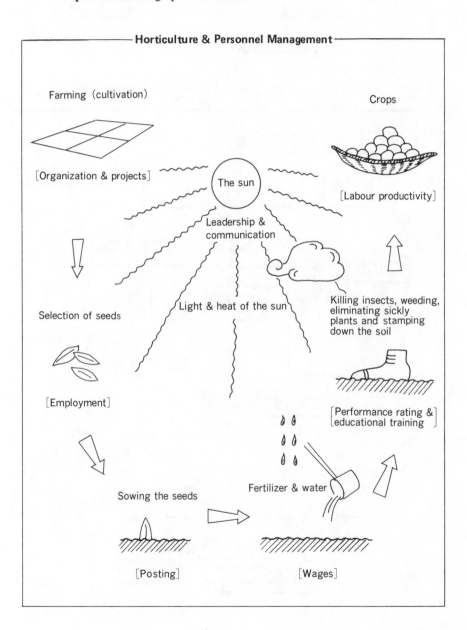

Organic Chart of Personnel and Organization Management Tools

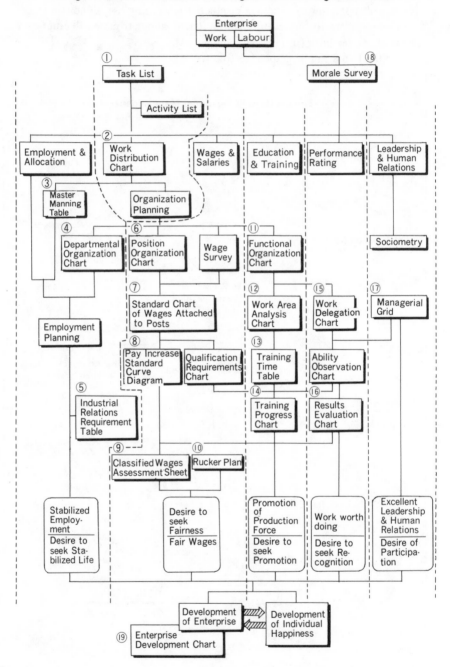

ORGANIC CHART OF ORGANIZATION AND PERSONNEL MANAGEMENT TOOLS

The true form of work allocation throughout the entire organization needs to be perceived accurately. Job analysis is the starting point or foundation for all the phases of personnel management.

First, compile a *job assignment chart,* following these three steps:

Draw up a *task list* (1) This is to be completed by each of the workers in the workshop. This list shows how many hours in each working week of 48 hours each worker spends actively performing his job. When the *task lists* for all personnel including the supervisor are completed, we make the list of principal work of the workshop workers.

When the *task lists* and *job descriptions* are drawn up, the mechanics will become routine. The work distribution chart (2) is a useful aid for organization planning. Without its help, the planning will never materialize because however logically we classify or arrange work on paper, it is impossible to devise concrete organization planning unless we have definite and reliable information.

In developing charts to be employed for organization planning, there are three kinds: *Departmental organization chart* (4), *position organization chart* (6) and *functional organization chart* (11).

A *departmental organization chart* (4) presents the system of organization units of a department, section, subsection and so forth. It is simple to make and often employed for practical use. When necessary, include not only the names of departments and sections, but also the names of personnel belonging to those departments and sections in the designated rectangular spaces.

Position organization chart (6). We put positions of workers in the rectangular spaces representing organization units. It is customary to enter the workers' names under the names of organization units.

The *functional organization chart* (11) aims at showing the principal work of a department or section, or an individual worker. In consequence, the rectangular spaces will be rather large and the chart itself will be a large one.

Work distribution charts and organization charts are an effective base for personnel and labour management. For example, consider them as the bases of recruitment, wage control, education and training, performance rating and leadership and human relations.

First, consider the various phases of recruitment. In order to perform employment and allocation activities rationally and scientifically, a *master manning table* (3) based on the work distribution chart must be prepared.

What qualification and ability a certain person has, at what stage we need such a person, how many such persons we need and also their ages, school careers and experience must be made clear here.

Recruitment and employment plans must be made simultaneously with a *departmental organization chart.* In order to deal very carefully with the problems of recruitment, we need a *recruiting and industrial relations requirements diagram* (5).

Wages are the basis of life for workers and as such, are very important. Morale and productivity of workers are strongly influenced by the rationality of the wage system.

Now, a wage survey should be made. Plot the wage levels of the company in a graph and compare them with that of all industries or the same industry. At the same time, study the standard cost of living and examine the cash flow in your company.

Next, draw up a *standard job classification chart* (7). The future direction of modern and rational wages is towards wages fixed by job evaluation or wages corresponding to a given position.

A *standard job classification chart* has a number of job classes as a basis. In the light of classification standards and the results of the study on wage rates, we will draw a *pay-increase standard curves diagram* (8). In short, it is the design for salaried personnel to progress up the salary ladder.

If there are six job classifications, six pay-increase curves are to be drawn. The next problem is where to put each worker in the pay-increase *curves.* Just like an address, wage classes and grades must be completely clarified.

To examine the classification, we draw up a *job evaluation and rating sheet* (9). Job grades are rated by the importance, difficulty and specialty of work and wage rates consider such human factors as school career, age, sex, and length of service. In a wage rates sheet, the result of a performance evaluation is to be taken into account. Therefore, all workers are classified on some point on the *pay-increase standard curves.*

Discontent and complaints of workers can be handled with a new system of wage incentives related to position and the *Rucker plan incentives and profit correlation chart* (10), which promises workers some additional payment as an incentive, is very useful. This incorporates the ideal of fair wages and appeals strongly to fair-minded workers.

Next, let us consider the phase of education and training. Here a *functional organization chart* (11) has already been drawn up. In the *functional organization chart,* the classification and division of work function have been already systematized to attain the objectives of the company. If this is represented as an organization system of purely duties and work, regardless of human elements, it will become a *work area analysis chart* (12). By dividing a work area into departments, units and individual tasks, a series of operational classifying systems will be formed.

The reason for having a *work area analysis chart* is that all on-the-job training (OJT) should be based on 'the principle of functional understanding'. Always be conscious of the relations between 'the whole and a part' or 'a part and the whole' and try to learn them. When we proceed a step farther with training based on such a principle, a *training timetable* (13) is used.

To show the progress of the training, *a training progress chart* (14) is used. "Who is being trained?" "What is he being trained for?" "What kind of training is given?" and "What kind of educational programme should be set?' A *training progress chart* will show all these factors and may prove ideal as a management method. Education and training contributes considerably to development of the production capacity of workers and greatly encourages their desire for job promotion.

Next comes the phase of performance rating. Reasonable rewards and fair penalties are the basic principles of personnel management. It is not fair to treat those who have the will to work on an equal basis with those who lack it.

From the functional organization chart there comes the *delegation of authority chart* (15). This will save resorting to the complicated literature of organization manuals or organization handbooks, and will enable top management to understand at a glance the kinds and degrees of authority they need to exercise.

The age of some classical organization theories has passed, and in the modern age of 'management by result' this chart method will be most convenient.

The basis of leadership and control on the part of management are the data obtained from observation of subordinates. For this purpose, *performance evaluation forms* (16A) and RADAR chart cards (16B) will prove useful. There are many methods of personnel evaluation, such as the Probst method, the comparison method, the general evaluation method and others. However, it is necessary for all the assessors to be well trained so that they do not make any errors or show any partiality.

As mentioned above, these results will be fed back into the job evaluation and rating sheet and will determine wage increases at the time of the annual pay raise. Workers are always striving to obtain their seniors' recognition. Overt appreciation by seniors promotes positive work attitudes.

In the area of leadership and the phase of human relations, good or bad personnel management will show in the rise or fall of morale and on-the-job spirit. They will depend on the ability of leaders and on the coefficient of group dynamics. Consequently, as efficiency factors of group dynamics, we must evaluate these two elements and continually strive to promote and strengthen them. For that purpose, all management should evaluate these factors by *Blake's managerial grid* (17). This is called a PM leadership chart, and it is used to classify management into five types and at the same time give us some useful hints on guidance techniques.

In addition when we evaluate a workshop as a group, it is convenient to employ sociometrics. In this way, the human relations dynamics comprising fine leadership and high morale will satisfy the desire of workers to participate.

Relative to the discussion of techniques of organization and personnel affairs, remember that a company cannot function without employees and that personnel management is wholly related to them. Therefore, it is desirable to make a *morale survey form* (18) (survey of attitude and the examination of mental inclination) by the NRK (Nihhon Rodo Kenkyukai — a study committee on labour) method at least twice a year. By means of this, a personnel policy with a definite target may be developed.

However beautiful a vision of the development of our business we may have, it will not materialize unless either the spiritual or material happiness of workers is realized through working for the company. If workers improve their lives, their company improves also.

When the vision is seen in the form of an *enterprise development chart* (19) its significance and persuasion grow.

VARIOUS PERSONNEL MANAGEMENT POLICIES TO PROMOTE LABOUR PRODUCTIVITY

Labour management consists of 'give and take' between workers and management. It aims at promoting workers' spiritual and material happiness and asks them for growth in productivity in return.

Workers   **Management**

Spiritual factors:	Patriotism. Love of company Morale. Creativity.
Material factors:	Quality of labour. Quantity of labour. Productivity. Improvement of operation. Cost reduction.

Spiritual factors:	Principle of human repect. Leadership. Communication. Education & training.
Material factors:	High wages. Ample bonuses. Benefits and welfare. Shortening of working hours.

Here are the policies of personnel management to promote increased labour productivity. The following is the table related to the above.

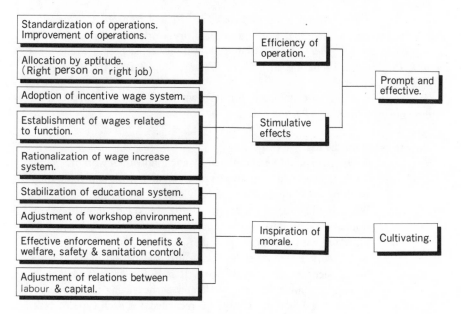

1.   TASK LIST

Purpose

To simplify organization and make it efficient, it is best to develop new organization planning. For the preparatory work we must draw up a *work distribution chart.* To do that, follow three steps: Step 1 Preparing a *task list.* Step 2 Preparing an *activity list* and Step 3 Drawing up a *Work distribution chart.*

A *task list* is not prepared for its own sake, but as a step toward drawing up a *work distribution chart.*

How to make up the list

    a.   A *task list* should be completed by each individual worker.

    b.   Work is classified into two types: Regular work and temporary work or work repeated periodically every few months.

    c.   Work hours must be converted into weekly or monthly work hours, divided into ½-hour units. Any overtime work must be indicated with a coloured pencil.

    d.   Total work hours must be set against the period of daily work hours recorded in a work diary. It is not necessary to include absences, coming late for work and early leaving in the record.

    e.   A task number must always be recorded for each type of task.

Various relations

When a *task list* is prepared, we make an activity list or job description as the secondary step according to the following points:

    a.   A supervisor prepares it.

    b.   Work to be done in a workshop is to be classified into a certain number of activities. In general the activities number approximately seven to 13. The order is decided according to the order of relativity, the number of work hours, the grade of importance, etc.

    c.   Classify jobs function-wise to facilitate the preparation of a flow process chart.

    d.   General business – any important work which cannot be put into any job classification item must be placed where provision has been specially made for it.

    e.   Job in group (subsection) – Some supplementary work to be performed to execute some main work, supply of materials and tools, mutual understanding, daily reports, benefits and welfare and other tasks related to work in the workshop, must all be included.

    f.   Other jobs. Indirect or not directly connected work (for example, work to be done at other workshops or personal work to be performed outside regular work hours) should be included.

(1) Task list (sampling)

Section: Employment section, Name: Jiro Nishikawa Position Clerk (Acting
Personnel Department name: section manager)

Classifi-cation	No.	Content of work	Volume of work	Time	Work evaluation	Activity No.
Regular work	1	Forming & adjustment of supplementary employment project.	Once.	4	A	4
	2	Forming of recruiting project.	Once.	3	A	1
	3	Forming of selection programme	Twice.	2	A	2
	4	Interviewing and selection.	13 times.	5	B	2
	5	Examination of the documents presented by applicants.	For 37 men	2	A	2
	6	Decision on employing applicants (substituted for section manager).	For 12 men.	1	B	2
	7	Substituted duties relating to general employment procedures.		5	B	4
	8	Decisions concerning the kinds of jobs and their initial salaries (substitute duties).	For 5 men.	1	B	3
	9	Explaining employment conditions to new employees.	For 12 men.	1	AB	3
	10	Preparing attendance record and report documents in subsection.	For 7 men.	1	C	5
	11	Workshop Meeting.	Once.	1	B	5
	12	Interviews with visitors and performance of liaison work.	4 times.	4	C	4
	Total.			30		
Special work	1	Making and keeping of records of consumers' cooperative society for employees.	Once.	5	C	6
	2	Issue of office identification cards for general employees and retirement certificates.	7 times.	4	BC	6
	3	Project and study of works specially ordered.	0.5 case.	5	A	4
	Total			14		

Investigation and from 6th July Week Total work Regular work hours (44h) Total (44h)
observation period: to 11th July Month hours: Overtime work hours (0h)

Remark: Activity number column shows activity numbers of the activity list and is filled in when we develop a work distribution chart.

[CHART 83]

2. WORK DISTRIBUTION CHART

Purpose

There are frequent accidents and mistakes; discontent is generalized among the employees; laziness has become common; workers' morale has begun to decline. All these developments are often due to poor or inappropriate *job assignment*. Many of these situations can be prevented by developing a work distribution chart. This is an improved method of allocating jobs and a systematic method of studying organization. In this way, what is going on, who is doing it and how many hours are spent on it can be determined at a glance. We can easily see where there are problems to be dealt with and, by making a single chart, we can study them.

How to draw up the chart

a. Supervisor prepares the chart.

b. We note what is written on the activity list in the job column on the left side of the chart. The *task list* of individual workers, from supervisors to workers are arranged from left to right. Those doing the same job, however, are classified under the same item heading.

c. The task of each worker must be classified and noted in the corresponding activity column.

d. Compute total work hours in each activity.

e. In the case of work such as repairs and security where the main operations at the workshop change extensively every few months, it may be necessary to draw up several charts.

Relations

Organization planning is a deductive method and a work distribution chart is an inductive method with regard to the study of organization. The inductive technique, however, can produce quick and sure results.

How to use the chart

Posing the following six questions we can study the chart which has been developed.

1. IS THERE ANY WASTE IN THE WORK OR OPERATION HOURS? Study jobs classified function-wise by drawing up a flow process chart. Evaluate the jobs classified content-wise according to whether the hours spent on them are reasonable or not.

2. DO WE SPEND TOO MUCH TIME ON UNIMPORTANT OR UNNECESSARY WORK? We should find out and eliminate any work, such as miscellaneous work in the job column, which shouldn't be performed in this workshop (improper means for predetermined objectives).

3. DO YOU EMPLOY ANY PERSONS UNDER OR OVER THEIR

CAPACITY? Evaluating intelligence and skills, we should examine whether we have given workers jobs most suited to them. If we find any inadequately assigned work, we should shift it to the right person. (Specialization of ability and suitability of work.)

4.   LIKE A "JACK OF ALL TRADES", IS THERE ANY PERSON WHO WORKS ON A LARGE NUMBER OF JOBS WHICH ARE NOT RELATED TO EACH OTHER? Is there anybody who does everything such as data gathering and statistics, arrangement and maintenance of reports, typing and shorthand, meeting visitors, etc? We should assign work of the same nature to one person. If possible try to find if there is any room for division of work. (Homogeneous job assignment and division of work.)

5.   ARE TOO MANY EMPLOYEES WORKING ON A SINGLE JOB DIVIDED INTO TOO MANY PARTS? If we let too many workers work on a single job which is minutely divided, it will invite various problems such as contradiction, avoidance of responsibility and excessive interference, (specialization of work = specialized ability).

6.   DO WE ASSIGN WORK EQUALLY TO WORKERS, GIVING CONSIDERATION TO NOT ONLY THE VOLUME OF WORK, BUT ALSO THE QUALITY OF WORK? We should study whether we have made a fair distribution of work according to workers' ability, the urgency of work, the degree of importance and the grade of difficulty (balanced work distribution = reasonable volume of work).

In addition, by means of a *work distribution chart,* we can enhance the interchangeability of jobs and a substitute system of work.

Employment Section, Personnel Department

Job No.	Job	Total man hours	Taro Higashiyama Employment Section Chief	Man hrs.	Jiro Nishikawa Deputy Section Chief	Man hrs.	Saburo Minano Clerk, Research Section	Man hrs.
1	Recruitment	26	Supervises recruitment Accepts labour union demand papers, gives explanations and listens to demands. Liaison work for recruiting	2 2 2	Making of recruiting chart	3	Liaison work for recruiting	9
2	Selection	96	Supervision of selection work. Interview and selection. Decision on employment of applicants.	3 3 2	Development of selection programme Interview and selection. Examination of documents presented by applicants. Decision on employment of applicants when the section manager is absent.	2 5 2 1	Exchanges of opinion with supervisors as to decisions on employment of applicants. Screening of application bio-data and testimonials.	2 15
3	Employment procedures	15	Supervising employment procedures. Deciding jobs and initial pay. Taking the new employees to the places of work.	2 2 2	Explaining working conditions to new employees Deciding jobs and initial pay. (When the section manager is out).	1 1		
4	General employment affairs	126	Supervising general employment operations. Reports to the personnel department manager concerning employment affairs. Various projects and studies. Interviews with visitors and others liaison work. Managers' conference (labour division)	6 2 4 4 1	General employment affairs. Preparation and adjustment of supplementary manning programme Projecting and studying jobs specially asked for by supervisors. Interviews with visitors and other liaison work.	5 4 5 4	On-the-job surveys and reports concerning supplementary manning programme Surveys and reports on matters specially orderd.	7 4
5	Sectional business	19	Guidance of employees. On-the-job conferences.	1 1	Preparation of attendance records and report papers in section. On-the-job conferences.	1 1	Taking change of accounts and maintenance of furniture and equipment. On-the-job conferences.	2 1
6	Other work	26	Handling complaints of general employees concerning personnel management.	5	Preparing and keeping of records on employees' consumers' cooperative society. Issuing office identification cards and retirement certificates to general employees.	5 4	Personal checks and reports on long-time or frequent absentees.	4
	Total	308		44		44		44

Distribution Chart

Shiro Kitada Clerk Statistics	Man hrs.	Hanako Haruno Clerk	Man hrs.	Reiko Natsukawa Clerk.	Man hrs.	Tsukiko Akiyama Typist	Man hrs.
Selection of wording and design for recruiting campaigns.	2					Typing the papers for recruiting campaigns.	3
Liaison work for recruiting campaigns.	3						
Preperation of necessary documents for selection (making drafts.) Keeping in contact with the workshop for technical examinations and providing information to applicants. Keeping in contact with the medical department for physical check-ups and providing information to applicants.	4 7 5	Logistic support to examination of candidates. Accepting applications. Interview and selection. Arrangement documents presented by applicants. Making of lists of various selection results (data for decisions on employment of applicants).	2 2 2 4 3	Completing application forms (Explaining how to fill out the forms) Administering aptitude tests and subject examinations and assessment of results. Assessing selection results from various angles and reporting thereon to section manager Assessment of biodata and testimonials of prospective employees are assessed (by mail).	3 8 3 5	Typing of necessary documents for selection Preparing of interview letters to applicants. Typing tables of various selection results Preparing notification cards for informing applicants of the results of selection	4 4 1 4
Orientation of new employees.	1	Taking new employees to personnel control clerk for the latter to take necessary action.	1			Preparing of employment notification and pay to be delivered to the parties concerned. Preparing of interview letters to prospective employees.	1 4
Preparing of various statistical tables for employment affairs. Intervieviews with visitors.	10 4	Sending out papers, receiving and handing receipts, etc. Filling and keeping of documents related to employment. Checking typed documents.	6 13 8	Collection of various statistical data on employment affairs. Checking typed documents. Mimeographing related documents. Delivery of related documents to parties concerned.	4 5 3 8	Typing documents related to general employment. Cutting of stencil paper.	17 2
Liaison with persons in charge of fire prevention. On-the-job conferences.	1 1	Serving tea to section members. On-the-job conferensces	2 1	Serving tea to section members. On-the job conferences.	2 1	Purchasing requests, arrangements and maintenance of reference books. Serving tea to section members,. On-the-job Conferences.	1 2 1
Sports club meetings concerning interdepartmental games. Making contact with the medical centre concerning periodical physical check-ups for general employees	2 4			Cutting up sensitive paper for use as writing paper.	2		
	44		44		44		44

[CHART 84] 281

3. MASTER MANNING TABLE

Purpose
Financially, employing a worker corresponds to buying expensive machinery. When you are going to purchase machines worth millions, you carefully discuss how to raise the funds and other matters pertaining to depreciation at the directors' meeting.

But when you employ a worker, you act according to the circumstances and necessities of the occasion, without the same consideration and prudence given to capital investment. You cannot expect a new worker to settle down immediately at work. To employ and educate a man and let him settle down at work requires a long-range plan. Personnel projects must be collected in a master sheet as an important link in the chain of long-range management planning.

How to draw up the table
Formulate the project in advance in the following form:
a. A *master manning table* shows how many workers are distributed by (1) department, (2) education and (3) age group over a period of five years.
b. An *age structure graph* to show changes in the age structure of personnel.
   A *five-year education-profile manning sheet* is used to project the changes in the personnel composition over the coming years.

Relations
Devise an employment project and put it into practice as a link in the chain of a long-range personnel plan.

Allowing management to take its natural course (drifting management) and letting employment problems resolve themselves are mismanagement.

How to read and use the table
Once your plan is decided, don't change it casually. Strive to obtain the necessary number of new employees, as originally planned in the *master manning table*. You mustn't leave this important matter to secondary consideration.

282

(3) Master Manning Table

Education	Sex	Age.	Marketing 234	General affairs 49	Engineering 139	Production 329	Laboratory 18
University graduate	Male	over 50	3	1	7	0	2
		50~40	1	1	2	1	1
		40~30	3	3	13	2	0
		30~	6	2	13	4	0
	Female	over 30	0	2	0	0	4
		30~	0	1	2	0	0
High school graduate	Male	over 50	3	7	2	1	0
		50~40	16	3	4	1	0
		40~30	51	5	27	4	1
		30~20	105	11	38	207	3
	Female	over 30	3	6	16	51	0
		30~	31	4	15	33	7
Junior high school graduate	Male	over 50	2	1	0	10	0
		50~40	1	2	0	3	0
		40~30	3	0	2	10	0
		30~20	0	0	0	2	0
	Female	over 30	4	0	0	0	0
		30~	1	0	0	0	0

Present number of personnel ———
Number of personnel in 5 years. ———
Capacity number in 5 years ———

[CHART 85A]

5-Year Education-Profile Manning Sheet

Classified		1980			1981			1982			1983			1984			1985		
		Head office	Factory	Total	Head office	Factory	Total	Head office	Factory	Total	Head office	Factory	Total	Head office	Factory	Total	Head office	Factory	Total
Administrative post		21	73	94	20	80	100	20	90	110	25	90	115	30	95	125	30	100	130
University graduate	Technical	0	51	51	0	55	55	0	60	60	0	60	60	0	70	70	0	70	70
	Clerical	23	0	23	30	40	0	40	0	40	50	0	50	60	0	60	70	0	70
High school graduate	Technical	0	410	410	0	430	430	0	450	450	0	470	470	0	490	490	0	510	510
	Clerical	241	0	241	250	0	250	260	0	260	270	0	270	280	0	280	290	0	290
Junior high school graduate		14	27	41	15	35	50	20	40	60	25	45	70	30	50	80	35	55	90
Total		278	488	766	295	465	760	320	480	800	345	515	960	370	540	910	375	565	960

[CHART 85B]

4. DEPARTMENTAL ORGANIZATION CHART

Purpose

There are four principles of organization, namely, "unity of command", "span of control", "homogeneous job assignment", and "delegation of authority".

A *departmental organization chart* is drawn up in accordance with these principles when an organization is initially established. After it is established, these will become the operating principles to guide the organization.

How to make the chart

The points are as follows:

(1) There is one level above and two or three levels below the key person, making four organizational levels in all.

(2) Concerning the size of rectangles, the key person is the largest and as they range up or down, they get smaller.

(3) Those of the same rank must be shown on the same level.

(4) The staff is usually drawn on the upper right of the chart.

(5) It may seem trifling, but I would suggest drawing thick lines at the base and right side of the rectangle, as box shape, as they will be easy to see and will look attractive.

Relations

An organization chart is a divided structural system of an objective or a target and is also a means to achieve it. For that reason, an organization must change in response to changes in objectives or targets. Frequent changes are troublesome, but rigid organization is worse in the long run.

How to use the chart

In the case of a company *departmental organization chart,* it should be printed and distributed throughout the organization. This will constitute the format of organizational activities. It will also serve as the basis of a target structural organization chart, and also of the establishment of the budget departments, cost centres and other control systems. However, the main purpose of its use is fundamentally organization planning itself.

(4) Departmental Organization Chart, ABC Co., Ltd.

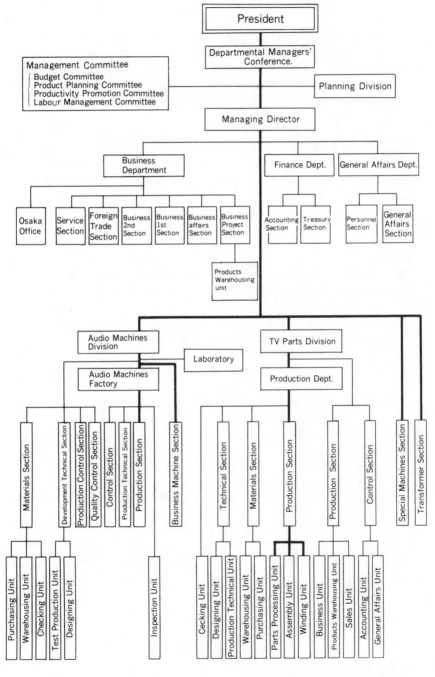

[CHART 86]

5. RECRUITING AND INDUSTRIAL RELATIONS REQUIREMENTS DIAGRAM

Purpose

Recruiting and orientation at work are two sides of the employment coin. It is impossible for either to exist alone. Being conscious of strong ties between recruiting and orientation, the process is depicted in a single chart and continues to proceed with the ideas one by one. This is a carefully planned strategic chart of employment and orientation.

How to make the chart

The industrial relations system may be adequate. However, to obtain good results by new ideas, the personnel section manager should meet and hold an idea promoting conference with those under him. The ideas which appeal to young workers will come from young people and it is important to have promising young workers among the "brain stormers".

Relations

Whatever measures are planned and implemented, we cannot expect good results unless we have central pillars to support them.

The three pillars are:

(1) A long-range management plan must be developed to give the workers a vision of the future.

(2) Management stands on the principle of human respect and a humanistic way of thinking.

(3) It must have excellent leadership and a good training system within industry.

How to use it

As we consider measures for employment and work orientation, colour the circles concerned with a red pencil and put it into practice. This diagram is a relative one and can be changed into a schedule table of the *Gantt chart* type.

The measures can be divided into 3 groups: (1) One-time measures, (2) measures used regularly, and (3) measures used for a long period. When an aim is accomplished, we can strike the corresponding measure off the *Gantt chart*.

(5) Recruiting and Industrial Relations Requirements Diagram

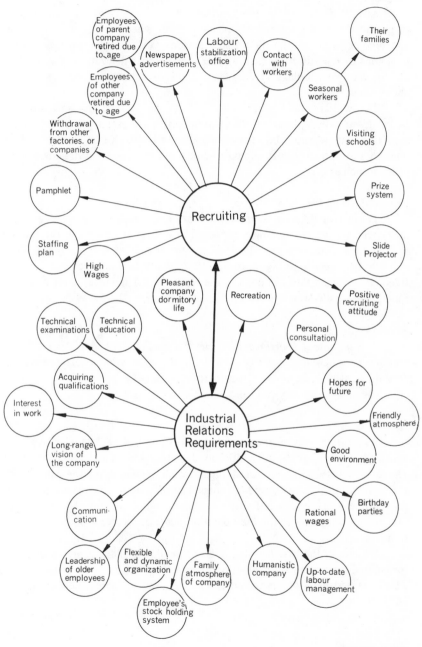

[CHART 87]

6. POSITION ORGANIZATION CHART

Purpose

All the rectangles in the *position organization chart* show positions (a position occupied by a single person), from whom and to whom orders and reports come and go, how many persons work under a supervisor, any omissions or repetitions in each worker's job, proper delegation of authority and so on. We should give members of the organization advice as to the above items.

This will also establish the relations between the lines and staff. Among the staff functions there are those functions such as advising, surveying, assistance and services, but these functions do not give any order to the lines. A *position organization chart* admits and represents an organizational premise such as this.

How to draw up the chart

The actual drawing method is the same as the *departmental organization chart,* but all the rectangles represent positions. The names of those who occupy these positions are added on the lower half of the rectangles. The important point in plotting an organization plan is to unify the classification standard of organizational units in the same level. Therefore, never mix the functional classification on the same organizational level.

Relations

A *departmental organization chart* shows all the departments and sections of a company, while a functional organization chart represents an individual and his work in a department. But this position organization chart has more versatility and can be used in both cases.

How to use it

A *position organization chart* has two uses. One is for analysis in which the present situation is faithfully depicted, probed and studied deeply. The other presents an improved organization system after the probe and study mentioned above, and an organization chart for management to standardize it. Thus one is for the designing and formation of an organization, while the other is for the operation and management of the organization.

Whichever the case may be, once we finalize a chart, it means we have formulated an organization plan. So after getting the approval of superiors, let all the personnel of the company know and post it somewhere conspicuous in the office.

288

(6) Position Organization Chart
First Production Section, Production Dept. of "ABC" Industries, Ltd.

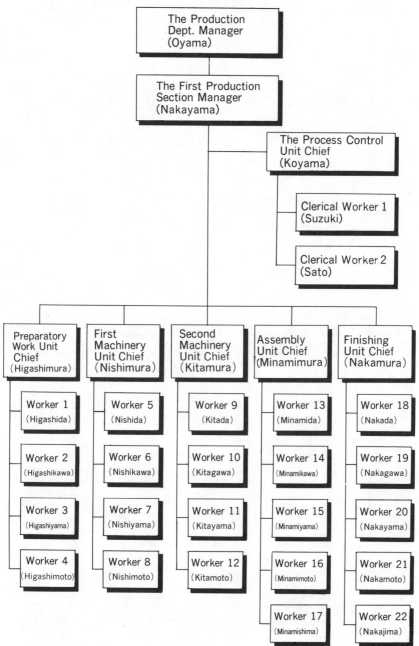

[CHART 88]

(7) Position Standard

Class	Position class	Supervising work	Non-supervising work
I	Primary class employee	None	Performs some auxiliary and apprentice work in departments.
II	Inter-mediate class employee	None	On the basis of knoweledge and experience of general bussiness he handles daily routioe work, but he will never go beyond the level of assistant to senior class employee.
III	Senior class employee	As group leader he sometimes undertakes supervising work, On such occasions he leads and gives orders to some of his men. Usually as leading worker or clerk he is engaged in non-supervisory work	On the basis of knowledge and experience of general business he performs routine work, but not always a definite type of work. He prepares for new job and plans work distribution in the shop.
IV	Primary class staff member	If in the post of group leader, he has ten or more men under him in a workshop and several men in the office. When necessary, he sometimes helps with routine work. He plans and controls the work of his men.	Even though he is not in the position of supervisor, he performs specific and difficult work as follows. (1) Work needs special techniques and knowledge. (2) Work as a whole needs special projects, design and flow of operation. (3) Work which cannot be completed without a creative, spontaneous and positive mind.
V	Inter-mediate class staff member	As middle management, he assists the section manager, and participates in the decision making partaining to their regular work and has authority to direct his subordinate workers.	Though he may not be in the position of unit chief, he does such important, difficult and specific tasks as follows: (1) Work needing high grade technical knowledge. (2) Work of special type needing specified projects, design and setting-up. (3) Work which cannot be completed without creative, spontaneous, positive ideas.
VI	Senior class staff member	He has authority of decision and direction as an employee in a senior management position, He formulates plans, gives directions and performs control on the work of his subordinates so that he can effectively and economically execute all the duties assigned to his section.	Whether in businees or in other operations, he performs regular duties as a section manager as follows: (1) Maintaining cooperation with other departments. (2) Planning effective and economical work of the section. (3) Cost reduction necessary for profitability. (4) Heightening employees' morale.

Classification

Control to be received	Qualification requirements	Representative positions	
Following regular procedures, he handles business under detailed directions.	Needs ability above that of junior high school graduate. Sound mind. Good health.	Business	Business clerk (Class 3)
		Technical	3rd class technical clerk.
		Material	Warehouse clerk (Class 3).
		Production	3rd class operator, production clerk, production staff member.
		Clerical	Apprentice account clerk general clerical worker, general affairs apprentice clerk.
Following regular procedures he handles business under detailed guidance.	Needs ability above that of a high school graduate. Sound mind. Good health.	Business	Assistant business clerk (class 2)
		Technical	Tracer, 2nd class technical clerk.
		Material	Assistant purchasing clerk, assistant materials clerk, 2nd class warehouse clerk.
		Production	2nd class operator, production clerk, production staff member.
		Clerical	Accounting clerk, general affairs clerk, key puncher (2nd class).
For the departmental policy of business procedures. He is given detailed directions and for the method of handling he is given instructions on important points. The results are reported and checked. As a group leader he cannot go beyond these limits.	Actual working experience of 3 years after graduation from junior high school or 1 year after graduation from high school or ability above that of a technical high school graduate, Sound in mind and body	Business	Business clerk, typist, business clerk (1st class).
		Technical	3rd class technician, 1st class technical clerk.
		Material	Purchasing clerk, materials clerk, 1st class warehouse clerk.
		Production	1st class operator, production clerk, production staff member.
		Clerical	Accounting clerk, general affairs clerk, guard, key puncher (1st class), equipment caretaker, operator.
He usually makes decisions on routine work of his men and leads, encourages, and enables them to perform their duties well. But he cannot go beyond the limits of departmental policy. For the results he reports on important matters only and is checked.	Having actual working experience of over 5 years after graduation from junior hihg school, over 2 years after graduation from high school or over 1 year after graduation from university. Sound in mind and body.	Business	Senior Business clerk, business supervisor.
		Technical	Senior technician, 2nd technician, 2nd class designer, technical supervisor.
		Material	Senior purchasing clerk, senior materials clerk, senior warehouse clerk.
		Production	Chief clerk (production, quality control, production engineering subcontructors management, material management).
		Clerical	Senior accounting clerk, senior personnel clerk, senior general affairs clerk, programmer.
He gets directions from department and section managers only on general opertging policy and key points. Gets directions on unusual and important matters. Gets checkups by department and section managers on the correctness of the work he has done.	Having actual working experience of over 8 years after graduation from high school or higher ability. He must have managerial ability as a unit chief. If he has no such ability, he must have expert technical knowledge and a strong sense of responsibility.	Business	Chief, Business Unit.
		Technical	Chief, engineering unit, 1st class technician, 1st class designer.
		Material	Chief, purchasing unit, chief, material unit.
		Production	Unit chief, (production, quality control, production engineering subcontractor's management, material management).
		Clerical	Chief, personnel unit, Chief, general affairs unit, Chief, accounting unit
Gets directions only on general policies and important points. Receive directions only on unusual and important matters. Concerning the quality of his work, results are examined by the departmental manager	This post needs over 10 years work experience after graduation from high school or higher ability. He excels in planning, organizing and leadership and has a strong sense of responsibility. He must have graduated from management training course with satisfactory results.	Business	Business section manager.
		Technical	Engineering section manager.
		Material	Purchasing section manager
		Production	Section manager (production, quality control, production engineering, subcontractor's management material management).
		Clerical	General affairs section manager, accounting section manager.

[CHART 89]   291

7.   STANDARD JOB CLASSIFICATION CHART

Purpose

This is the first step toward rationalization of wages. There may be enterprises which cannot avoid the seniority wage system and traditional wages, but it is the desire of every worker to get equal pay for equal work. To introduce the standard job classification system, all the workers must be graded. The basis for grouping classes is the *Standard job classification chart* shown on preceding pages 290 and 291.

To classify straggling basic wages into six or seven finite classes, we must define each of them clearly so that no doubt will occur as to the classification of positions.

How to make the chart

When the types of business, the forms of enterprises and the sizes of companies differ, the content of work and the ranking of job systems should differ accordingly, and the chart alone cannot satisfy every case. In your company you must draw up a *standard job classification chart* suitable for your own particular company. Therefore, this chart should serve as a general model, so you must draw up a chart to answer the peculiarities of your business.

The point to keep in mind when first introducing standard job classification is to have a system not too contradictory to the existing organized classes of your company.

Relations

After making a *standard job classification* for all the workers, the salaries and wages are decided by the importance, speciality and difficulty of work performed by them.

Besides this, some consideration must be given to personal factors to some extent. This is necessary in Japan due to the practices existing between labour and capital in Japan's industrial world. To incorporate this, a classified wage survey table is employed.

How to use this chart

When we classify all the workers, it is desirable to prepare the job analysis (or *task list*) of all the workers. The contents of all the items in this chart should be analyzed thoroughly to classify the workers.

A task is the classified fragment of an activity, but does not directly recognize workers' ability and talent. If we classify jobs, the problems of promotion and placement of personnel remain to be addressed.

8. PAY-INCREASE STANDARD CURVES DIAGRAM

Purpose

To what degree are we qualified and talented? What degree of effort do we make? What job can we get? If we find out what standard of living will be guaranteed in future, we'll be more motivated in our work. This is the salaried man's way to success.

On the pay-increase standard curves diagram, the classified wages are graduated. According to good or bad marks for work evaluation, workers are placed in grade II at worst and in grade VI at best. Work is rated by job class, while workers are rated by such grades as on the classified wage line.

How to draw up the diagram

First of all, it is important that we know the wage standard of our company, and then we must adjust it.

The programme requires the following four steps:

Step 1 . . .   With the basic wages of the company on the vertical axis and the ages on the horizontal axis, we plot actual wages of employees on the graph and evaluate them according to the model wages (Comparison of actual wages with the model wages, wage market, and standard living costs).

Step 2 . . .   The desirable pay-increase standard line is drawn freehand on a graph. Estimates are made from the standard living costs, wage market and paying ability of enterprise.

Step 3 . . .   Prepare the classified wage table by job classes and personal grades. This pay-increase standard rough line will include and consider the slanting angle of the standard line which calculatively will make both ends meet, adjusted ages, notches of classified wages and work evaluation.

Step 4 . . .   The *pay-increase standard curves* are completed. Now we shall make a master table of classified wage amounts by job classes, and personal grades.

Relations

Standard curves for pay-increase by job classes are products of dialectic evolution between the American job classification system and Japanese wage practices (for example, regular pay-increase system and year-end bonus).

How to use the curves

When the diagram is drawn up, a job classification sheet will be employed. By employing it, we count every one of the workers and their job classification and classified wages will then be decided.

(8) Position Classification-Pay-Increase Standard Curves

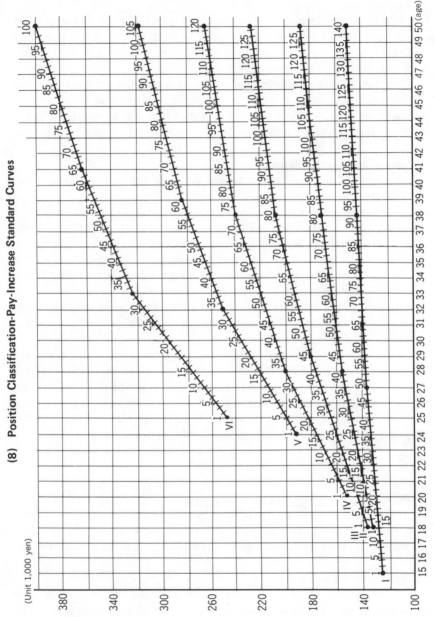

(Unit 1,000 yen)

[CHART 90]

294

9. PERSONAL GRADE ASSESSMENT SHEET BY JOB CLASS

Purpose

When we shift from the old wage system to the new wage system based on the job classification system, it is necessary for us to correct unbalanced conventional wages and change to rational ones.

As a technique to construct this new wage system, we often employ a naked counting system. Ignoring the conventional factors and practices for deciding wages, we can stabilize a wage system based on a completely new concept. For that purpose, a job classification and rating sheet will be employed.

Explanation

Under the new wage system introduced here, an employee's job class will be categorized as explained earlier. The new wage system is the dialectic evolution between the American system and the Japanese conventional (seniority) system, and the next step is to determine the personal grade.

As personal grades are assigned according to the evaluation of the personal factors of workers in each job class and assess their abilities as shown by work results, we use one form for each worker and treat it concretely and objectively on an individual basis.

In rating, plus or minus x, (x = absolute figure) is assigned for personal grade.

Relations

When job classes and personal ratings have been set, the basic wages of workers can be determined by means of the master table of wages. We then put the names concerned on the *standard pay increase curves diagram*.

How to use it

In this example we include personal matters such as (1) education; (2) years of service; and (3) past experience. Next, we assess clearly existing factors of ability of workers such as (4) service efficiency and (5) performance. We then evaluate workers by a points system.

However, we must not overlook the fact that each rating factor has been given a range of weights. Moreover, the weight will differ according to each class. In the sample sheet, Mr Kitajima is a deputy section manager and in the 5th class his weight multiplies each point by 0.1, 0.2, 0.1, 0.2, 0.4. Here, when his wage is found to be the 5th class 57th grade, we can compute his basic wage from the master table of wages and from the pay increase standard curves diagram.

(9) Personal Grade Assessment Sheet by Job Class

Name: Shiro Kitajima	Position to be given:	Class:
Date of entry: 1 April 1976	Deputy Section Manager.	V
Date of birth: 11 November 1955		

		Weight	1	2	3	4	5
Educational career	I	0.1	Junior High School graduate	High School graduate	Technical High school graduate	Junior College graduate	University graduate
	II	0.1					
	III	0.1	2	4	6	⑧	10
	IV	0.1					
	V	⓪.①				0.8	
	VI	0.1					
Years of service	I	0.3	1 year	2 years	3 years	4 years	Over 5 years
	II	0.3					
	III	0.3	2	4	6	8	⑩
	IV	0.2					
	V	⓪.②					2.0
	VI	0.2					
Vocational career (The same line as vocation)	I	0.1	1 year	2 years	3 years	4 years	Over 5 years
	II	0.1					
	III	0.1	2	4	6	8	⑩
	IV	0.1					
	V	⓪.①					1.0
	VI	0.1					
Efficiency rating	I	0.4	Poor	Fair	Good	Excellent	Outstanding
	II	0.4					
	III	0.3	2	4	6	⑧	10
	IV	0.3					
	V	⓪.②				1.6	
	VI	0.1					
Work result	I	0.1	Poor	Fair	Good	Excellent	Outstanding
	II	0.1					
	III	0.2	2	4	⑥	8	10
	IV	0.3					
	V	⓪.④			2.4		
	VI	0.5					

Points	2	2.5	3	3.5	4	4.5	5	5.5	6	6.5	7	7.5	⑧	8.5	9	9.5	10
±Rating	−8	−6	−4	−2	4	+2	+4	+6	+8	+10	+12	+14	+16	+18	+20	+22	+24

Assessed rating	41	Adjusted rating	+16	Final rating	57

Class:	V	Final rating:	57	¥280,300

[CHART 91]

10. INCENTIVES AND PROFIT CORRELATION CHART BY RUCKER PLAN

Purpose

The basic principle of remuneration is to give workers consistent and continuous incentives to guarantee their compensation relative to their joint efforts.

Therefore, in management theory, it is desirable that remuneration be paid in accordance with productivity converted into monetary value. If the productivity (value added) is low, both labour and capital must make every effort to raise it. When productivity grows, it is important to reward the labour sector by raising remuneration. For that purpose the introduction of the *Rucker plan* is desirable.

The *Rucker plan* advocates the unity of destiny between workers and management, placing strong emphasis on the necessity of collaborating efforts of both parties in maximizing the total added value of the entire company.

Instead of being counterproductive, the introduction of a modern technical revolution — new products, new methods, improvement techniques and new management ideas — will promote incentives for the future.

Explanation

The chart shows in three dimensions the mutual relations of value added, wage sources and profits. More concretely speaking, an increase in additional value leads to an increase of profit for both labour and capital as shown in the graph. On both the vertical and horizontal lines, sales amounts are shown in scale. The amount remaining, after subtraction of ¥1.8 million for supplementary materials and ¥3 million for processing expenses for subcontractors from sales, is the added value. (Direct material cost has been already subtracted.) In the chart, "OAA" is the accounting area of the company, while "OBB" is that for the workers.

With a fluctuation of sales volume, this chart will show at a glance how incentive wages will change with increased production, and consequently, how profit will increase or decrease.

Relations

If you use this *Rucker plan* method, together with the job classification system previously mentioned, good results will be obtained. The remaining part of wage sources, excluding basic wages, in the name of additional wages for production, will be settled month by month and soon returned to the pockets of the workers. Needless to say, the fruit of this system is marvelous.

How to use it

This chart should be printed and kept by workers and management. People have doubts if we try to hide the truth. Fair practice by corporate management represents the only path to success.

(10) Incentives & Profit Correlation Chart

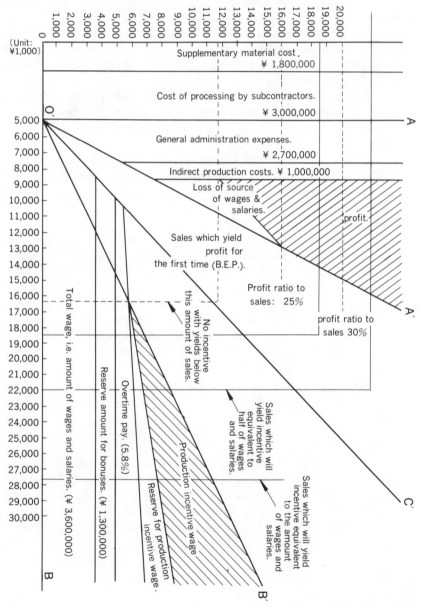

[CHART 92]

11. FUNCTIONAL ORGANIZATION CHART

Purpose

The *departmental organization chart* and the *standard job classification* mentioned previously indicate the position held by the people in an organization, prescribe the relations of command and subordination, and also indicate the routing of reports.

However, the *functional organization chart* also indicates the responsibilities and duties to be carried out by the members of the organization and hence its extent of use is much wider. In other words, by whom in what position in the organization, by whose command and what duty is to be performed, are clearly indicated by this chart.

If this chart is completed, it will be easy to find out how homogeneous work is to be alloted and it can be constantly checked to see whether there is performance failure and/or an overlapping of duties.

How to construct it

It is most desirable to make this chart on the basis of the work distribution chart mentioned previously.

By doing so it will be possible to realize the following:

(1)   Allotment of time to important jobs in order of priority.

(2)   Rationalization of the use of labour.

(3)   Rearrangement of duties in accordance with technical level of employees.

(4)   Elimination of overloading one person with various unrelated jobs.

(5)   Avoidance of excessive division of labour.

(6)   Completion of the *functional organization chart* after elimination of disproportionate job allotment.

The *functional organization chart* can be completed after all jobs are assigned.

Relations

On the basis of the above, the *work area analysis chart* is drawn up.

Although work area analysis is a system of purely logical division of labour, it cannot overstep the scope of practical job assignment.

How to use

The chart should be copied and given to all members of different departments and sections to inform each individual regarding their duties and their organically connected relationship.

Teamwork in the real sense can be generated only when each worker understands the nature of the work, its extent, its speciality and the difficulty of others' jobs.

(11)   Functional · Organization Chart

Ichiro Yokota, Chief, Comptroller Division

1. Plotting long range management plans.
2. Setting overall budget making policy and supervising budget control.
3. Supervising preparation of Financial Statement and cost accounting Reports.
4. Deciding accounting matters of the company.
5. Controlling fund operation.
6. Management analysis and comparison.
7. Supervising and leading the Accounting Section.

Takashi Ohyama, Chief, Accounting Section

1. Plotting profit planning.
2. Making management

1. Plotting profit planning.
2. Preparing and controlling overall budget.
3. Making management comparison and time series comparison with other companies in the same industry.
4. Making a Financial Statement and cost accounting reports.
5. Controlling taxation.
6. Reports to governmental and public offices on accounting matters.
7. Controlling the accounting work of the headquarters.
8. Management of the general affairs of the section.

Takashi Ohyama, Chief, Management Accounting Unit

1. Making of overall budget and controlling business.
2. Management analysis and guidance in making management comparison table with other companies in the same industry.
3. Guidance in preparing cost accounting reports.
4. Budget Variance Analysis.

Mamoru Suzuki, Chief, Accounting Unit

1. Study of balance sheets & Profit & Loss statement of branch offices.
2. Calculation of corporation tax and guidance on business tax, metropolitan and ward taxes, application papers.
3. Guidance in preparing various data on Financial Statement.
4. Guidance in preparing accounting business reports and application papers.
5. Keeping of various books and documents on accounting and control of the Unit.

Yoshimura, Chief, Cost Accounting Unit

1. Checking of the slips from the head office.
2. Supervision of the accounting business of the head office.
3. Development and operation of cost accounting system.
4. Guidance on calculation and Accounting of various cost data.
5. Control of the Unit.

Sadao Maruyama

1. Assistance in planning overall budget.
2. Assistance in preparation of expenditure budget and its control.
3. Preparation of budget and comparative table of actual result.
4. Budget Variance Analysis.

Kiyoshi Nakagawa

1. Preparation and summation of provisional Financial Statement.
2. Preparation of balance sheet and various data.
3. Preparation of business tax and metropolitan tax application papers.
4. Preparation of reports relating to accounting matters.

Hiroko Nakao

1. Detailed check ups of all accounts from head office.
2. Preparation of a table of comparison between the budget and the actual results of the head office.
3. Keeping of the ledger of primary materials.

Ken Uehara

1. Preparation of cost accounting reports.
2. Cost Varience Analysis.
3. Preparation of cost table for comparison with other companies in the same industry.

Tatsuya Kishigami

1. Preparation of various data for B/S & P/L.
2. Preparation of reports on accounting matters.
3. Preparation of month-end overall day programme and details on month-end balance.
4. Assistance with keeping various books and documents relating to accounts.

Jiro Yasuda

1. Keeping of ledger of prime materials.
2. Summation of direct material costs and stock inventory.
3. Summation of direct labour costs.
4. Keeping of various statistics on direct expenses.

Hideo Toyama

1. Calculation of target profit.
2. Preparation of break-even point chart.
3. Summation of branch profit and loss estimates and preparation of chart for analysis of difference between estimates and actual results.

Matsuyo Shirato

1. Preparation of various data for B/S and P/L.
2. Preparation of mid-month overall day schedules.
3. Preparation of overall average balance detailed table.
4. General affairs in the section.

Hanako Haruno

1. Summation of manufacturing expenses.
2. Summation of general administration and selling.
3. Summarizing of daily work reports.
4. Preparation of daily production schedule.
5. Handling of production slips and receipts.

[CHART 93A]

12. WORK AREA ANALYSIS CHART

Purposes

When 'on the job training' is carried out, always bear in mind that 'functional understanding' is one of the principles of learning.

Effectiveness of studies is attained only when the organic relationship between the whole and the part is fully realized and recognized. When work area analysis is conducted, one can learn clearly what one knows and does not know, which is the first step in learning.

How to prepare

First of all, the work area needs to be defined. The attached diagram comprises the total work of the First Sales Section.

The system is made by dividing the total job into blocks, units, jobs, and operations. In this case, the basis of classification should be considered. There are various types of classification: 'purpose-wise', 'function-wise', 'technique-wise', 'equipment-wise', 'area-wise', 'technological process-wise', 'clientele-wise', etc. However, at the same level, it is recommended to employ the same basis of classification.

Relationship

This chart, at first sight, looks very much like the *functional organization chart,* but actually there is a big difference. The *work area analysis chart* is an organization chart for strictly logical work. On the other hand, the *functional organization chart* is an organizational chart for those who take partial charge of a function.

How to use

The purpose of drawing up the *work area analysis chart* is to logically systematize the main themes of job training. For instance, the studies for obtaining a driver's licence include 'actual driving ability', 'laws', 'mechanics of the vehicle', etc. 'Mechanics' deals with engine, oil system, electric ignition system, battery and cooling system, clutch, transmission, etc. Furthermore, 'transmission' is subdivided into 'mechanics', 'disassembly', 'detection of trouble', 'assembly', 'adjustment', etc. Thus, in this manner, the trainee learns systematically and effectively.

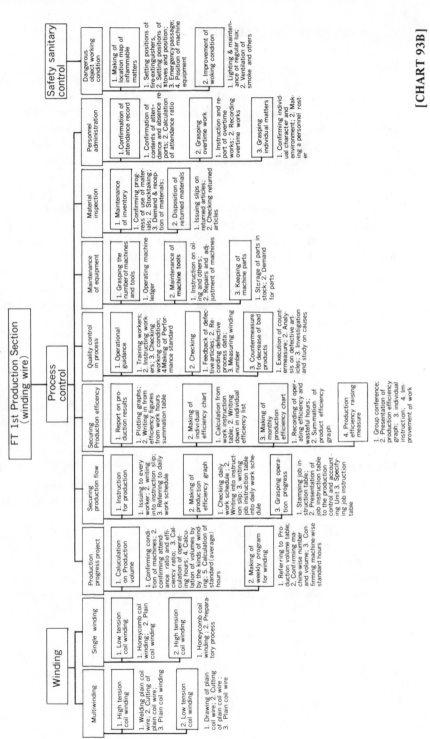

(12) Work Area Analysis Chart

[CHART 93B]

13. TRAINING TIMETABLE

Purpose

Training in a business organization is not merely for education purposes, but is primarily geared to obtain practical results.

For this purpose, it is necessary to identify the training needs. This can be done by the following formula:

$$\text{Training needs} = \text{Volume and Quality Required for present and future work} - \text{Qualitative and Quantitative ability for the present work}$$

For this purpose, the *training timetable* shown here can be used. Its main characteristic is that it is meant not only for making schedules and planning but also for isolating the training needs. The training timetable is used to enhance the ability of workers on a given job rather than for specialized training.

How to construct

Step 1 . . .   First of all, the main subjects of training are to be written from left to right on the upper part of the table. It is recommended that they be arranged in order, progressing from easy to learn to more difficult to learn.

Step 2 . . .   The names of the trainees are to be written in the left column, top to bottom, preferably in order of seniority.

Step 3 . . .   On the cross points of the table of different subjects for each trainee, those subjects that have been already mastered are to be indicated with a check mark.

Step 4 . . .   Those that need not be taught, are to be noted by a dash — mark. In this manner, it can easily be checked which items have not been done by different individuals, and thus the training needs for certain subjects can be found.

Step 5 . . .   The blank columns, remain to indicate training needs, and scheduled dates of completion of training are to be entered.

Relations

This table can be used together with the *training progress chart* (14). For this purpose, at the completion of step 4, the training timetable copies can be used as a *training progress chart* by simply changing the date notations.

How to use

In order to use it as an official training timetable, it is recommended to obtain a signature of approval from a superior. After this, training should be carried out strictly in accordance with the timetable.

(13) Training Time Table

[CHART 94]

Group	Task / Remarks	Junji Ozawa	Sampei Hibi	Masaharu Fugawa	Tomio Watase	Yoshiharu Okutsu	Katsuji Inouye	Tomosaburo Akiyama	Sono Aikawa	Shigeru Shimizu	Kiyoji Watanabe	Makoto Okuyama	Tokuichi Morohashi	Yoshizo Fujimoto
	Remarks (per person)	Served for 12 years	Production control (additional work)	Scheduled to retire at the end of July			Scheduled to be promoted to Class 3 before long				Physically weak			
Transportation	Transportation by hoist	>	>	>	>	>	>	>	6/20	6/20	6/20	6/20	6/20	6/20
	Transportation of trucks	>	>	>	>	>	>	>	>	>	>	>	>	>
	Transportation of subframes	>	>	>	>	>	>	>	6/15	6/20	>	6/15	6/15	6/15
	Transportation of bodies	>	>	>	>	>	>	>	>	>	>	6/11	6/11	6/11
	Transportation of chassis	>	>	>	>	>	>	>	6/7	6/7	6/7	6/10	6/10	6/10
	Transportation of parts	|	|	>	|	>	>	>	>	>	>	>	>	>
Finishing	Cleaning & Clearing	>	>	>	>	>	>	>	>	>	>	5/25	5/25	5/25
	Deburring	>	>	>	>	>	5/16	>	5/16	5/16	5/16	5/16	5/16	5/16
	Sand finishing	>	>	>	>	>	>	5/15	5/15	5/16	5/16	|	|	|
	Grinding finishing	>	>	>	>	>	>	>	5/5	5/5	5/5	|	|	|
	Washing & cleaning	>	>	>	>	>	>	>	>	>	>	5/3	5/3	5/30
Electric wiring	Connection	>	>	4/23	4/23	4/23	4/23	4/23	4/23	>	>	4/23	4/23	4/23
	Placement	>	>	4/20	4/20	4/20	4/20	4/20	4/20	>	>	4/20	4/20	4/20
	Leading electricity from sources	>	>	>	>	>	4/20	4/20	4/20	4/20	4/20	4/20	4/20	4/20
	Basic knowledge of electricity	>	>	>	>	>	>	>	4/20	4/20	4/20	4/20	>	>
Welding & cutting	Oxyacetylene cutting	>	>	>	>	5/17	>	>	5/17	5/17	>	5/17	5/17	5/17
	Electric arc welding	>	>	>	>	>	>	>	>	>	>	>	>	>
Methods: Processing	Prop making	>	>	>	>	4/25	4/25	4/25	4/30	4/30	>	|	|	|
	Boring	>	>	>	>	>	>	>	>	4/16	>	|	|	|
	Bending	>	>	>	>	>	>	>	>	>	>	|	|	|
	Arc welding	>	>	>	>	>	>	>	4/15	4/15	4/15	|	|	|
	Cutting by oxy acetylene cutter	>	>	>	>	>	>	>	>	>	>			
Parts & methods of Installation	Oiling	>	>	>	>	>	>	>	>	>	>	5/10	>	5/10
	Adjusting	>	>	>	>	>	>	>	>	>	>	5/10	>	5/10
	Assembling & fixing	>	>	>	>	>	>	>	>	>	>	5/7	5/7	5/7
	Welding	>	>	>	>	>	>	>	>	>	>	5/10	>	>
	Bolt fastening	>	>	>	>	>	>	>	>	>	>	5/3	5/3	5/3
	Removing	>	>	>	>	>	>	>	>	>	>	5/1	5/1	5/1
	Operating method	>	>	>	>	>	>	>	>	>	>	4/15	4/15	4/15
Structure	Body	>	>	>	>	>	>	>	>	>	>	4/10	4/10	4/10
	Cylinder	>	>	>	>	>	>	>	>	>	>	4/8	4/8	4/8
	Operating lever	>	>	>	>	>	>	>	>	>	>	4/6	4/6	4/6
	PTO.	>	>	>	>	>	>	>	>	>	>	4/6	4/6	4/6
	Subframe	>	>	>	>	>	>	>	>	>	>	4/5	4/5	4/5
Production control	Delivery work	|	>	>	4/12	|	|	|	|	|	4/12	|	|	|
	Progress control	|	>	>	4/10	|	|	|	|	|	4/10	|	|	|
	Routing & reception of parts	|	>	>	4/1	|	|	|	|	|	4/1	|	|	|
	Keeping of pro-trol charts		>	>	4/1	|	|	|	|	|	4/1	|	|	|
Operational group / Unit	Unit	4	4	4	3	2	2	2	2	2	2	1	1	1
	Number	1.	2.	3.	4.	5.	6.	7.	8.	9.	10.	11.	12.	13.

Proposition classification

Legend: > = Finished learning | = no need for further learning 4/10 = prospective date for completing training.

14.   TRAINING PROGRESS CHART

Purpose

After ascertaining the necessary points of training according to the training timetable, it is necessary only to implement the training programme. However, in contrast with the manufacture of products, the training of personnel (particularly when it concerns the job itself) is difficult to confirm with data how much progress has been made.

Due to such problems, there is a need to make entries and keep records to show progress in training. The training progress chart is designed for this purpose.

How to construct

It is made identical to the *training timetable* through Step 4. Wording of the training columns, entering of names of trainees and the method of indicating the particular training by entering a $\sqrt{}$ mark and noting the training that is not applicable with a − mark, are as shown for the *training timetable*. (The difference is that in the *training progress chart*, the indication is □ instead of $\sqrt{}$, and X instead of −). The extent of training progress can now be recorded. In this case, on-the-job training consists of the following 5 steps and the symbols mentioned below are to be employed according to the progress made.

Step 1	Preparation	:
Step 2	Presentation	I
Step 3	Application	L
Step 4	Examination	U
Step 5	Discussion	□

Relations

Managers and supervisors are those who accomplish jobs through the efforts of subordinates. Therefore, the advancement of production efficiency of the subordinates through training is one of their most important duties. Today's business, therefore, require managers who perform the role of trainers.

How to use

This table is designed to be used by managers/training instructors for control of their training activity but, if necessary, it can be shown to all subordinates and be used as a stimulus for attaining the targeted aims.

(14) Training Progress Chart

[CHART 95]

Operation group	Position classification	1 Junji Ozawa (4)	2 Sampei Hibi (4)	3 Masaharu Fugawa (4)	4 Tomio Watase (3)	5 Yoshiharu Okutsu (2)	6 Katsuji Inouye (2)	7 Tomosaburo Akiyama (2)	8 Sono Aikawa (2)	9 Shigeru Shimizu (2)	10 Kiyoji Watanabe (2)	11 Makoto Okuyama (1)	12 Tokuishi Morihashi (1)	13 Yoshizo Fujimoto (1)	Remarks
Transportation	Transportation by hoist.														Served for 12 years.
	Transportation of trucks.														Production control (additional work)
	Transportation of subframes.														Scheduled to retire at the end of July.
	Transportation of bodies.														
	Transportation of chasssis.														Scheduled to be promoted to Class 3 before long.
	Transportation of parts.	×	×		×										
Finishing	Cleaning & clearing														
	Deburring														
	Sand finishing										×	×	×		
	Grinding finishing.										×	×	×		Physically weak.
	Washing & cleaning.														
Electric wiring	How to bind wires.														
	How to connect wires.														
	How to lead in electricity from its source.														
	Basic knowledge of electricity.														
Arc welding and cutting	Oxyacetylene cutting.														
	Electric arc welding														
Processing methods	Prop making.										×	×	×		
	Boring.										×	×	×		
	Bending.										×	×	×		
	Arc welding.										×	×	×		
	Cutting by oxyacetylene cutter.										×	×	×		
Parts & their fixing methods	Oiling.														
	Adjusting.														
	Assembling & fixing.														
	Welding.														
	Bolt fastening.														
	Removing.														
Structure	Operating method.														
	Body														
	Cylinder.														
	Operating lever.														
	PTO.														
	Subframe.														
Production control	Delivery work.	×				×	×	×	×	×		×	×	×	
	Progress control.	×				×	×	×	×	×		×	×	×	
	Routing & reception of parts.	×				×	×	×	×			×	×	×	
	Keeping of Pro-trol charts.	×	×			×	×	×	×	×		×	×	×	

15. DELEGATION OF AUTHORITY CHART

Purpose

In recent times, bureaucratically dominant-type leaders, managing on the basis of complex company rules and regulations, are in vogue. It is known that when this manner of business administration escalates and reaches the extreme, it breeds bureaucratic evils.

Leaders today also know that even if organizational manuals are compiled and the rules of authority are worked out, they tend to be very complicated by an abundance of juridical terms. Consequently such manuals and regulations are rarely referred to in actual work. The activities of present-day business are possibly too dynamic and fluid, with many exceptions to rules, so that rigid regulations are not of much use in actual business. However, manuals and rules are the norms for company activity and cannot be totally eliminated.

This chart will prove helpful in simplifying responsibilities.

How to construct

This chart shows how the delegation of authority is carried out in practice. First, at the top of the chart is shown the positions of the persons in the firm and from top, left down, are listed the duties of top management. Then, in the appropriate columns of the table, the type of authority to be exercised by each individual is marked with the abbreviated symbol shown at the bottom of the page. For instance, those with authority of participation in planning, authority of planning, authority of assessment and checking, authority of decision, authority for approving and authority of execution and control, are entered with the appropriate symbols. However, the last-mentioned authority is actually nominal and in practice it shows responsibility in the line of authority for the implementation of the project.

Relations

When such a table is made, a lengthy organizational handbook is not required, and legal experts become unnecessary for handling everyday organizational activities. 'Management by objectives' helps to minimize bureaucracy and eliminate a false sense of sphere of influence that is not to be encroached upon.

How to use

This table should be distributed to all concerned. Each should then mark off the appropriate columns with red or blue pencil and place the table on his desk for daily guidance.

(15) Delegation of Authority Chart

Positions (column numbers):
1. Board of Directors
2. President, Vice President
3. Managing Directors Meeting
4. Representative Managing Director
5. Management Planning Committee
6. Labour Management Committee
7. Chief, Management Analysis Section
8. Sales Meeting
9. Containers Control Committee
10. Business Department Manager, Deputy Manager
11. Business Branch Manager
12. Saitama Plant Manager, Deputy Manager
13. Administration Department Manager, Deputy Manager
14. Administration Section Manager
15. Accounting Section Manager
16. Containers Section Manager

Classification	No.	Item to be decided	1	2	3	4	5	6	7	8	9	10	11	12	13	14	15	16
Management in general	1	Long-range basic policy	–	AP	D	EX	P	–	PP	–	–	PP	–	PP	PP	–	–	–
	2	Long-range management planning	–	AP	D	EX	P	–	PP	–	–	PP	–	PP	PP	–	–	–
	3	New enterprise project	D	EX	P	PP	AS	–	PP	–	–	P	–	PP	P	–	PP	P
	4	Equipment planning	–	AP	D	EX	AS	–	P	–	–	P	P	P	P	P	P	P
	5	Profit planning (calculation of target profit)	–	AP	D	EX	AS	–	P	–	–	PP	PP	PP	EX	PP	PP	PP
	6	Budget formulation and budget control	–	–	AP	D	–	–	PP	–	–	PP	–	–	EX	–	P	PP
	7	Organization planning	D	PP	AS	PP	–	–	–	–	–	PP	–	–	P	–	–	–
	8	Stocks	D	–	AS	EX	AS	–	–	–	–	–	–	–	EX	–	PP	–
	9	Law suits	D	–	AS	P	–	–	–	–	–	–	–	–	P	–	–	PP
	10	Overall management statistics	–	AP	–	D	AS	–	P	–	–	PP	–	PP	EX	–	PP	–
	11	Establishment and utilization of report control system	–	AP	–	D	AS	–	P	–	–	PP	–	PP	EX	PP	PP	–
	12	Items concerted with related companies	AP	D	AS	EX	–	–	–	–	–	PP	PP	PP	PP	–	–	–
	13	Liaison with the industry	–	AP	D	EX	–	–	–	–	–	PP	PP	–	EX	–	–	PP
	14	Liaison with taxation offices and National Taxation Agency	–	AP	–	D	–	–	–	–	–	–	–	–	EX	–	P	–
	15	Liaison with labour standards offices and other labour organs	–	AP	–	D	–	AS	–	–	–	P	–	PP	EX	P	–	PP
	16	Liaison with controlling government offices	–	AP	–	D	–	–	–	–	–	P	PP	PP	EX	–	–	–
Finance	1	Fund operating plans	–	D	AP	EX	–	–	–	–	–	PP	PP	PP	AS	–	P	–
	2	Short-range financial results accounting (monthly profit and loss statement)	–	AP	–	D	–	–	AS	PP	–	PP	PP	PP	EX	EX	PP	PP
	3	Preparation of financial statements	–	AP	–	D	–	–	AS	PP	–	–	–	–	EX	EX	PP	–
	4	Analysis of financial statements	–	–	AP	D	AS	–	PP	PP	–	PP	PP	PP	EX	EX	PP	PP
	5	Calculation of product-wise marginal profits	–	–	AP	D	AS	–	PP	PP	–	P	–	–	AS	–	P	–
Marketing and Sales	1	Demand forecast	–	–	AP	D	AS	–	PP	PP	–	PP	PP	–	EX	–	–	–
	2	Sales analysis (by section and branch officers)	–	–	–	AP	–	–	AS	–	–	PP	P	–	EX	–	PP	–
	3	Sales analysis (overall)	–	–	AP	D	AS	–	P	–	–	PP	PP	–	EX	–	PP	–
	4	Product mix	–	AP	D	EX	AS	–	PP	P	–	P	–	–	–	–	PP	–
	5	Setting sales target	–	AP	D	EX	AS	–	P	P	–	P	PP	–	–	–	PP	–
	6	Fixing the amounts of sales quotas	–	–	AP	D	AS	–	PP	PP	–	P/EX	PP	–	–	–	–	PP
	7	Selling prices of chief products	–	AP	D	EX	AS	–	–	–	–	P	PP	PP	–	–	–	–

			–	AP	D	EX	AS	–	–	–	–	–	P	PP	PP	PP	–
Marketing and Sales (Cont'd)	8.	Product development (deciding new products)	–	AP	D	EX	AS	–	–	–	–	–	P	PP	PP	PP	–
	9.	Distribution channels (establishment of sales network)	–	AP	D	EX	AS	–	–	–	–	–	P	PP	PP	PP	–
	10.	Rationalization of delivery charges	–	AP	D	EX	AS	PP	–	–	–	–	P	PP	PP	–	PP
	11.	Advertisement and publicity	–	AP	D	EX	–	AS	–	–	–	–	P	PP	PP	–	PP
	12.	Comparison of sales results by branch offices	–	–	AP	D	–	AS	–	–	–	–	PP	–	–	–	PP
	13.	Credit sales control (including credit research)	–	–	–	AP	–	AS	–	–	–	–	D	P/EX	–	–	PP
	14.	Preparation of sales statistics	–	AP	–	D	AS	PP	–	–	–	–	P/EX	PP	–	–	–
	15.	Handling dead stock	–	AP	–	D	–	–	–	–	–	–	P/EX	P	–	–	PP
Purchasing	1.	Monthly purchasing plan	–	AP	–	D	–	–	–	–	–	–	P/EX	PP	PP	–	PP
	2.	Deciding on the companies to purchase from (vendors)	–	AP	D	AS	–	AS	–	–	–	–	P/EX	PP	PP	P	–
	3.	Unit price of purchases (principal articles)	–	–	AP	D	–	AS	–	–	–	–	P/EX	PP	PP	P	–
	4.	Value analysis	–	AP	D	AS	–	PP	–	–	–	–	P/EX	PP	PP	P	–
	5.	Giving orders (purchasing in large quantity)	–	–	–	AP	–	–	–	–	–	–	D/EX	P/EX	P/EX	P	–
	6.	Expediting delivery (purchasing in large quantity)	–	–	–	–	–	–	–	–	–	–	AP	D/EX	D/EX	EX	P
	7.	Preparation of purchasing statistics	–	AP	–	D	–	AS	–	–	–	–	P/EX	PP	PP	PP	–
Labour and personnel	1.	Basic labour policy	–	AP	D	EX	AS	–	–	–	–	–	PP	–	P	PP	PP
	2.	Various labour management plans	–	AP	D	EX	AS	–	–	–	–	–	–	–	P	PP	–
	3.	Various problems between labour and capital	–	AP	D	EX	AS	–	–	–	–	–	–	–	P	PP	–
	4.	Deciding the source of salaries and wages	–	AP	D	EX	AS	PP	–	–	–	–	–	–	P	PP	PP
	5.	Wage and salary systems	–	AP	D	D	AS	–	–	–	–	–	–	–	EX	P	–
	6.	Wage and salary levels	–	AP	D	EX	AS	PP	–	–	–	–	–	–	PP	PP	–
	7.	Recruiting plans	–	AP	D	EX	AS	–	–	–	–	–	PP	PP	P	PP	PP
	8.	Placement plans	–	AP	D	EX	AS	–	–	–	–	–	PP	–	P	PP	–
	9.	Working regulations	–	AP	D	EX	AS	–	–	–	–	–	PP	PP	PP	P	–
	10.	Performance rating (above the section managers)	–	AP	D	P/EX	–	–	–	–	–	–	PP	–	–	–	–
	11.	Wages and salaries above those of section managers	–	AP	D	P/EX	–	–	–	–	–	–	P	P	P/EX	P/EX	P
	12.	Wages and salaries below those of section managers	–	AP	D	D	P	AS	–	–	–	–	P	P	P	P	P
	13.	Transfer of personnel above the level of section manager	–	AP	D	P/EX	–	–	–	–	–	–	PP	–	–	–	–
	14.	Education and training programmes	–	AP	D	D	PP	–	–	–	–	–	PP	PP	EX	EX	–
	15.	Benefit and welfare projects	–	AP	D	–	AS	–	–	–	–	–	PP	–	EX	EX	–
	16.	Preparation of labour statistics	–	–	AP	AP	AS	PP	–	–	–	–	PP	PP	P	–	–
	17.	Company regulations	–	–	–	AP	AS	P	–	–	–	–	PP	PP	D/EX	D/EX	PP
	18.	Book control	–	–	–	AP	AS	P	–	–	–	–	PP	PP	D/EX	D/EX	PP
	19.	Various office management systems	–	–	–	AP	AS	P	–	–	–	–	PP	PP	D/EX	PP	PP

Authority to participate in planning . . . . PP
Authority of drafting and planning . . . . P

Authority to participate in planning . . . . PP
Authority of decision . . . . D

Authority of drafting and planning . . . . P
Authority of approval . . . . AP

Authority of assessment and inspection . . . . AS
Authority of execution and control . . . . EX

[CHART 96]

309

16.   PERFORMANCE EVALUATION FORMS AND CARDS

Purpose

It is difficult for a person to judge or evaluate another human being. Regarding the theory and method of performance rating, there are divergent views and no decisive definition. However, if things are taken too seriously, one dares not risk anything and the result is that plans are only envisaged but not carried out.

There are quite a number of methods for a performance rating system, among which are:

1. Output registration method
2. Periodic checks method
3. Attendance record method
4. Ranking according to results method
5. Comparison method
6. Marking results method
7. Distribution limitation method
8. Graphic ratings method
9. Personal specification method
10. Evaluation of standard performance method
11. Business reported method
12. Multi-item evaluation method

All these have their merits and drawbacks, but the method introduced here is truly a rational one which is a blend of the merits of marking results method, the Probst method and graphic ratings method.

How to construct

Performance evaluation forms and *cards* are interrelated with each other, but each is designed for a different purpose. The first is a sheet of paper, while the latter consists of a slightly thicker type of paper. Such forms should be printed beforehand.

Depending on the type of work performed and the position of those who are to be evaluated, even in the same company, several forms may be made for various purposes.

First of all, entries are made on the evaluation forms and then posted on the cards. This should be done within as short a period as possible. In this company, this is done once every two months.

Relations

The important thing in the system of performance rating is that there should be sufficient preparation and training in order to prevent possible distortion of rating by those who make the evaluation. In particular, efforts should be made to be aware of and eliminate:

1. The tendency to be lenient

2. The tendency to concentrate
3. The tendency to disperse
4. The tendency to be strict
5. The 'halo' effect
6. Dialectical errors

How to use

Performance evaluation forms and *cards* are intended for evaluation of results themselves.

This aim consists of:

a. justification for wage raises and advancement
b. training of subordinates
c. references for appropriate placement
d. decisions concerning the right amount to be given as bonus

(16A) Performance Evaluation Form

18th, December 1985

For supervisors

Name: Shiro Kitajime	34 years old	Section: the 3rd Production Section	Position: Deputy section manager	Basic salary: ¥74,800 per month		
Classifi- cation	No.	Evaluation factors	Remarks	Marks	Weight- ing	Points
Achievements	1	Work results	Management effectiveness—whether skillfully employing the management techniques acquired at MTP and bringing about good results.	4	4	16
	2	Leadership	Understanding of the nature of his men, trust and respect from them and effectiveness of organization of section.	5	4	30
	3	Development	Whether he is skillfully leading and developing his men. Whether he is good at fostering his men's talents. Whether his training technique is good.	4	2	8
	4	Team work	Whether all the members of the organization are cooperating with each other. Whether the members are factious. Is morale high?	5	2	10
	5	Planning	Whether he spends enough time plotting plans. Whether he acts after giving matters due consideration. Are his plans of high quality and practical use?	3	2	6
	6	Improvement	Whether he is handling every matter constantly with a desire to effect improvement. Whether he has implemented improvement projects and got good results from them.	3	2	6
	7	Promotion of sales	Whether he is obtaining business from new customers or not. Whether he is skillfull at selecting subcontractors and purchasers and is proceeding with business favourably.	4	2	8
	8	Reduction of operating cost	Whether he has taught his men the real meaning of production cost. Has the production cost actually come down? Are there any actual results from his cost reduction programme?	5	2	10
Ability	1	Knowledge of work	Whether he has good knowledge of management and organisation. Whether he has enough knowledge of his own and his men's work.	5	3	15
	2	Guidance	Is he fond of teaching? Is he keen on education?	4	2	8
	3	Leadership	Is he capable and motivated to lead all his men?	5	3	15
	4	Labour management ability	Does he handle his men skillfully? Is he good at setting problems? Does he criticize his men wisely?	5	2	10
	5	Negotiating ability	Is he sociable? Is he persuasive? Is he reliable?	4	2	8
	6	Planning ability	Is he capable of plotting projects? Is he good at plotting projects?	3	3	9
	7	Will to work	Has he will to work? Can he get over difficulties? Has he got the courage of his convictions?	5	3	15
	8	Creative ideas	Is he always conscious of problems? Is he spontaneous? Has he creative ideas?	3	2	6

Points: Full mark = 200 points.　　　　Total points: 170. Rated by Ichiro Minamishima, signed.

[CHART 97A]

(16B) Performance Evaluation Card with RADAR Charts

name:	Age:	Section:	Position:	For supervisors
Shiro Kitajima	34	the 3rd Production Section	Deputy Section Manager	Basic salary: ¥174,800

October, 1985

(Work results chart)

Management effectiveness — Leadership — Development — Team work — Success or failure of planning — Improvement — Promotion of sales — Cost reduction.

(Ability chart)

Knowledge of work — Guidance — Leadership — Labour management ability — Negotiating ability — Planning ability — Will to work — Creative ideas

Special items

- Are there any striking signs of improvement in overall points as a supervisor.

- Through good team work he has reduced consumption of secondary materials by 25%. This is a meritorious achievement on the part of the deputy section manager.

- His planning ability is still weak. He acts before he plans. Moreover, he lacks ideas.

- His leadership for the group of worker is distinct and outstanding relative to all the supervisors in the Production Department.

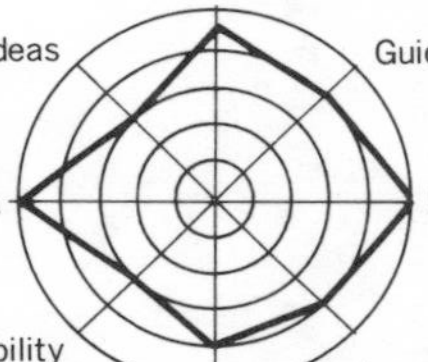

December, 1985

(Work results chart)

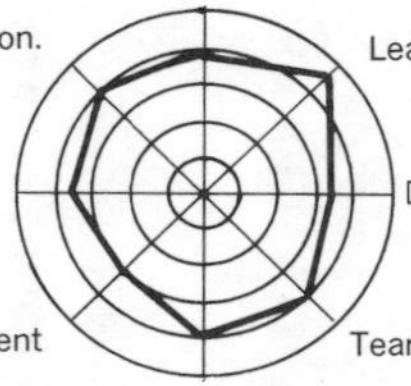

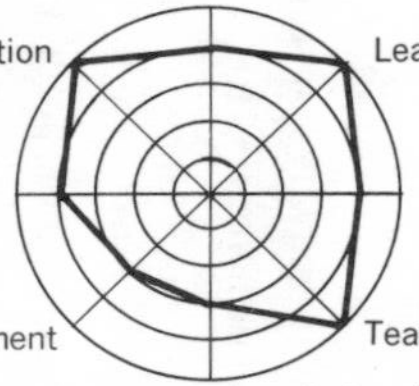

Management effectiveness — Leadership — Development — Team work — Success or failure of planning — Improvement — Promotion of sales — Cost reduction

(Ability chart)

Knowledge of work — Guidance — Leadership — Labour management ability — Negotiating ability — Planning ability — Will to work — Creative ideas

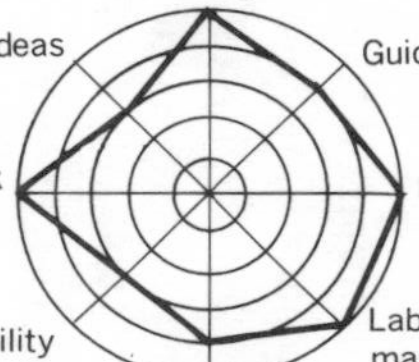

[CHART 97B]

313

17. MANAGERIAL GRID (SELF-EVALUATION SHEETS FOR MANAGERS)

Purpose

The core of modern managerial ideas is management by objectives. This means that each worker is given an objective in accordance with the company objective and allowed leeway or discretionary power to make decisions and thus he takes responsibility for results and can practice self-control to reach the set objective.

When an organization or system is made in accordance with this new approach, the way of thinking, the character (personality) and the ability of the managers in the various positions play an important role. Accordingly, a former professor of Texas University, R.R. Blake, suggested making a managerial grid by which all managers perform self-appraisal in promoting management by means of objectives. According to Blake, the manager should fundamentally have basic concern regarding two fundamental matters. One is concern for production and the other is concern for people. If the former is expressed with a horizontal line and the latter vertically and the degree of the concern is scaled from 1 to 9, it will yield a grid-like pattern. Blake called this a managerical grid and by combining the horizontal and vertical scales, five types of typical managerial images are obtained and vertical scales, five types of typical managerial images are obtained. This is shown in chart 17-B.

In the system of management by objectives, the most desirable combination is type 9-9. All managers should set this as their goal and accordingly should devote themselves to self-enlightenment and engage in self-training.

The method of self-appraisal

Notations should be made in Tests I and II. First of all you should become thoroughly familiar with the contents of Test I a, b, c, d, and e and write in parenthesis ( ) the figures 1, 2, 3, 4 and 5, starting with the item most appropriate to yourself. In Test II, put a O mark in the most appropriate items in each element. In each element there should be only one O mark respectively.

(17A)   WHAT KIND OF A MANAGER ARE YOU?

Test I

(   ) a   Listen to others' decisions. Consent to the views, attitudes and ideas of others, or avoid taking sides. If there is a conflict, try to be neutral or take the position of an observer. By being neutral, avoid becoming emotional. My character is regarded by others as being subtle (weak, vague).

[CHART 98A]

314

(   ) b   Highly evaluate the desire to work smoothly with others. Prefer to adopt the views, attitudes and ideas of others rather than insist on my own. Try not to make conflicts, but once there is a conflict, try to calm emotions and make efforts to reconcile. If, through disputes, feelings of indignation occur, try to make efforts to suppress my feelings. Aim to work smoothly with others. If there is tension, try to evade serious problems.

(   ) c   Highly evaluate decision making, if I think I am right. Even if the feelings of others are hurt, insist on my views, ideas and way of thinking. If there is a conflict, try to stop it by all means or try to enforce my own opinion. If things do not go smoothly, I get irritated. My character is straightforward.

(   ) d   Seek to make decisions which are practical although they may not be perfect. If there are different views, ideas and approaches, I try to take a neutral position (the third person attitude). If there is a conflict, I try to be fair and to achieve a just solution. Rarely become upset (or rarely lose my temper) except on rare occasions, but if things do not go smoothly, there is a tendency to become irritated. I have a tendency to run through my ideas and make an approach.

(   ) e   Highly evaluate sound and original settlements which bring about understanding and agreement. Try to seek and listen to different views, ideas, and approaches. Although I may possess a clear-cut conviction, I still respect the sound ideas of others to the point of altering my own way of thinking. If there is a conflict, I try to find out the reasons and settle it at the source. Even if provoked, I rarely become upset. Can adapt myself to circumstances. Even under stress, do not lose my sense of humour.

Test II

Element 1   **Decisions**

(   ) a 1   Respect the decision of others.

(   ) b 1   Highly evaluate smooth working relationships with others.

(   ) c 1   Highly evaluate my decisions if I think I am right.

(   ) d 1   Seek a solution to problems laying stress on practical possibilities although they may not make a perfect solution.

(   ) e 1   Highly evaluate decisions which are sound and original and which bring about the consent and understanding of all.

[CHART 98A – continued]

Element 2 **Conviction**

( ) a 2 Follow others' views, approaches and ideas, or avoid taking sides.

( ) b 2 Prefer to adopt the views, ideas and the way of thinking of others rather than insist on my own.

( ) c 2 Even if the feelings of others are hurt, I insist on my own views, way of thinking and ideas.

( ) d 2 If different views, approaches and ideas are aired, I try to adopt a neutral position (third person attitude).

( ) e 2 Try to seek and listen to different views, ideas and ways of thinking although possessing clear-cut convictions, I still respect the sound ideas of others.

Element 3 **Conflict**

( ) a 3 If there is a conflict, I take a neutral position or the attitude of an observer.

( ) b 3 I try not to start conflicts and if there is a conflict, I try to smooth feelings and seek an amicable settlement.

( ) c 3 If a conflict occurs, I try to stop it forcibly, or force my own approach on the parties concerned.

( ) d 3 If a conflict arises, I try to reach a fair, just, and sound solution.

( ) e 3 If a conflict arises, I try to find the causes and eliminate it at source.

Element 4 **Emotions**

( ) a 4 By adopting a neutral position, I rarely become upset.

( ) b 4 If I feel indignant as a result of a dispute, I make efforts to suppress my feelings.

( ) c 4 If things do not go smoothly, I become irritated.

( ) d 4 Rarely become upset, but if things do not go smoothly, I have a tendency to be irritated.

( ) e 4 Even if provoked, I rarely become upset.

Element 5 **Disposition**

( ) a 5 My disposition is regarded as subtle by others.

( ) b 5 My disposition enables me to work smoothly with others. If there is tension, I try to evade the serious issues.

( ) c 5 My disposition is straightforward.

( ) d 5 My disposition is such that I try to transmit my views or my approach to others.

( ) e 5 Can adapt to different situations. Even under stress, do not forget my sense of humour.

[CHART 98A – continued]

Example
Test Answers

Test I a—type 1.1 b—type 1.9 c—type 9.1
        d—type 5.5 e—type 9.9
Test II In the order a, b, c, d and e of each element,
         1.1, 1.9, 9.1, 5.5, 9.9, in order.

(17B) Blake's Managerial Grid

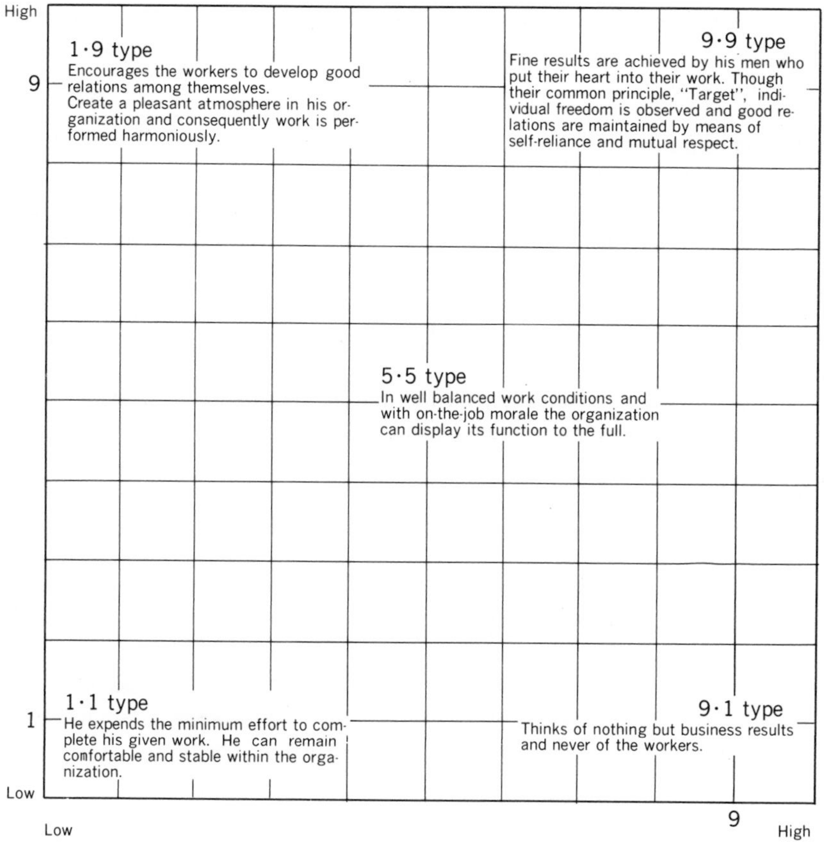

High

1·9 type
Encourages the workers to develop good
relations among themselves.
Create a pleasant atmosphere in his organization and consequently work is performed harmoniously.

9·9 type
Fine results are achieved by his men who
put their heart into their work. Though
their common principle, "Target", individual freedom is observed and good relations are maintained by means of
self-reliance and mutual respect.

9

5·5 type
In well balanced work conditions and
with on-the-job morale the organization
can display its function to the full.

1·1 type
He expends the minimum effort to complete his given work. He can remain
comfortable and stable within the organization.

9·1 type
Thinks of nothing but business results
and never of the workers.

1

Low

Low   9   High

Concern for production

Concern for work results.

1-1 type ·········· Unsuitable as manager (Irresponsible type).
1-9 type ·········· Undesirable manager (Cheerleader type).
5-5 type ·········· Practical type of manager (Compromising type).
9-1 type ·········· A work results priority type of manager (Authoritarian type).
9-9 type ·········· The most desirable type of manager (Ideal type).

[CHART 98B]

18. MORALE SURVEY FORM (NRK SYSTEM)

Purpose
The prescription for success in an enterprise lies, first of all, in giving employees the desire to work. To this end, what can be done so that an employee can feel at ease and have the will to do a job? To answer this, it is imperative to know exactly what employees grievances are and what they entail. In line with opinions given, appropriate reforms should be carried out. These complaints usually cannot be heard through the organization of the office and therefore it is recommended to use the following *morale survey form* which is to be passed around among the employees and filled in. The NRK system of morale survey, as a method for labour analysis is used throughout Japan.

Method of putting into operation
This survey can be completed in about 50 minutes.
1. First of all, the survey forms are given to employees who are requested to fill them in. (Answers are to be given marking with O one of three alternatives given.) Employees' names are not requested and therefore frank views may be given. These forms are then to be collected as soon as the answers are written in.
2. After the forms are filled in, the answers are to be collated.
3. The results are entered into the diagnosis sheet.

Various relations
A morale survey is similar to a physical check-up at the office and has the following two effects:
1) The employees can air their views and their complaints and thereby ease feelings of tension. The survey itself serves as a measure for solving labour problems.
2) On the basis of diagnosis, corrective measures can be taken.

As a result, the atmosphere in the office or at the work site is improved, the will to work is increased and employee stability is enhanced.

How to use
It is recommended to make a periodic survey at least twice a year. This survey should be taken at any time if there are the following signals:
- Employees quit their jobs often.
- There are complaints regarding wages and promotion.
- There is general dissatisfaction among employees.
- The feelings of employees cannot readily be comprehended.
- The level of production efficiency is not as desired.
- Attendance is poor.

(18)   Morale Survey Form

MORALE SURVEY FORM

Name of work place	On-the-job worker	Clerical worker	(person to be surveyed: unit chiefs and below.)		
Names are not necessarily written. This sheet is not to be shown to the executives.					

No.	Item	Answers. (Put a circle mark on the corresponding answer and write your comment in the blank)			
1	Have the policies and directions of your company been well brought home to every member in the shops and offices?	Yes	Ordinary	No	
2	Do you think your work is worth doing?	Yes	Not Much	No	
3	Do you find it difficult to follow as there are many who give you directions?	Yes, often	Yes, sometimes	Never	
4	Are you dissatisfied with the unfair way of distributing work?	Yes	Not much	No	
5	Do you find the directions and guidances given by your direct supervisors adequate and suitable?	Yes	Not quite	No	
6	Do you think it would be better for you to acquire more knowledge or technique for executing your work?	Yes	Not much	No	
7	How much do you get tired in your daily work?	Very much	Not very much	Not at all	
8	Can you make full use of your recess?	Yes, fully	Not so much	Not enough	
9	Do you think you can improve your efficiency with the present equipment?	Yes	Not much	No	
10	Do you think the wage rating in your company is fair?	Yes	Normal	No	
11	Do you know the details of your wage or salary?	Yes	Yes, but rough.	No	
12	Do you think the wage calculation method is complicated?	Yes	Not much	No	
13	Do you find any dangerous and harmful spots in the factory?	Yes	I don't know	No	
14	What points do you find most inconvenient?	W.C.	The place to wash face & hands.	A place of rest	
		Bathroom	The place to change clothing.	The place to take meals	
		Lockers for personal effects			
15	What do you want to improve to raise operational efficency?	Shortage of materials	Irregular tools	Machine troubles	
		Taking too much time to transport production materials.	Poor communication among workshops.	Bad working environment as to lighting ventilation & such.	
		Others			
16	Are the feelings and thoughts of workers well understood by the executives of the company?	Yes	Ordinarily understood	No	
17	Does the atmosphere of the workshop fit you well?	Yes	Ordinarily	No	
18	Do you want to continue to work in this company?	Yes	Not keenly	No	
19	Do you sometimes consult with your foreman (senior) as to your work?	Yes, often	Yes, sometimes	Yes, but seldom	
20	Do you sometimes consult with your foreman (senior) about your personal matters?	Yes	No		
21	Do you want to have an occasional meeting with the men in administrative positions?	Yes	No		

[CHART 99]

19. BUSINESS DEVELOPMENT CHART

Purpose

A proverb says: "You cannot return from where you have not been" or "You cannot realize anything which you have not planned".

An enterprise is founded on the ideas and vision of its creator. However, ideas and visions are of little value when unaccompanied by practicality. But when raised to the level of concrete planning and realization, they can be of great value.

The 1980s will also be the decade of discontinuity with the past. It is time to escape from the illusions of the past and develop a new concept for enterprises. First of all, it is necessary to express one's vision on paper and not merely say that the matter can readily be achieved by management.

The illustration given in (19) shows product diversification strategies developed by executives in a pulp industry.

How to use

For constructing this, there are no definite rules and regulations. As the concept of management broadens, it is only necessary to construct more rectangles and draw more lines.

It can reasonably be said that a man of integrity should not indulge in reveries or dreams which cannot be realized. He should be engaged in more practical work. However, as far as management is concerned, idealism is an important factor. It is by idealistic management that one can win the hearts of employees and develop new initiative in business, thus bringing into realization a new type of modern management.

To give an illustration of a concept, only a sheet of paper, a pencil and intelligence are required. But to implement an idea, much more is required. Ideas in written form can have great persuasive power but determining whether they can be realized or not depends on further investigation.

(19) Illustration of Business Development

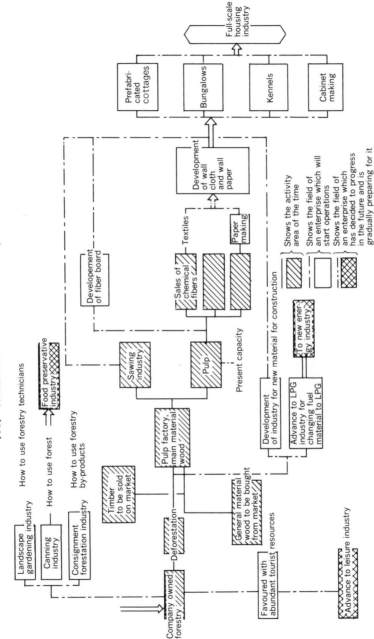

Shows the activity area of the time

Shows the field of an enterprise which will start operations

Shows the field of an enterprise which has decided to progress in the future and is gradually preparing for it

(Quoted from data on management, Kyushu Productivity Center 1969)

[CHART 100]

INDEX TO CHARTS

The numbers in brackets refer to the Chart numbers that appear in the lower right corner of each Chart; other citations are to page numbers.